A CELL OF GOOD LIVING

A CELL OF GOOD LIVING

THE LIFE, WORKS AND OPINIONS OF ERIC GILL

Donald Attwater

GEOFFREY CHAPMAN

LONDON DUBLIN MELBOURNE 1969

Geoffrey Chapman Ltd
18 High Street, Wimbledon, London SW19

Geoffrey Chapman (Ireland) Ltd
5-7 Main Street, Blackrock, County Dublin

Geoffrey Chapman Pty Ltd
44 La Trobe Street, Melbourne, Vic 3000, Australia

First Published 1969

© 1969, Donald Attwater

SBN 225 48865 5
This book is set in 10 on 12pt. Juliana with exception
of prelims
Printed in Great Britain by Clarke, Doble and Brendon, Ltd.,
Plymouth, Devon

CONTENTS

LIST OF ILLUSTRATIONS

(between pp. 128 and 129)

7

Apology is made for any inadvertent infringement of copyright

SOURCES AND ACKNOWLEDGEMENTS

The chief printed sources for the life of Eric Gill are his *Autobiography*, published by Jonathan Cape in 1940, his *Collected Letters*, edited by Walter Shewring (Cape, 1947); and *The Life of Eric Gill* by Robert Speaight (Methuen, 1966).

Evan R. Gill's *Bibliography* of his brother's writings and his inventory of the *Inscriptional Work* are invaluable for reference; both were published by Cassell & Co., 1953 and 1964. Other relevant books and articles are mentioned in my text.

Through the kindness of Mr A. Douglas Millard and of Mr Devin A. Garrity I have been able to revise and incorporate herein the greater part of my memoir *Eric Gill: Workman* (James Clarke & Co., London, 1945; The Devin-Adair Co., New York, in *Christian Revolutionaries*, 1947). I am grateful to the publishing house of Jonathan Cape for allowing me to make such extensive use of Eric Gill's own words from the *Autobiography* and *Letters*.

I must here thank Eric Gill's surviving daughters, Mrs Denis Tegetmeier and Mrs René Hague, with his eldest sister, Mrs Enid Clay, and his youngest brother, Dr Cecil Gill, for their goodwill and patience with my importunities; other relatives and friends and many other persons have also been most kind in supplying information, reminiscences and opinions.

I was emboldened to undertake this book by the encouragement and generous financial help of The Homeland Foundation, Inc., of New York; I welcome this opportunity publicly to thank the Foundation and its trustees.

With them I must bracket two personal friends; for months on end, a niece of Eric Gill, Mrs Evelyn Cox, sheltered, fed and befriended me, so that I might have the services in Sussex of Miss Lilian Cox, who was eyes and hands to me throughout, and a sympathetic critic of what I dictated.

D.A.

9

TO

THE MEMORY OF

THE FAMILY

AT

LITTLE GIDDING

1625-1646

TO

THE MEMORY OF

THE FAMILY

AT

LITTLE GIDDING

1625–1646

"The work which I have chiefly aimed to do in my life is this:
to make it well of peace in me in the place of our world."

JOHN FERRAR

Chapter One

BRIGHTON
1882-1897

Eric Gill was by birth a Victorian. To an Englishman of the eighteen-eighties the England of the beginning of the nineteenth century seemed a long way away. But though considerable and important changes had taken place, his own time was a recognizable sequel to and development of what had been in existence before, and the differences were not startling differences: it was the same world. The man of today who looks back to the 'eighties sees something almost unrecognizable, another world. A revolution, or series of revolutions has taken place, touching fundamental values, ways of life and thought, even, it would seem, "the laws of nature". Once, environment (good or bad) at least seemed stable and secure, with perhaps a hopeful future; now all things seem in a perpetual state of movement and uncertainty. With ever-increasing leisure, the last thing most people feel is leisured; social security brings also a feeling of insecurity.

Among the striking differences between those days and these which affect the whole of society and the individual lives of its members, two are of special interest: the Victorian times were an era of domesticity, and one in which the influence of religion was powerful at all levels.

Generally speaking, home was the centre of every man and woman's life and interests. Families tended to be large, unmarried children normally lived at home, and those who were themselves married returned frequently to the parental roof. Furthermore, families of only moderate means were able to employ one or more domestic servants, and these not infrequently were very much part of the family. Of such an establishment the father was in theory the undisputed head, and the mother the undisputed heart; they were

13

both conscious of having to exercise authority in their several ways, and the children were made conscious of their duty to defer to that authority, even sometimes after they had come of age. For neither side was authority necessarily synonymous with tyranny. Divorce was rare, and was looked on with horrified disapproval by high and low and not by religious people alone, for divorce by its nature broke up the home. Social intercourse took place principally at home. Holidays—much less common than now—were as often as not a period spent in somebody else's home. Recreation was normally domestic; if the winter evenings or summer afternoons were long, how to pass them had to be devised at home. (A quarter of a century was to pass before an advertisement in magazines adjured parents to "buy a bagatelle board and keep your boys at home".)

As for religion, it animated individuals and institutions, and through them was brought to bear on the life of the nation as a whole in every aspect, in civil affairs as well as in moral and personal ones. The idea that religion is every man's private business and of no public consequence was unheard-of. Christians in England were divided on matters of theology, church order and worship, and these differences were frequently buttressed and embittered by sectarian prejudice and complacency. But underneath was a basis of fundamental Christian faith and standards of conduct held in common. Allowing for all the divisions and disagreements, there had yet come about a curious unanimity of religious outlook and life, whose strongest emphasis was on personal uprightness and social good works.

Christianity was not reduced to a system of ethics, or made a religion of humanitarian "works" : it was in fact religious, the belief in, worship of, and obedience to the God of Abraham, Isaac and Jacob, the following of his Christ, and watchful attention to the promptings of the Holy Spirit. This religion was inspired and animated by the reading of the Bible; from that book it was deduced that earthly life is simply a preparation for another after death, in which the virtuous would be rewarded and the wicked punished. The proper business of life was duty, not pleasure. The effects of such considerations were evident in politics and business, as well as in domestic life; the resulting moral qualities were seen as much among the growing number of agnostics and free-thinkers as in anybody else. For example, they accounted for the high reputation for honesty enjoyed by English merchants, which made a large contribution to the prosperity of English commerce; even to business men "the Last Judgement seemed as real as the week's balance-sheet" (R. C. K. Ensor, *England 1870-1914*). Accordingly as it was interpreted, the fruits of this religion could be narrowness and bigotry, oppressiveness and gloom; or they could be a gentle self-discipline and cheerful certainty in a pervading atmosphere of evangelical piety.

The end of the Victorian Age can be dated with more precision than is usual in such convenient divisions of history. It came about, not with the death of Queen Victoria, but thirteen years later, on 4 August 1914. By that date Eric Gill had already lived over half of his life. He was, as are most people in varying degrees, a man of his time. But his time was two times, before the war of 1914-18 and after that war; and this twofold aspect is one of the keys to his character and life, to his work and thought.

Eric Gill was born, at No. 32 Hamilton Road, Brighton, on 22 February 1882. His parents were the Reverend Arthur Tidman Gill, who was born in the South Seas, and his wife Rose King, who was partly of French descent. Eric was their second child and eldest son, and at the time of the boy's birth Mr Gill was assistant minister at the Brighton chapel of the Countess of Huntingdon's Connexion, a small select body of Dissenters. Eric wrote of his father that "he was from a high-brow, intellectual, agnostic point of view a complete nonentity". If so, then the high-brows and agnostics would be mistaken: Mr Gill could be taken as a type and representative of a large section of the rank and file of clergymen and other professional men of his time; devoted to his duties, a zealous visitor of the poor and aged, a painstaking and effective preacher, who spent hours in the preparation of his discourses. A man, too, of culture and wide interests—two of his heroes were Lord Tennyson and Mr Gladstone; and he was himself a painter of some ability. In person, he was a good-looking, bearded man, in whom some detected a certain likeness to Tennyson; there were sharp-eyed young people among his parishioners later at Bognor who said that he cultivated this likeness. They may have been right, and it may have appeared that Mr Gill, hard-working clergyman as he was, was inclined to indolence if compared with the ceaseless activity of his wife. But the chief complaint of Eric Gill, who respected and loved his father, was his sentimentality and emotionalism, which the other children also found trying. All who knew him lay great stress on this characteristic of Mr Gill; it is remembered by one who heard him preach Sunday by Sunday at Bognor that on one occasion he recited the whole of George MacDonald's "Where did you come from Baby dear?" in the pulpit, with appropriate emphases.

Perhaps it seemed that Mr Gill took his wife's care and attention, her protection of him from outside disturbance, too much for granted. But he was not a self-centred or selfish man; he had a just estimate of his duties and responsibilities as the head of a household and as a minister of religion, and to carry them out effectively was his daily object. Nor can he have been unconscious of the burden, even in those days, of providing with decency for a wife and ever-growing family on £150 a year. He was a man faced by a man's job, and he did it, refusing to be diverted from it by outside interests or speculative questions: he never argued. The quality above all which Eric admired in his father was this single-minded attention to the job in hand, which must be done for its own sake, from composing a sermon to peeling an apple smoothly and in one piece. The state of life to which it had pleased God to call him was to be a husband, a father and a minister; and he never lowered his standards of the seemly and becoming, either for himself or his family.

In his later years, Mr Gill had Maurice Hewlett, novelist and poet, as a neighbour at West Wittering. On 3 April 1916 Hewlett, writing to E. V. Lucas, referred to Mr Gill as "as kind a soul as ever wore a cassock, and *most* prolific. A quiverful. Seven sons and four fair daughters. He shall not be ashamed when he meets his enemy in the gate".*

The mother of this brood was the daughter of Gaspar King, who was the manager of a timber-yard at Brentford in Middlesex, a modest and unassuming man, living contentedly in his poverty. Eric used to remind his brothers and sisters that "Mother has riz", that is, she had married above her station; this was not a derogatory statement, for he wrote that to this side of his parentage they owed "the inestimable blessing of good 'working-class' blood". But there was also music in the King family; Rose's sister Lizzie was a good pianist, and at the time Mr Gill first met Rose she was a professional

* *The Letters of Maurice Hewlett* (1926), page 154. I owe this reference to the kindness of the County Librarian, at Chichester.

singer, and she had or acquired other cultural interests in common with her husband.

In character they were contrasted. Whereas Mr Gill appeared detached and tried to avoid whatever might disturb his equilibrium, Mrs Gill was lively, combative and vigorous. The work she did for a family which eventually numbered thirteen children was prodigious, and she gave herself to it without reserve; to be completely tired out was all in the day's work, and even when domestic help could be afforded servants did not stay long—they got in Rose's way and vexed her by inefficiency. The strains and stresses of so hard an everyday life of course sometimes made her hard and irritable, but she was none the less loving towards and loved by all her children. It has been said above that Mr Gill would not argue in favour of his own convictions, but Rose did it for him in verbal battles, chiefly with the children, defending opinions most of which had been learned from her husband and made her own. Rose could be witty, and had a strong sense of fun. She was once standing at an upper window with the latest baby in her arms; in the garden below stood her husband, looking up and rhapsodizing at the sight. Suddenly Rose turned inward, laid the baby on the bed, quickly wrapped its shawl round a pillow, and, calling out "Catch, then!" threw the bundle out of the window.

She was forthright and down-to-earth in her speech, and impatient of wasted time. Once, after listening to her daughters' chatter about clothes and hats and materials and so on, she said to them, "Thank goodness your brothers will be here at the week-end, and we shall have some manly talk". And she found comfort in the assurance that "In my Father's house are many mansions" because she said, "There are some people whom I feel I could never get on with, even in Heaven".

In so far as these things may be attributable to heredity, it seems clear that, while he owed his passion for system and order to his father, Eric in most other respects took after his mother in temper and disposition, not least in his vigorous energy and capacity for work. When his mother died in 1929, Eric Gill put on her memorial card, "Her children rose up and called her blessed, and she shall laugh in the latter day", meaning in the end of time. These words are taken from the Book of Proverbs (Douai translation) where in Chapter 31 there is a long passage detailing and praising the qualities of "the valiant woman"; Rose Gill in the nineteenth century may well be taken as an incarnation or example of the ideal woman so eloquently praised by the Hebrew writer over two thousand years before.

It is worth recording that these two very earnest religious people were not puritanical. For instance, they were not teetotallers; and if Mr Gill disapproved of "The Belle of New York", or, later on "The Beggars' Opera", it was not because they were stage performances but because they were frivolous. When it was proposed to build a music hall at Brighton they objected, but on social grounds, because it was proposed to put it in the same street as the theatre. Mr Gill was a smoker, and he once remarked to his son that "smoking a cigarette in a holder is like kissing a lady with her veil on"; Eric became a heavy smoker of cigarettes—in a holder.

The nominal-roll of Arthur and Rose Gill's children is a clear testimony to their literary predilections. They were: Enid Rose, Arthur Eric Rowton, Cicely, Leslie MacDonald (Max), Stephen Romney Maurice, Lilian Irene, Madeline Beatrice, Gladys Mary, the twins Evan Robertson and Vernon Kingsley, Kenneth Carlyle, Margaret Evangeline (Angela), Cecil Ernest Gaspar. Of these, Irene died when a baby, and Cicely when she was fourteen. Eric was deeply attached to this younger sister, and her sudden death was a shock so great to him that he was able to record and re-create it forty years later in two eloquent and moving pages of his autobiography.

Eric tells us that his father's object in giving the names of his contemporary heroes and heroines to his children was the hope that they would be inspired by their illustrious namesakes. It is not for us to inquire to what extent this hope was realized, but it may be said with some confidence that it was not realized in any degree in the case of Eric. That any father should name his son after the priggish hero of Dean Farrar's Eric, or Little by Little is a matter of surprise today, but it was not so at all in 1882. Another twenty years was to elapse before my own father, having bought this popular book to read to me, noticed my yawns after a few pages and threw the book aside, saying, "Yes, this is very dull rubbish". Not so little Eric; when he was asked to suggest a name for one of the new twins, he chose "Vernon", out of that book (which his elder sister recollects she used to refer to as Eric, Gradually).

After what has been said, there would seem to be no need to emphasize that the Gills of Brighton (where they had three different addresses) were a happy family; like any other, they had their ups and downs, their internal squabbles, the usual clashes of temperament, but these did no lasting harm, and it seems true to say that every one of the eleven children who grew to maturity looked back to his or her childhood with gratitude and affection. There was an intense feeling of family solidarity, which for most of them lasted throughout life, and gave rise to the quip that "to marry into the Gill family is to undertake a career". That member of the family with whom this book is concerned, Eric, singles out for special mention two things that he owed to his upbringing: a recognition of religion as the fundamental basis of life, and the need not merely to accept poverty but even to seek it.

The religion was that combination of evangelical teaching and upright conduct, joined to both strict domestic discipline and dissenting independence, that at its best had been so valuable a factor in making the English character. The "Nonconformist conscience" was despicable only in decay. The young Gills were brought up on virtuous principles, and those principles were put before them in such a way as to win both heart and mind. "We took religion for granted, just as we took the roof over our heads . . . But taking things for granted doesn't mean you aren't interested in them, or that, on occasion, you won't be very interested indeed." There is no reason to suppose that they were specially docile children, so it is interesting to notice that there seem to have been no rebellious feelings even about forty minute sermons in chapel; referring to these in his autobiography, Eric says that the children did not attempt to follow the sermons, supposing—rightly enough—that they were intended for the grown-ups. The long services as a whole do not seem to have been irksome to them, but this was not due altogether to a precocious devoutness: there is evidence of a precocious spirit of professional criticism of how the services were conducted, especially services in other places of worship than their own. On the occasion of a revivalist mission, the children were brought down from their privileged position in the gallery behind the pulpit, and were seated among the ordinary sinners in the pit; and here one day young Eric raised his hand in witness that he was saved. Nearly fifty years later, he commented, "I see no reason to doubt that I actually was saved", making the analogy of the ignorant small boy with the soldier who went over the top in trench warfare without really knowing why he was doing it.

But religion did not begin early on Sunday morning and end at

bedtime; as well as public worship in chapel, they prayed together at
family prayers, and individually at their bedsides, and not only that:
they were taught to lead the whole of daily life with all its triviali-
ties with the consciousness that God's eye was upon them, not
simply the watchful eye of a Judge, but even more the loving and
careful eye of a Father. All in all, it was during the years of childhood in his home that the foundation was securely laid of Eric Gill's
deep conviction that all that ultimately matters in man's life, the
one thing necessary, is his love for God and God's love for him.

Poverty and poor are difficult words; there are endless gradations
of poverty, and such things as making and mending or the reputed
hardship of clothes being handed on from one person to another
were, are, the practices of many households which are in no sense
in want. There are states of indigence and destitution which have
always been so common that no description of them is necessary:
that is bad poverty. There is a state of having just enough, a decent
sufficiency for one's reasonable needs, and no more: that is good
poverty. And that is the poverty which has been commended to
Christians from the gospels onwards; that is the poverty of which
Eric Gill was a tireless advocate.*

The Gill family at Brighton was poor, really poor, from the point
of view of ways and means. So far was this from having an embitter-
ing effect on Eric (or, I believe, on any of them) that it was the
practical starting-point of his own repudiation of worldly wealth
and his attachment to a decent poverty as a fundamental necessity
for any renewal of western society. The poverty of the Gills was in
fact a bad poverty; at Brighton the family income was £150 a year,
and afterwards for a time it was substantially less, when it gave an
average of £7 a head a year for the two parents and eleven children.
After making all the necessary allowances, for sums earned by Mr
Gill's occasional jobs of tutoring, the generous practical help of
friends and parishioners, and for the greater buying power of money
in those days, this is still severe poverty. It is not surprising that
Eric wrote, "Sometimes we really did go hungry and underclothed—
as when, with infinite patience and pride in his skill, father would
cut one breakfast sausage into such a large number of thin slices as
to give each one of us ten or more children three or four slices each

* Eric sometimes indulged a mild inconsistency when he showed a
retrospective self-pity for himself and his brothers and sisters as being
"poor relations".

for our breakfast". Yet such was the spirit of the parents, the uncomplainingness of the father and the devoted diligence of the mother that out of that evil good was brought.

It appears that Eric was an intelligent, observant, sensitive boy, in no way freakish, vigorous and active, whose favourite author was G. A. Henty. With two of his sisters, Eric went off and on to a kindergarten school in Montpelier Crescent, conducted by two sisters of the Dickens illustrator Hablot K. Browne, "Phiz". Whatever these ladies taught him, they did not quite succeed in teaching him to read, and when he was about nine he was sent on to another local school where he remained until his schooling ended when the family left Brighton. This was Arnold House School, whose head master seems to have had a contempt for books but was a genius at the producing of outstanding games teams from his small number of pupils. The few years spent here represent the total of Eric's school education. In his own words, it consisted solely of "learning things out of little books and being able to remember enough to answer questions"; mathematics was the only school subject in which he took any sort of interest. For the rest, he was in later life thankful that his school-masters had been too timid or too uninterested to try to coerce his mind or to mould him against his proper nature.

His schooling then would appear to have been so much time wasted. But it was not, for it included games, and games were one of the two enthusiasms of Eric's boyhood. He and his fellows played cricket and football, studied them, talked about them, with all that interest and assiduity which fond but undiscerning parents might prefer to see given to school work. For when he was older, Eric gave considerable importance to what games had meant to him, not as competitive contests, still less as a sort of moral gymnasium, but as things worth doing and enjoying for their own sake. The boys were sometimes able to watch county cricket at Hove, and every cricketer must be touched by the lyrical passage in Gill's autobiography about Ranjitsinhji's batting. So games were one enthusiasm; and the other was drawing locomotive engines. For ten years Eric's great employment was drawing, and the subjects of his drawing were locomotive engines, and bridges and signals and tunnels, and then back to engines. He came to have special facilities for this, as the last house which the Gills occupied at Brighton overlooked the railway sidings

and the tracks as they entered the town. He used ruler and com-
passes when drawing, but for measurements and proportions he
trusted to his eye; what attracted and held him was the shape of
locomotives, he was fascinated by the character and meaning of
engines, "and as this character and meaning were manifest in their
shape, it was their shape I was determined to master". A by-product
of this activity was his first attempts at lettering, made necessary by
the fact that every locomotive had its own name inscribed on its
sides.

   This was, too, the beginning of the attraction which machines
had for Eric, an interest which he kept throughout his life; more
importantly perhaps, it was the unconscious beginning of an understanding of the significance and importance of the word "form" as
meaning the soul of a thing as well as its shape. In the circumstances,
it was inevitable that friends and relatives should assign an engineering career to the boy, and he had some such hazy idea himself. It
was taken sufficiently seriously for his father to arrange an interview
with a civil engineer, but this was not a success from Eric's point of
view. Writing of it nearly fifty years later, he does not make the
matter altogether clear, but he certainly underwent a disillusionment, slightly softened by an almost unformulated hope that the
engineer might be mistaken about his own profession. All this came
to an end when the Gill family moved to Chichester, but some of
its effects remained.

   Mr Gill's father and uncle had been Congregational missionaries
in the Pacific Islands, and he himself had begun his clerical career by
being called as minister to a Congregational chapel in Burnley. Here
a disagreement had arisen between the minister and his congregation. One of the later results of Victorian optimism was a growing
tendency to question that doctrine of eternal punishment which had
hitherto been taken for granted. Mr Gill, who avoided controversy,
had nevertheless repudiated this doctrine from his pulpit, and his
hearers had been scandalized. He had to resign, and he joined the
Countess of Huntingdon's Connexion.

   Selina Hastings, Countess of Huntingdon (1707-1791), was active
in spreading the teachings of John and Charles Wesley among the
nobility and gentry of her day, this of course being at a time when
the Methodists still were a group within the Church of England. She

formed her followers into congregations, to which she appointed Anglican clergymen as chaplains, and this led to difficulties with the Anglican authorities in 1779. Thereupon she had her chapels registered as dissenting places of worship, thus establishing what came to be known as the Countess of Huntingdon's Connexion. Because of its origin, this body used the Book of Common Prayer in its public worship; accordingly, although by now the Connexion was regarded simply as a small Nonconformist body, Eric from the beginning was accustomed to a fixed form of liturgical worship.

Then, when Eric was about fourteen, his father determined to make another change, and asked to be received into the Church of England. The reasons for this are unknown. Eric records categorically that his parents never spoke of the matter to their children, either then or subsequently, but he allows himself to speculate, rather tendentiously, in the *Autobiography*. It does appear that some people at the time imputed to Mr Gill motives of social advancement and financial improvement. From what we know of Arthur and Rose Gill, the truth of this is antecedently most improbable, though a consciousness of such possibilities need not be excluded. In the event, these consequences did not follow, his first Anglican appointment carrying with it a stipend of £90 a year.

The first hint which Eric got that something might be in the wind was one Sunday morning after service in the North Street chapel. His father, instead of as usual joining the church parade for a blow on the sea-front, took him in a different direction, and into St Peter's Church in The Steyne. Why his father did this Eric never knew; there was a service going on, and presumably they stayed to the end. This incident made a curious undefinable impression on the boy; it was the first time he had been into an Anglican church except as a building to be looked at, and he noticed the austerity of its furnishing when compared to his father's chapel, and that many members of the congregation were obviously poor. But it was not these things that gave him a sense of mystery, and he does not attempt to explain it in the autobiography.

However, it was soon followed by more understandable things, and the children saw that their father had ceased to minister at the chapel, they were now taken Sunday by Sunday to the nearby parish church of Preston, and Mr Gill went away to Chichester Theological College. Those of them who were old enough to have any opinion in the matter agreed that this new religious alignment was an improvement on what had gone before; though he can hardly have known it at the time, there was for Eric himself an element of relief at being no longer burdened by the personality of an officiating minister and by a select and well-to-do congregation. The summer of 1897 was barely over before Mrs Gill and her family left Brighton for Chichester.

Chapter Two

CHICHESTER
1897-1899

Eric Gill wrote of Brighton as "a shapeless mess", a collection of "more or less sordid streets, growing like a fungus, wherever the network of railways and sidings and railway sheds would allow". He was writing about the Brighton that he knew best, the outer suburbs in which his childhood had been spent, and he was not unmindful of the dignity and decencies of another and older Brighton. But more especially he was thinking of his home town when seen in the light of what he regarded as the earliest of his "revelations", the blinding light of the urban nobility of the City of Chichester.

It is possible to enter Chichester for the first time by North Street, and to get off the bus at a stop almost immediately opposite a small Georgian colonnade. In the wall at its back there is a large rectangular slab of stone, and on that stone is an inscription cut by a mason in the later part of the first century of the Christian era. It is the dedication stone of a temple of Neptune and Minerva formerly standing at that place, the offering of a gild of craftsmen for the safety of their overlord the Roman Emperor. Here at once is laid bare the origin of that town which so entranced young Gill: a Roman city, which has kept the main lines of its pattern through the days of Anglo-Saxon devastation, through the centuries of the earlier and later middle ages, which Eric saw before the building of suburbs outside its walls had disguised it. Today when much change has come over the city, when in particular its quiet streets are jammed with the noisy traffic of a new age, that original pattern can still be plainly seen, four quadrants formed by the intersection of North, South, East and West Streets. Subsequent ages have brought to the south-west quadrant a cathedral whose spire challenges Salisbury, and to the south-east quadrant the quarter called The Pallants whose four elegant streets of eighteenth century and earlier houses reproduce the plan of Chichester in miniature.

After the "mess" of Brighton, it was Chichester's ordered shape, its meaningfulness, that at once captured Eric. The first time he saw it was when he cycled over from Brighton to visit his father at the Theological College. He at once realized that it was not a picturesque town in the sense that a dozen other English cathedral cities are picturesque, it was something better than that; it had grown and developed and changed, there had been destruction and building, but the whole process had gone on in an orderly, coherent, understandable way; the result was a place "where life and work and things were all in one and all in harmony. Here was something as human as home and as lovely as heaven". He rode back to Dyke Road and its purlieus in a glow of excitement.

Opposite the cathedral in West Street stands the church of St Peter, and here Mr Gill, now ordained in the Church of England, served as a curate at £90 a year. He lived with his family a little farther up the street at No. 2 North Walls, a pleasant house, but rather constricted for eleven children; it is now demolished. On the ramparts just beyond it, Eric could stand looking inwards over the roofs, and see the cathedral spire, like a finger of light against a pale sky, or a spear against threatening cloud. Looking outwards over the wall, he saw green fields and ploughland and trees. "Fairyland", he called it. Railway engines and signal boxes were forgotten; his love was transferred to the heart of the city, the cathedral church of the Holy Trinity.

He explored the cathedral to the most inaccessible parts, the spire, the clerestory, the space above the roof vaulting: and wherever he went, he drew. His aim was to make records of what he saw; he had been well trained in the art of perspective by his father, and now put it to good use. Once again he was enthralled by shape, form, the conformity of a building with its meaning, dimly apprehending that the meaning of a church great or small is the whole people's worship of God. He writes that "I wasn't interested in sculptures or carvings, I was only interested in buildings". This raises an interesting point.

In the south choir aisle of the cathedral there are two large stone carvings, perhaps the most beautiful of their time in the whole of England. That time is somewhere between the years 1000 and 1130, and the subjects of the carvings are Christ's meeting with Martha and Mary, and his raising of Lazarus to life. Eric must have seen these scores of times, then and later, yet I never heard him refer to them in conversation and so far as I know they are not mentioned anywhere in his writings. The admission that as a boy he was interested only in buildings explains why he made nothing of these carvings then, but the later silence remains a puzzle. Perhaps he became tired of being told that some of his own carving owed much to the work of the Chichester masons, and he himself would doubtless have maintained that any unconscious likeness was due to the fact that he worked in the same way as those masons and with a similar mental background.

His being able to spend so much time in the cathedral and to get to know every nook and cranny of it was in great measure due to the kindness of the sacristan Henry Holding Moore, who owned a flourishing plant nursery in the city. He imparted to Eric all his knowledge of the building and its history, and let him go about wherever he liked. Another friend to whom he owed much, of a different kind, was the assistant organist, Osmund Daughtry. The word friend is justified, for Eric records that Daughtry treated him as an equal, weaned him from his liking for the music of Mendelssohn, Stanford and Dykes, and was the first to introduce him to the earlier English church composers, to say nothing of Bach, Beethoven and Mozart. These musical discoveries made a great impression on him, and he added to the more usual ways of hearing music that of listening to the organ through holes in the bosses of the vaulted roof.

Eric naturally became a well-known figure about the place and its precincts; he played football with the choristers, made friends with the lay vicars, and sat in the choir stalls, where he was more regular in attendance at the daily services than the canons themselves. This brought him to the notice of one of the prebendaries, Dr Robert Codrington, who invited him to tea at his little house just outside the cloisters. Dr Codrington had been a missionary in the South Seas, and like so many clergymen who have worked in the foreign mission fields he had a better understanding of the relative significance of things than have many clerics whose experience of life has been more limited. In Dr Codrington's case, in so far as it affected Eric, it was manifested in a critical attitude towards contemporary ecclesiastical architecture in England, and particularly the activities of church restorers. His criticism was well-informed and always expressed with gentle urbanity, but he made it quite clear that an opinion which is in general unquestioned is not therefore necessarily right. No doubt he was not trying to teach Eric this principle as such, but this was the lesson that Eric learnt from him. It was perhaps his first step on the road to rebellion.

Meanwhile, Eric had been meeting another new experience. After being allowed to run wild, as it were, for a while, his father entered him as a regular student at the Chichester Technical and Art School. The art master at this school, George Herbert Catt, seems to have at once recognized Eric's ability, and he certainly liked him personally. He gave a lot of out-of-school time to the boy, taking him for long walks in the country, identifying birds and flowers, explaining the technicalities of building, and implanting in him a temporary enthusiasm for Tennyson's "In Memoriam"—yet not so temporary that he did not quote a relevant passage from it on a mountain top at Capel-y-ffin twenty-five years later. He supplemented these walks by long bicycle rides over the neighbouring country, in the course of which he made drawings of village churches, cottages, barns, windmills.

Eric's attitude to Mr Catt became one of adoring respect. But if he liked and admired his teacher, he had reserves about the school and what was taught in it. Instead of the freedom offered him in the cathedral, he had to conform to the rules, conventions and current fashions of an official curriculum. But he appears to have conformed with a good grace, and no little success. He carried off a prize for perspective drawing, and when a picture of the church was required for the cover of the Portfield Parish Magazine, it was Eric who was asked to do it. This was his very first job, in the sense of work for which he was paid. It was, too, at the art school that the practice of lettering, begun as an adjunct of drawing locomotives, became a much more conscious interest; it is true that he was taught "the most monstrous perversions and eccentricities of 'new art' lettering", but he showed himself good at it, and was encouraged to invent new forms of these decorative abortions. Indeed, he became in his own words "mad on lettering", for he had discovered that letters were something special in themselves.

However, this contented situation did not last long. It gradually dawned on Eric that the art school course was simply a preparation for becoming an art teacher, and a teacher was the last thing he wanted to be; he wanted to do, and to make. His teacher Mr Catt noticed his pupil's waning interest, and this was aggravated when

Eric became attracted by one of his fellow students. He thought he was in love with her; but his feelings were not reciprocated, and the affair was nothing but a friendship. Nevertheless Catt took it seriously, seeming to think that Eric's behaviour would bring his school into disrepute. Eric was conscious of his own innocence, and the suspicions of his teacher destroyed Eric's affection for him. This upset came at a moment when he had already become rather discontented and rebellious. It is not clear to what extent religion at this time was a reality to him, a thing to be realized in one's self in the first place. His attraction was clearly to a large extent external, and when other things about the Church of England did not measure up to his first experiences at Preston parish church and Chichester Cathedral he felt he had been let down, and deprived of one more illusion. He was then eighteen.

At this critical juncture, it was in fact a clergyman who came to the rescue, Prebendary Codrington again. Through his good offices Eric was offered a place, at a reduced premium, in the London drawing office of W. H. Caröe, architect to the Ecclesiastical Commissioners. This opportunity was as agreeable to his father as to Eric, for he had long hoped that his son might become an architect. Just at this time Mr Gill was appointed to a curacy at St John's Church in Bognor, and in the late summer of 1899 the family moved from Chichester to what Eric called "that remarkable place (truly remarkable because it's so difficult to know why it exists)". Eric himself left his native county for London very soon after.

But before leaving Chichester, he had given his heart irrevocably to Ethel Moore, "Ettie", daughter of his old friend the sacristan of the Cathedral.

Chapter Three

LONDON
1899-1907

Eric Gill's own account of his earliest years in London represents them as a period of disintegration, disillusionment and revolt. These are strong words to describe a very commonplace process which is liable to occur whenever an intelligent young man—or young woman —from the provinces migrates for the first time to a big city, leaving behind the shelter of a more or less integrated community with its limited vision, its safeguards, its props and stays. In the particular case of young Gill, it brought about the immediate undermining and eventual collapse of his acceptance of architecture as a profession, of religion as he had experienced it, and of his uncritical view of contemporary society.

At first, helped by the generosity of Dr Codrington's brother, Oliver, he lodged at 68 Victoria Road, Clapham, a church club adjoining St Saviour's church, and from here he went up every day to Mr Caröe's office in Whitehall Place, Westminster. He travelled by horse-tram or bus to Victoria, and sometimes chose to walk the whole distance. The Caröe firm was a large business establishment, and its principal was unable to, or did not, concern himself with individual pupils. Gill found himself one of a score of draughtsmen, pupils and clerks in a basement drawing-office. They were under the control of the head draughtsman, who allowed a good deal of time to be spent in casual conversation and argument which had an immediate impact on Gill. One by one all the things he had been taught to believe and put his trust in were called in question, ridiculed, and contemptuously dismissed—family life, religion, art, architecture, morals.

When a boy, Gill had once heard somebody refer to him as "easily led". At first this rather upset him, but after a time he came

to think it was rather a good thing to be easily led—provided you
make a good choice of the leaders whom you will follow. He certainly did this in the drawing-office. His respect for the head
draughtsman, C. C. Wilson, a tolerant, kindly man, together with
his own upbringing, his impecuniousness and shyness, helped to keep
him from the grosser transgressions. More than to anyone else, however, he owed the benefit he derived from his time in the drawing-
office to a fellow-pupil, George Carter. The devotion which he had
had for Mr Catt and Dr Codrington was now transferred to Carter,
and he could not have done better. It was this young man, Gill's
senior by only a few years, who encouraged him to work outside
office hours by taking him to sketch in Westminster Abbey and
other places, who talked with him with more seriousness and understanding than was to be found in office discussions, and who eventually put him in the way of finding his vocation in life. Gill
recognized Carter's quality and his own debt to him: with
Chichester the integral city, and Lincoln's Inn the integral life, he
always bracketed George Carter the integral man.

Gill had not come to Mr Caröe's office with any high ambitions
in his head: he intended to start at the bottom, and aimed at being
able to build an "ideal cottage, four square, three or more up and
one down, i.e. one big living-room and lots of little snug bedrooms
in a high roof" (what about the kitchen?). This modest object was
not attained. It was largely through George Carter's sensitive conscience and clear mind that Gill came to see that architecture was
not the same thing as building, and that the tyranny of the architect in his office had reduced the working mason and builder to the
mere copying of things designed on paper in the smallest detail by
other people. Such irrational and inhuman division of labour was
not for him: he wanted to be a workman with a workman's rights
and duties, to design what was to be made and make what he had
designed.

That good building depends on the quality of the life and religion
of the society concerned is an idea nearly as uncommon in the third
quarter of the twentieth century as it was in the first quarter. This
idea was engrossing Carter and Gill, and was given considerable
support by the opinions both on religion and society expressed so
freely in the drawing-office. These young men in the service of an
official ecclesiastical architect were particularly contemptuous of the
Established Church and its clergy. Gill found nothing at St Saviour's,

Clapham, to counteract the irreligious influence of his young companions: "nothing in the outward show of that Christianity could possibly hold me—the frightful church, the frightful music, the apparently empty conventionality of the congregation. And nothing that the parson ever said seemed to imply any realization that the Church of England was in any way responsible for the intellectual and moral and physical state of London". So, on the basis of an insufficient, external experience of Anglicanism he slid out of it into a vague and hungry agnosticism.

Furthermore, it seemed to young Gill that professional politics was as much a sham as a great deal of professional religion, that Parliament did not really represent the people, and that politicians took no more responsibility for the state of society than did the clergy; laws about this and that were decided behind the scenes, and private interests were often served at the expense of the public good. So he became in an equally nebulous way a socialist.

But he did not get all his ideas from drawing-office gossip or the long talks with Carter. In a letter* to his sister Enid written at the end of 1901, he said, "You know Omar. Well, the theme of his writing is, I take it, 'let us eat drink and be merry for tomorrow we die'. Is it not so? . . . I wanted to discuss a point or two with thee on the points of difference and similarity in the moralities of Omar, Browning and Tennyson, as to which points in each are untenable, and which sound, and which 'indifferent honest'. But I'm not in the mood". This is indeed an example of the pre-occupations proper to a serious-minded young man at the turn of the century. He even read Carlyle at breakfast day after day, and was suitably excited by that sage's discomfort at the sight of a clerical hat. He read the tracts of the Fabian Society and the Rationalist Press Association pamphlets with care and attention, but got more profit and inspiration from Ruskin and Morris; these two were the real sources of his youthful socialism. He referred to Morris as "that most manly of great men", and that Morris anticipated some of the ideas that are associated with Gill's name is nothing new. But the degree of anticipation, as shown in Morris's published letters, is remarkable; no less remarkable is their frequent expression in a similar sort of way to Gill's, and with like turns of speech. Was Gill more influenced by Morris

---

* A postscript to this letter reads, "Balance, Dec. 16. A meat pie, some raisins, and 4d".

than he realized? It seems to have been his opinion that he owed more to Ruskin.

The pupils in Caröe's drawing-office were expected to attend evening classes in architecture; at George Carter's suggestion, Gill rejected this exercise, and instead went to learn masonry at the Westminster Technical Institute, and to classes in writing and lettering at the Central School of Arts and Crafts. Here his teacher was that great calligrapher Edward Johnston. Johnston himself was then only twenty-seven, but he was already an acknowledged master, and Gill was instantly captivated by his work, his teaching methods and his personality. In the *Autobiography* he becomes lyrical when he describes the effect on him when he first watched Johnston write: here was another "revelation", here was another man by whom he must let himself be led. He declared that Johnston's influence both in art and thought altered the whole course of his life.

On the other hand, Johnston was well-disposed towards Gill, so much so that in April 1902 he invited him to share his lodgings at 16 Old Buildings, Lincoln's Inn. Gill accepted with delight, and found his new surroundings to be something even better than he had imagined. He likened this experience to that of an eager young man who for the first time lives in college at Oxford or Cambridge: the beauty and dignity of the buildings and their setting, the formalized life of the Master and Benchers of the Inn (though Johnston and Gill, being simply tenants, were debarred from dining in hall), the decorum which had to be observed in relation to the whole institution, and especially a newly-found integration. Talk and discussion were no longer graceless arguments and the airing of prejudices and predilictions. Above all, there was the company of Edward Johnston himself.*

At the beginning of this year 1902, Gill began a diary which he kept to the end of his life. For years he used a small annual pocket diary, but later home-made books which would give more room, some twenty-five books and booklets in all. The contents were very largely factual jottings, but there is also a considerable amount of comment and reflection.†

* There are interesting references to Gill in *Edward Johnston* (London, 1959), by his daughter Priscilla. In her experience, Eric Gill was "the kindest and gentlest of men".

† Most of these diaries are in the William Andrews Clark Memorial Library at Los Angeles.

". . . to design what was to be made and to make what he had designed." That was now Gill's watchword, but what work that he could do was wanted? All things had been hiddenly working together towards one end, an end which now became clear: lettering in stone.

He soon was receiving several small commissions from churches and private persons; a tombstone among them took him three months to do in his spare time, and he was paid £5 for it. Then a more considerable opportunity came to him in a rather roundabout way. Early in 1901 there was a proposal on foot to restore the medieval market cross which stands at the crossing of the four principal streets of Chichester. This drew from Gill a long letter to the *Chichester Observer*, of which the kind of content and manner were to become so familiar in years to come. It was his first letter to the press, and many a harassed editor might well have wished it might have been his last. It was concerned with the difference between restoration and repair; the cross certainly needed repair, but in doing it no attempt ought to be made to reproduce the work of the original masons. He signed himself A Cicestrian in London, and in subsequent issues of the paper the letter received the support of the architect Edward Prior. No decision was reached, and nearly two years later, in January 1903, a writer to the *Chichester Observer* suggested that the cross should be pulled down and possibly re-erected elsewhere, since it was obstructing the traffic of the streets. At this, Gill and George Carter put their heads together and concocted another anonymous letter; it was rather heavily weighted with sarcasm, but the main point is sound, that is, that once a monument has been pulled down, its historical interest is almost entirely destroyed in whatever place it may be put together again. This produced another supporting letter from Prior, which emboldened Gill to seek his personal acquaintance. The upshot was that Prior invited him to undertake the lettering on the new Medical Schools then being built at Cambridge.

This was an important commission and one that could not be carried out at odd times after office hours. To accept it would mean leaving the architect's office, but Gill lost no time in making up his mind what he was going to do. He went to Cambridge, and from there wrote apologetically to say that he would not be able to return to the office. Mr Caröe replied in an exemplary, not to say generous, way: he returned Gill's articles, duly endorsed for three years' apprenticeship, and promised to send him work when anything suitable should turn up. Thus Eric Gill became a letter-cutter and monumental mason, and from that day was never out of a job. At the end of a year on his own he had earned £75, and his prospects were encouraging by his modest standards. He and Ethel decided that the time had come for them to marry.

The wedding of Eric Gill and Ethel Moore* took place on 6 August 1904, at the Sub-deanery Church of St Peter in Chichester. Mr Gill had been no more pleased by his son's engagement to the Cathedral sacristan's daughter than he had been by his attraction to the girl at the Art School. But he had waived his objections, and he officiated at their wedding assisted by the Vicar of St Peter's and Prebendary Codrington. They were respectively twenty-two and twenty-six years of age. They could not afford to go away for a honeymoon.

They made their first home in a working-class district of Battersea. This choice of neighbourhood was deliberate, for Gill had already a horror of any sort of respectable urban suburb. It helped to confirm his chosen status as a workman, and to identify him and Mary with that serious, unsentimental, straightforward estimate of marriage which still often characterizes working people. They took it for granted that marriage meant babies, and that the coming of children imposes the ready acceptance of fresh and over-riding responsibilities. Their first child, Elizabeth, was born on 1 June 1905. As there were difficulties about workshop accommodation in or near Battersea, they moved in the autumn of that year to 10 Black Lion Lane, Hammersmith. Here another girl, Petra, was born on August 18 the following year. Gill's optimistic estimate of his chances of immediately making an adequate living were more than justified; helped by teaching engagements at the Central School and the L.C.C. Paddington Institute, he was even able to afford a maid for the household, and a short holiday in Rome with Mary. The year 1906 was marked, too, by the taking of his first apprentice. This was Joseph Cribb, who after serving his articles continued to be Gill's principal assistant for twenty years, and became a considerable sculptor on his own merits.

* When later she became a Catholic, Ethel took the additional name of Mary, as she was always called thereafter. For convenience, I use that name from this point onwards.

Life in London was very full. The tombstone and lettering business prospered, and took him about the country a good deal. Soon he was to begin to make small carvings in stone, with the encouragement of W. R. Lethaby, and to try his hand at wood engraving. His lettering became very generally known through the signboards he lettered for the shops of W. H. Smith and Son. A special friend and patron at this time was the painter William Rothenstein : there is a long series of Gill's letters to him, but an estrangement eventually grew up between them. He continued to be in close touch with Edward Johnston, and it was chiefly through him and Rothenstein that he made the acquaintance, sometimes more than the acquaintance, of some of the best-known artists and men of letters of the day. Among them were Ambrose MacEvoy, Roger Fry, Augustus John, Sidney Cockerell, A. R. Orage, Cecil and G. K. Chesterton, H. G. Wells, George Bernard Shaw, the Webbs. It was now that for the first time he met Douglas (Hilary) Pepler, a young man of very varied experience, to whom he gave lessons in stone carving.

Gill entered into the life and interests of all these people, and more, with an enthusiasm which was as yet uncritical. Together with Mary he attended endless lectures and discussions on art, politics and religion and their inter-relation; they were keen theatre-goers; Eric read Nietzsche's *Thus Spake Zarathustra*, and was duly impressed, and listened while Edward Johnston read Plato to them in the workshop. (Mary, who had been trained in gold-leaf work, also had a little workroom in a loft.) Consideration of the relationship of the workman to his work necessarily led to a deepening interest in industrial organization and so to politics. It was almost inevitable that Gill should be drawn into the Fabian Society,* and he was in fact deeply involved in its ideas and activities.

To those who knew Gill in later life it is odd and amusing to think of him at this period, short as it was, when he was not merely full of political enthusiasms but acted on them; he supported socialist candidates at elections, even writing a pamphlet on behalf of one of them, and was sympathetic towards the Independent Labour Party. This led to his involvement in the so-called riot in London one

---

* The Fabian Society is an organization for the promotion of Socialism by constitutional means, founded in 1884. It has always been distinguished for its high standard of scientific inquiry, and its publications are still influential.

Sunday in July 1907, when there was a large gathering in Trafalgar Square to protest against the Liberal Government's coming to an understanding with the despotism of Tsarist Russia. Among the speakers was that picturesque firebrand R. B. Cunninghame Graham, who just twenty years previously had got himself jailed on a similar occasion. After the speeches, an impromptu procession was formed to march to the Foreign Office, assurance having been given by the police that they would not be interfered with if they behaved themselves; the police in fact marshalled the procession. However, at the corner of Downing Street reinforcements of police suddenly appeared from every direction, and roughly and effectively broke up the orderly demonstration. This example of official perfidy made a lasting impression on Gill; to break one's word is a thing "that no fellow should do", and the authorities had done it. More potent perhaps was the memory of a policeman's compelling hand on the back of his neck—his attitude towards the police always tended to be impatient.

Although he had abandoned the religion of his upbringing and to some extent its standards of behaviour, Gill had entered into marriage with excellent dispositions, holding it ideally to be a lifelong and exclusive partnership. But at this time Grant Allen's *The Woman Who Did* was still being read and acclaimed as a portent of a new age, and Wells's *Ann Veronica* was soon to follow it up, and young Gill was not untouched by current notions of sexual freedom. Early in 1907 an event occurred which he records unambiguously in his autobiography; I may therefore refer to it here without impropriety.

Eric became enthralled by a girl he had met at the Fabian Society. They went about together, she gave him a copy of *Thus Spake Zarathustra*, he gave her lessons in writing. For several weeks there was a very unpleasant situation, with long discussions between Mary, her husband and the girl. Eric at last made up his mind to break with the girl, but instead he went off with her to France for a week. It was in these equivocal circumstances that he first saw the cathedral at Chartres, which he ever afterwards coupled with Ajanta (a place he never saw) as man's supreme expressions of worship in stone. After returning to England Eric quickly brought the association to an end. Mary was soon reconciled with the girl, who for a short time was even given lessons in stone-carving in Gill's workshop.

Eric took this affair very seriously and it caused him acute suffering and searching of heart. Thirty-five years later, a young American soldier on service in England visited Mary at Pigotts. When in the course of their conversation reference was made to this and other matters touched on in the recently published *Autobiography*, Mary looked at him levelly and said, "These things don't matter when a woman loves a man and knows that he loves her". They had lived happily ever after.

I know of no more adequate appreciation of Mary Gill than Robert Speaight's paragraphs on pages 113-114 of his biography of Eric; it is sensitive, penetrating, understanding, and—in my experience and from what others have told me of her—accurate. It is perhaps worthwhile to put beside it the spontaneous words of a young man who knew her in the early days of her widowhood. Like so many others, the American soldier referred to above speaks of her eyes, shining and as it were speaking behind the spectacles, the impression she gave of quiet strength, her determination (she could be obdurate), her gentleness. "Always there was a serene quality about what she had to say. She was, I think, the most mature person I have ever known. She was no artist, no intellectual, but she was the seed-bed of Gill's art and thought. She was sure of herself, knowing what she had been, what she was and what she would be. These massively feminine women, powerful and quiet, who succeed in being a man's wife and mother are rare indeed." Mary Gill was a woman in her own right : she was never just "Mr Gill's wife", however efficient and devoted. There are some who have referred to her as "poor Mary" or "his poor wife" : the implications of these phrases of condescending commiseration are grotesque to a degree. Eric and Mary were made for one another, they lived in a way which they both wanted, and he was a considerate man and a most considerate husband.

Chapter Four

DITCHLING VILLAGE
1907-1912

During 1907 the Gills decided to leave London and make a home in some rural part of their native county. They went to Ditchling, the most easterly of the string of villages at the foot of the Wealden face of the Downs from north of Brighton to Steyning. Those villages were a great deal quieter and less sophisticated then than some of them are now; Sussex speech was predominant instead of the urban whine, and a dog could sleep in the middle of the road at mid-day; but Ditchling was already attracting artists of one sort or another. Here Gill succeeded in renting a dignified detached house, Sopers, fronting the main street, and in October they moved in.

One over-ruling consideration prompted this move: the conviction from experience with two growing daughters that a big city was no place to bring up children. In addition to the primary consideration, Mary welcomed the move because at all times and wherever they went it was she who looked for and undertook whatever farming activities were practicable: her domestic interests did not stop short at the kitchen door. Precisely in relation to this first move, Eric wrote: "I hadn't any theory about all this domestic and farmyard development. In a general way it frightened me and I put a brake on it. But it was entirely in tune with all our other notions of life and work, so I couldn't but see that it was good. And if they had the courage, which I lacked, I was thankful, and not a little proud."

Eric himself always loved the life of the earth, "the earth that man has loved, for his daily work and the pathos of his plight," but there was no back-to-the-land sentiment in this move to Sussex and later to Wales. Here as elsewhere he was quick to discard irrelevancies, in this case irrelevancies such as "the beauty of the countryside". The city, he said in effect, is the crown of man's civilization; the country exists to help maintain it, and the city cannot exist without a contented and flourishing countryside around it. Cities and towns have become what they have become, and so the country is increasingly depopulated or urbanized and life in it becomes more and more insufficient. This situation is abnormal: "because Babylon is vile it does not follow that Jerusalem is vile also". Children can play in the streets of Jerusalem, they cannot play in the streets of London; children can pick flowers in the gardens of Jerusalem, they cannot pick flowers in the park in Leeds. While sympathizing with and admiring the courage of those who follow a call to undertake an agricultural "simple life" in groups and associations, Gill refused the gross over-simplification of regarding this as a cure-all to be urged on people indiscriminately. In particular did he protest against "any attempt to make out that a certain kind of self-supporting country life is the only life for good Christian people".*

After moving to Ditchling, Hammersmith in fact continued to be Gill's working centre, and even after he had a workshop at Sopers he continued to go to town for several days every week. But a different home atmosphere was beginning to have its effects; exercise in the open air—long walks on the Downs, playing tennis—was helping to clear his mind. After all, the atmosphere of much of his socio-artistic experience in London was rather rarefied, there was so much comfortable high-mindedness—as he put it himself, there was "no smell of burning boats". Soon after coming to Sopers he resigned from the Fabian Society; he found he "could not believe that charity was the flowering of justice, but, on the contrary, justice was the flowering of charity".

At the same time he was in full flight from the Arts and Crafts movement. W. R. Lethaby ("who shall measure the greatness of this man?") told him that he was "crabbing his mother"; but Gill was not begotten of that movement, though it was natural enough that he should have been mixed up in it. He came to see its two great weaknesses: being unable to compete in price with mass-production, its products were luxury articles, bought only by the well-to-do; and it positively helped the mass-producers, who copied

---

* In a long letter to G.K.'s Weekly in 1927 (Letter 145) he put forward some telling objections to the social and economic advantages claimed for these experiments by their upholders.

its designs in their factories and thus started a flood of shams which still further corrupted people's judgement. So Gill escaped from arts-and-crafts: "I'm no gentleman and I don't understand loyalty to lost causes when the causes deserve to be lost."

Mary was about to give birth to another child. The sexual restraint forced on them by Mary's pregnancy was the occasion of a further step in the development of Eric's carving. For the first time, whether on paper, on wood or in stone, he made an image of a naked woman. Hitherto his great delight had been in cutting letters; he now experienced that delight translated into different terms. "And this new job was the same job, only the letters were different ones. A new alphabet—the word was made flesh", in fact, a sort of incarnation. In the *Autobiography* he describes his excitement at the discovery, but he did not think much of the carving that resulted. What, then, was his surprise when both Count Kessler and Roger Fry warmly commended it, and strongly encouraged him to go on. This was just the opposite of what he had expected to be told, and he "went home very much bucked and determined to do it again as often as possible".

Gill had no sooner fought off the dangers of arts and crafts when a new trap opened for him in another direction. He had already done work from time to time for Count Harry Kessler. This wealthy nobleman, son of an Irish mother and a German father, was a patron of the arts and a publisher of books from his Cranach Press at Weimar. He was critical of the Hohenzollern regime, and became known as "the red count"; later on he was to be an opponent of Adolf Hitler.

Kessler had been very much struck by Gill's first essays in stone carving, and he now conceived the idea that it would be a good thing for both men if Gill worked with the French sculptor Aristide Maillol for a time. Maillol worked in the then usual way of modelling in clay and then having the model reproduced in stone; Gill on the other hand worked directly on the stone: it was Kessler's particular idea that each could learn from the other in respect of these methods. Eric had his doubts about this, but he agreed to meet Kessler and Maillol in Paris for a discussion. Kessler acted very impulsively, and before the two sculptors even met he signed a three years' lease of a house for Eric and Mary near Maillol's home at Marly-le-Roi, and advanced a quarter's rent. Towards the end of January 1910 Eric crossed to Paris, and the matter was duly discussed that afternoon. Eric was getting more and more depressed about the whole prospect of an exile from home which he was convinced in his heart could serve no useful end, greatly though he admired Maillol. He had an appointment to meet Kessler again in the evening, but when he was alone his respect for Maillol and consideration for Kessler were swamped by forebodings of disaster. The whole scheme seemed mad. He scribbled a note of apology to Kessler, took a taxi to the railway station, and caught the night boat for home.

In his subsequent letter to Count Kessler Eric emphasized how much his work depended on carving directly in stone, and that on other matters he and Maillol were in such strong agreement that there could have been none of that benefit which Eric always found in the friction of minds. In the event, the understanding and generosity of both Kessler and Maillol were equal to the occasion, and the mutual relations of the three were undamaged. Gill recognized their forebearance with deep gratitude, but continued to be thankful that he had drawn back just in time. A few days after this happening, on 1 February 1910, Gill's third daughter, Joanna, was born.

The conjunction of an Eric Gill and a Jacob Epstein at this time might be expected to produce fireworks, and it did. The pair of them devised a scheme to endow the Island of Britain with a gigantic stone monument in the form of a cemetery in some suitable place, a new Stonehenge or Avebury. This modest proposal was enthusiastically received by Rothenstein and others; Augustus John wanted a temple in addition and designed a tomb for himself in the proposed Valhalla. The site was actually chosen: it was Asham House, an empty building standing in some six acres of land in a dip of the Downs below Eddington Hill, near Alfriston. Negotiations for acquiring this property were begun, Gill went to Portland and then into Derbyshire to inspect the stone of various quarries, and even serious people were optimistic that something would come of the scheme. The negotiations were for a lease of the property, but why anyone should want to build a new Stonehenge on land held on a fourteen years' lease is not obvious. Gill and Epstein in fact wanted to buy, but when the owners offered to meet them the price proved too high; and after a few months of glorious anticipation the scheme collapsed.

In January 1911 Gill showed some of his carvings in an exhibition at a London gallery, the Chenil. These called forth a very appreciative account by Roger Fry in *The Nation*, though one or two of his particular interpretations could probably be taken as apt illustrations of Gill's frequent remark that "the artist does the work and the critic gets the inspiration". Fry's approval was a promising start for the new year, which in fact was a fruitful one for commissions of several kinds. But if he was now regarded as a rising sculptor by the fine-art world, Gill was more and more retreating from that world. The small quarrels and more serious disagreements among these artists were too often allowed adversely to affect their personal relationships with one another, and Gill was finding this out; after more than one dispute, he and Epstein parted in a huff during this year, and Rothenstein's friendship for him had noticeably cooled. The London side of Gill's Ditchling life was being eroded.

Let Gill speak for himself.

I think it might not unfairly be said that [the artists whom I knew] all believed in beauty, were interested in truth, and had doubts about the good . . . I was so very much not the artist as they were artists, and though I was an agnostic in those days I was so very much not the sceptic as they were sceptics . . . They most certainly believed in something called Art and I most certainly did not, and I came more and more to detest the whole art world. I believed in religion and was desperately trying to find it, and they seemed to regard religion as being essentially nonsense but valuable as a spur to aesthetic experience and activity . . . I say I did not believe in Art or the art world. But of course I believed very much in the arts—with a small a and an s— whether it be the art of cooking or that of painting portraits or church pictures. But that's a very different matter and puts the "artist" under the obligation of knowing *what* he is making and *why*. It ranks him with the world of workmen doing useful jobs. And as for the art *world*, well, that is even more sickening, especially when all the snobbery of intellectual distinction comes in . . . Everybody was extremely kind and refined—and distinguished, but "I'd rather be a heathen suckled in a creed outworn . . ." On the other hand, in yet another sense, I believed in art very much indeed. The artist as prophet and seer, the artist as priest—art as man's act of collaboration with God in creating, art as *ritual*—these things I believed very earnestly. But here

again I was generally at variance with my high-art friends. Their
views were both more simple and more mysterious than mine.
They were essentially aesthetes: that was the awful truth. They
played about with religion and philosophy and labour politics, but
that was all very superficial; what they really believed in and
worked for was aesthetic emotion as understood by the art critics.
But art as the ritual expression of religion I did indeed believe in
and they did not . . . So I gradually escaped from the high-art
world which for a time seemed to be closing round me. Doubtless
I never was a serious artist as serious art was understood in that
world.

(*Autobiography*, pp. 172-174)

There were seven events in Gill's life which he called his
"escapades". This escape from the art world was the last of them.
The others had been his escaping from the art school at Chichester,
from architecture in Caröe's office, from Anglicanism as he knew it,
from London, from the Arts and Crafts Movement, and from the
Fabian Society and socialist politics.

The hour produced the man. It was precisely at this time, towards
the end of the Ditchling Village period, that Gill first met Ananda
Coomaraswamy, in London. Coomaraswamy was a Hindu from
Madras, a man of great learning both in the wisdom and the art of
India and in the philosophies alike of East and West. He later became
curator of the Oriental section of Boston Museum of Fine Arts, and
Gill's personal meetings with him were very few, in fact he did not
see him again after 1917. But they read one another's writings and
kept up a lively correspondence, and the influence on Gill was
profound. One aspect of this influence may be summed up in Gill's
belief that "an artist is not a special kind of man, but every man is
a special kind of artist"—an often-repeated aphorism which he took
directly from Coomaraswamy. But the influence was much wider
and deeper than that; indeed, in an article in *Good Work* (Summer,
1966; Cambridge, Mass.) Sir Herbert Read goes so far as to claim
that "all Gill's most dogmatic ideas about art and religion" were
derived from Coomaraswamy, either directly, or indirectly through
Jacques Maritain, who also was strongly influenced by Coomaraswamy; and behind all three men, the Hindu, the Frenchman and the
Englishman, can be discerned the figure of St Thomas Aquinas.

This is all very well; no doubt there is much truth in the general lines of Sir Herbert's argument. But surely a word of warning is called for. Is it not common that men who are using thought and study on the same subject should, even from different standpoints and experiences, reach identical conclusions independently of one another? Many of us from our childhood onwards have been pestered, for example, by literary critics to believe that if two poets said the same thing, one of them necessarily derived his thought from the other. The general question cannot be easily answered. Of Coomaraswamy, Gill himself wrote: "I believe that no other living writer has written the truth in matters of art and life and religion and piety with such wisdom and understanding". Of Gill, Coomaraswamy wrote, "We were in very close agreement about fundamentals . . ." Their correspondence from a relatively early age was so close that Coomaraswamy says, "It would not be untrue to say we went to school together and grew up together, though apart". In the same introductory essay to It All Goes Together (New York, 1944), Coomaraswamy wrote: Gill "said himself that he invented a religion and found that it was Roman Christianity: he might also have said that he re-invented a way of working, and found it was that of all traditional societies and Plato's way . . . This amounts to saying that Eric's was not a personal point of view, but simply a true one that he had made his own. He was not 'thinking for himself', but assenting to credible propositions; and he was, accordingly, a man of faith."

The relation between life, religion and work; the metaphysics of Hinduism and Buddhism side by side with the metaphysics of Christianity; the relationships of the true and the good and the beautiful; the real significance of erotic images; the artist as priest and seer; art as a ritual expression of religion; art as man's collaboration with God in creating—at such points as these the mind of Eric Gill and the mind of Ananda Coomaraswamy met. Coomaraswamy was the eastern pole of the Chartres-Ajanta* axis. And, as Mr Speaight points out, "whenever Eric was inclined to confuse art with usefulness, Coomaraswamy was there to emphasize its sacred foundations".

* Near the village of Ajanta in Hyderabad, South India, there is a series of some thirty halls and dwellings excavated in the rockface of a ravine. The interiors are covered with stone carvings and wall paintings dating from 200 BC to about AD 650: an extraordinary collection of examples of ancient religious art.

Gill wrote to Coomaraswamy, "It almost seems as though you and I and [Graham] Carey were a kind of secret society founded to 'put across' a certain point of view. The way we bag things from one another is, in a manner of speaking, jolly fine. It really is a wonderful phenomenon that with 3,000 miles between us we should be moved, as we seem to be, to say the same things, though I am not alone in thinking that you say them better than anyone else in the whole round world." And in what was apparently his last letter to Coomaraswamy (16 February 1940) he said, ". . . . I can only add that I do send you much love and deepest gratitude—the gratitude you can pass on to God to whom it is due".

"I was the son of a nonconformist parson, the grandson of a missionary. Life was more than art." These sentences are among the most significant pieces of self-revelation in all Gill's *Autobiography*. And before his repudiations could be complete, before he could become a citizen of a new and whole world, another and final crisis —"the end is the beginning"—had to be passed.

Gill was at this time in the process of solving for himself the problem of work; and he was also faced with the problem of social injustice. There was the evil of having too little material goods and the evil of having too much, of bossing and being bossed : where did this evil arise and what was the remedy? He knew that socialism could answer neither question adequately, but was convinced that somewhere, somehow, religion could. But he had cut himself off from the religion of his childhood, and he had no reason to suppose that the Christian religion could be the cure for the world's sickness. "The churches seemed to be concerned solely with their sectarian games—they hardly seemed interested even in feeding the hungry. And if you could not count on the parsons to help to redress even common cruelties and injustices, how much less could you count on them in deeper matters?"

For instance, it is no good agitating for municipal housing till you have made up your mind what sort of a being it is that has got to be housed; "is it conceivable that he is a temple of the Holy Ghost? But what the devil is that? And what kind of housing can possibly be his suitable shrine?" Religion is the first thing necessary; without it there is no answer to the primary and fundamental questions, What is man, and why? But Gill had no religion, and all the ready-made ones were wrangling among themselves, so that even of the Christian churches no two seemed to answer the questions alike. There was therefore nothing for it but for him to make up a religion to fit the situation. And then he began to discover, very slowly and gradually, that his new invention was an old one. "To invent" means to come upon, to find, to uncover; and what Gill was inventing was, to his surprise and indeed alarm, stripped of all real or assumed irrelevances, Roman Catholicism. "I did not think so to start with, in fact I thought I was doing quite the opposite. I thought the Christianity of the churches was dead and finished, and surely one can be forgiven for thinking so. The effect of Christianity in the world seemed non-existent, and I knew of Roman Catholicism only by repute. I did not know any Roman Catholics and I hardly ever went into any Roman Catholic churches or even read Roman Catholic books;* moreover what little I knew of Roman Catholicism from outward appearances was, in a general way, revolting . . . I suppose nothing on earth is more completely and efficiently camouflaged than Peter's 'barque', which, from a short distance, looks exactly like the Ritz Palace Hotel." But "I found a thing in my mind and I opened my eyes and found it in front of me. You don't become a Catholic by joining the Church; you join the Church because you are a Catholic."

The exact characteristics of this religion that Gill "invented" are a matter of some uncertainty, as are the precise stages by which he came to turn his attention to the Roman Catholic Church as a possible embodiment of them. His references to these matters are disconnected and sometimes oblique, and are far from complete. On 5 December 1910 he wrote a rather mysterious but certainly relevant letter to William Rothenstein in which he says, ". . . it is too splendid, if it's true, and so splendid that I hesitate to write about it. I will just hint it to you—there is a possibility that religion is about to spring up again in England. A religion so splendid and all-embracing that the hierarchy to which it will give birth, uniting within itself the artist and the priest, will supplant and utterly

* It does not appear that Gill's curiosity was stirred by orders for a headstone in 1909 for Father George Tyrrell, in the graveyard of the parish church of Storrington in Sussex, and in 1919, for the recumbent tombstone of Father Arthur Francis Bell, in the same place. In 1934, at Tolpuddle in Dorset, he cut an inscription for the grave of James Hammett, a Tolpuddle martyr.

destroy our present commercial age." It is a curious letter: there is
a quasi-prophetic ring about it, as though the writer were moved by
some strong stimulus, inward or external: but there is no evidence
about the nature of any such stimulus.

There is no doubt that Gill wanted a world in which all power
and influence, political, economic, intellectual, cultural and scientific,
should be ultimately answerable to a universally accepted religious
philosophy, embodied in a supra-national institution authorized to
exercise its power in the name of God. The later medieval church in
Western Europe comes to mind, Christendom in the sense the term
then had, and Gill was not ignorant of the theory behind the Holy
Roman Empire. Even in his "agnostic" days he confessed to a
suspicion that the evils he saw everywhere were fundamentally due
to deficiencies in established religious bodies, and that the more
Christianity was "de-institutionalized" the more ineffective it became.

Gill refers to the good impression made on him by Browning's
poem "Bishop Blougram's Apology", which a fellow-draughtsman
at Caröe's had put into his hands with the opposite intention. But
now, in 1911, he knew no more about the Roman Catholic Church
than he had done then. Nor did he find it easy to acquire information when he made up his mind that he must do so; presumably his
shyness and unwillingness to be a nuisance kept him from the
obvious course of calling on the nearest parish priest. But he was
working on an inscription for the tomb of Francis Thompson, and
this brought him into touch with the Meynells, at Greatham, where
his visits are still remembered; in consequence he made the acquaintance of the rector of St Etheldreda's church, Ely Place. At the
same time he started attending Mass regularly, while continuing his
discussions on religion in general with such diverse people as
Augustus John, Francis and Frances Cornford, and Rothenstein.

The turning-point in his quest appears to have come when in the
spring of 1912 he visited the Benedictine monastery of Mont-César
at Louvain, to which he had been invited to lend a statue for an
exhibition. There he had a long conversation with one of the monks,
Father Anselm, a conversation in which neither party knew the
other's language, and so had to be carried on with the help of goodwill and a dictionary. Their main topic was the historical, factual
truth or otherwise of the events chronicled in the gospels, many of
which Gill resolutely, obstinately, maintained to be simply sym-

bolical. Father Anselm countered by a reiterated simple denial, "Pas symbolique. Pas symbolique".

This exchange shows how far Gill still was from traditional Christianity. When he said that it did not matter to him whether or not Jesus actually rose from the dead, that the story was at any rate true symbolically, he was reducing the Resurrection to the level of Jonah's sojourn in the belly of a fish. "If Christ be not risen . . . your faith is vain," wrote St Paul. *Pas symbolique:* Father Anselm was adamant.

But this was not the only thing that happened at Mont-César. Eric attended one of the conventual offices in the church.

> At the first impact I was so moved by the chant, which you must remember I had never heard a note of in my life before, as to be almost frightened . . . This was something alive, living, coming from the hearts and minds and bodies of living men. It was as though God were continuing the work of creation here and now, and I was there to hear, to see—even almost to touch . . . There, at Louvain, after the slow procession of incoming monks and the following short silence when I first, all unprepared and innocent, heard "Deus in adiutorium . . .", I knew, infallibly, that God existed and was a living God—just as I knew him in the answering smile of a child or in the living words of Christ.

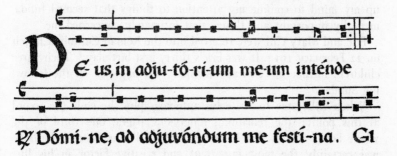

Dᴇ us, in adju-tó-ri-um me-um inténde

℟ Dómi-ne, ad adjuvándum me festí-na. G1

"O God, come to my help. Lord, make haste to save me."

It is easy enough to write such things off as mere emotionalism. But human feeling and experience can be vehicles of grace, and it is not unlikely that in the abbey church of Mont-César the bodiless hand of God, clothed in the materiality of public worship, touched Eric Gill. However, when he got back to England he put the emotion aside and "remembered only that Christianity was 'pas symbolique' ".

At this time Gill was rather hard up, and was working strenuously to clear his debts; his workshop was now in Ditchling, but he had often to go to London and elsewhere, on business and to keep in touch with his friends. With all this, he was trying to get light on his religious difficulties by assiduous reading, but he came to realize that the help he needed could not come that way. He got into touch with an English Benedictine, Abbot Edmund Ford, and their meetings were more fruitful, but still not decisive. Gill was apparently keeping up a correspondence with the monk who first invited him to Louvain, Bruno Destriers; and in July Father Bruno wrote urging him to by-pass his difficulties, questionings and self-communings, and to take the plunge of faith. Six weeks later, Gill wrote to Abbot Ford definitely asking for formal instruction in the Catholic faith, and towards the end of the year he and Mary started regular visits to Hove for this purpose, he going to Canon James Connelly and Mary to a convent. He was now prepared to answer the question, the all-inclusive and final question, "Do you believe all that holy Church believes and teaches?" with an unhesitating "Yes". "But as to *what* she teaches on all the multiplication of funny subjects that we worry ourselves about, well, at the great risk—or rather certainty—of being thought both lazy and unscrupulous, I made up my mind to confine my attention to things that seemed fundamentally important and things that intimately concerned me."

Eric and Mary Gill were received into the Roman Catholic Church on 22 February 1913. It was Eric's thirty-first birthday.* Their three children, Elizabeth, Petra and Joanna, were baptized on the following Sunday.

When Gill came to write his autobiography, he ends the record at this point: the remaining ninety-one pages, one third of the whole book, are labelled Postscript. Eric Gill's becoming a Catholic was certainly the most important and creative factor in his life. This is not merely a pious cliché or an expression of sectarian par-

---

* On this same day, on the island of Caldey off the coast of Pembrokeshire, a community of Anglican Benedictine monks officially informed the bishop of Menevia (Mynyw) that they wished to be received into the Roman Catholic Church. Ten years later Gill was to come into contact with these monks, with important consequences for himself and for many others.

tiality, but a plain fact which must be patent to anyone who knew him or who studies his work.

Gill was not, at any time of his life, an ecclesiastically-minded layman, in a depreciatory sense of that expression; he was not "interested in religion", he was passionately in love with God. Religion means the rule of God, and Gill had a vision of a holy church ruling the world in the name of God—not a theocracy in a political but in a personal sense. A church, then, speaking as one having authority, not answering every difficult or tom-fool question, but saying quietly and firmly to herself and to her children, "This is the way of the Lord", and putting the responsibility on her children to walk in it. So it was not professional apologetics or intellectual wrestling, or that mythical aesthetic appeal, or that escape into an imposed certainty (of which so much is heard) that persuaded Gill he had found the Church of God.

How then did he become convinced? "I would not have anyone think I became a Catholic because I was *convinced* of the truth, though I *was* convinced of the truth," he tells us. "I became a Catholic because I fell *in love* with the truth, and love is an experience. I saw. I heard. I felt. I tasted. I touched. And that is what lovers do."

And there were the gospels. He had been brought up on the Gospel, but he was not prepared to say whether this gave them an antecedent advantage in his mind or not: "it is impossible to tell. But the mere fact that you've been brought up with a thing doesn't necessarily give it an unfair pull over your mind. It might work just the other way." "All I know is that I felt like the prodigal son. I had been away, squandering my substance in riotous living—not with women and wine, though that would have been nice, but with riotous young minds and the wine of strong words—and now I was, in a manner of speaking, coming home."

Chapter Five

DITCHLING COMMON

1913-1924

On 11 November 1913 the Gills left the house called Sopers in Ditchling village and migrated to the Common a couple of miles to the north. This move was simply a further stage in their move away from London and its life; they needed a bit of land and more space generally to enable them to produce more of their own daily needs, and to have a house which could be regarded as a permanent home. They found what they wanted, and borrowed money to buy it: the house was situated in the angle between a side road and the main road across the Common on the west side, and was accordingly known as Hopkin's Crank after a previous owner. It was a plain foursquare Georgian building, with outbuildings, and two acres of land went with it.

Eric soon had a workshop ready in these more spacious surroundings, but he still had to maintain some close ties with London, where an exhibition of his work was in preparation at the Goupil Gallery. Before long, too, he had to go to Pickering in Yorkshire, where he had been asked to make a font for the Roman Catholic church. This was a modest commission compared with the unexpected one which soon followed.

There is in the Roman Catholic Church a service, originating in the later middle ages, called the Stations of the Cross. It consists of a short reading, prayers and a verse of a hymn, having a relation in turn to each of fourteen happenings, mainly recorded in Scripture but some simply matters of popular belief, during the passion and death of Jesus Christ. These happenings are now usually represented on the walls of churches, by carving, painting or in some other way, and the service takes place before each representation in turn. In the summer of 1913 Eric Gill was invited to submit designs for the fourteen Stations of the Cross in the new Catholic cathedral at Westminster, and in the following spring these preliminary designs were accepted. They consisted of fourteen sketches, each $2\frac{3}{16}$ inches by $2\frac{1}{4}$ inches, drawn in pen and ink on a single sheet of paper, within a gilded border. The haloes also were gilded, the body colour was white, and the inscriptions were lettered in red.*

In those days Roman Catholic churches in England were almost invariably built according to the fashions of the Gothic Revival or, less frequently, of the Classical Revival or Renaissance—St Philip Neri at Arundel, St Chad's at Birmingham and the Brompton Oratory are among the more ambitious examples. But the cathedral at Westminster was an innovation. The archbishop who initiated it, Cardinal Vaughan, had called for a large building which could be brought to a usable state with the least possible delay, and which would be no more costly than was absolutely necessary. The architect J. F. Bentley had suggested that these requirements—with the added advantage of not appearing to enter into competition with the ancient English cathedrals—could best be met by an adaptation of the Byzantine building of Greece and Asia Minor which could be decorated and finished at leisure; this was approved. By 1914 the building had been in use for some time, but still consisted substantially simply of a great shell of dark red brick walls and piers, roofed by high, shallow concrete domes. For this impressive edifice it was Gill's task to provide fourteen carvings of Hoptonwood stone, 5 ft 8 ins square, in low relief, to be affixed to the massive brick piers separating the narrow side aisles from the nave. The making of these in his workshop and in the cathedral was his principal work for the next four years.

They were the occasion of one of the best known Gill anecdotes. As he told it to me, he was working in the cathedral on one of the panels when a lady came up, watched him intently for a few moments, and then said:

"Young man!"

"Yes, madam?"

"Are these the stations of the cross?"

"Yes, madam."

---

* This sketch was bought in 1918 by the British Museum, whose Department of Prints and Drawings kindly supplied me with full particulars of it. Working drawings of the carvings are in the Victoria and Albert Museum.

"Are they all going to be like this one?"

"As near as I can make them, madam."

"Well, I don't like them."

"I'm sorry, madam."

"I don't think they're nice."

"Madam, I don't think the subject is *nice*."

This was not the only exchange of the sort that took place; Gill always rose to the occasion good-temperedly but effectively.

Gill became a well-known figure in the great church, and he made several friends there, among them the doorkeeper who presided at the main entrance. Eric loved to relate how this man said to him one day, "Mr Gill, this cathedral will never be filled until they go back to Mozart". This was at the time when Richard Terry was organist and choirmaster there, and making it well known for the rediscovery of Tallis, Byrd and other English masters, as well as for the singing of the great continental polyphonists.

As in tens of thousands of other English homes, the beginning of war in August 1914 had only marginal immediate effects on the Gill family. By now, Eric had no interest whatever in politics, least of all foreign politics, and he was the last man to be carried away by popular enthusiasms. This does not mean that he was devoid of patriotism as popularly understood; he loved his country and its people, and it seemed to him that these were indeed gravely threatened. But the personal obligations he had undertaken and immediate responsibility for his wife, children and household still had the first call on him. "If things get so bad that they need me," he said in effect, "they will send for me, and I will go"; meanwhile, he got on with his job. There was not a trace of that opposition to war which was later to distinguish him. As a young man in London, he had been a volunteer with the Queen's Westminsters, enjoying their exercises, and was a good shot with a rifle. Now he joined the predecessor of a later Home Guard, in which he carried out his duties ungrudgingly and improved his shooting in the process. But what kept Eric most in touch with the war was the fact that he had four brothers serving in the armed forces, the twins Evan and Vernon with the Canadians.

When the call did come, Gill did not personally apply for any temporary exemption; but an influential friend insisted on doing so for him, specifically that he might finish the Westminster stations. So it was not until immediately after this was done in August 1918 that he was drafted into the mechanical transport section of the R.A.F. and posted to Blandford. He was Pte A. E. R. Gill 295744 for less than four months, for part of which he was incapacitated by sickness. For the rest, he did the normal fatigues and was instructed in rough, very rough, and ready fashion in the driving of a lorry. He said it was "exactly like being in prison", and at that stage of the war—by now "everyone, officers and men, were utterly fed up and discontented and impatient"—there was little alleviation in the rigours of the recruit's life. He makes the most of them in the *Autobiography*, but dismisses the whole of his military service in those two pages; like the war itself, his few weeks in the R.A.F. were something that happened during Gill's lifetime rather than something that happened to Gill.

To catch glimpses of what went on at a deeper level, to see what really occupied his mind and heart at this time, one has to turn to his letters. He had left Desmond Chute as his "stand-in" at Ditchling, and his letter written from Blandford and dated October 5 is a remarkable essay in exhortation and instruction from a master to a just steward: the whole letter is divided into 23 numbered items, ranging from the exact method of entering carvings in the ledger and jobs book to the ethics of insurance, and from the number of 1½" letters an apprentice should be able to draw in half an hour, to Desmond's own progress in letter cutting. This with other letters which have been printed was written by a man who was tired, dispirited, unwell and at odds with his whole surroundings. It was a feat of concentration and faith.

Immediately after the armistice on November 11 Gill was transferred to the Admiralty as a draughtsman, and was sent on indefinite leave to await recall. He was home by Christmas, and the recall never came.

During the years from 1916 to 1919 a great change came over Eric Gill's life and work, and this change was unconnected with the war. In his own words, his quiet independent existence on Ditchling Common came to an end under the influence of two friendships. Those friendships were with Hilary Pepler and Desmond Chute.

The Johnstons had been living at Ditchling since October 1912, and after the Gills left Sopers that house was occupied for a time by Hilary Pepler, a friend of theirs whom Gill had already met at Hammersmith. Pepler belonged to a Quaker family and had been educated at the Friends' School at Bootham in York. At the time of his first coming to Ditchling he was thirty-seven years old, and was married to Clare Whiteman; they eventually had three boys and three girls. Pepler's experience had been very wide and varied; in his earlier years he adventured in commerce, handicrafts and land surveying. He then took up social work in London, where he was associated with William (afterwards Lord) Beveridge, Dick Sheppard and Frederick Rowntree. He founded at Hammersmith the Hampshire House working men's club, and later there was combined with this the Hampshire House Workshops for war refugees. He was a member of the Labour party, and the L.C.C.'s first organizer of school meals for children, and among his multiplicity of interests children's welfare always had a high place; in 1912 he published his *The Care Committee, the Child, and the Parent*, followed by *Justice and the Child* in 1915. It was in this last year that he moved his family to Ditchling, and for precisely the same reason that the Gills had left London, because of the difficulty of bringing up a family there. A further reason was that he was becoming increasingly interested in printing and publishing, and these activities could be carried on in the country. He had already issued several publications in London, printed at the Westminster Press; one of these, a sociological satire written by himself, *The Devil's Devices*, was the first book for which Gill made wood-cut illustrations, and another was a reprint of Cobbett's *Cottage Economy*, a handbook which was later put to considerable practical use in the Ditchling community. So he established himself in the workshop which Gill and Cribb had vacated, and started with a single Stanhope hand-press and a fount of Caslon Old Face.

At this time Hilary Pepler's friendship was probably still primarily with Edward Johnston, with whom Gill too maintained his close contact; but a couple of years later Pepler moved to a house he had built not far from the Crank, at the southern end of the Common, and his press was accommodated in some adjoining farm buildings, Halletts, of which the Johnstons occupied the house; the press had expanded by then, and was known as the St Dominic's Press. Had anybody thought of such a thing as a "community", the possibility was for the first time within sight.

Pepler had a private income, and that may account in part for the fact that, when contrasted with Gill's rigorous care and exact methods, he appears to have been rather casual. For example, he took up printing in the belief that "any fool can print"; he learned and corrected his error the hard way. Personally, he was a man of considerable charm, and his activities were pursued with a light touch and an engaging cheerfulness. His wit, sometimes biting, and sense of fun can be seen at their best in his topical verses: he was a ready rhymster and could write more seriously as well. He wrote and produced plays, and was interested in puppetry; but his great love was mime, and his ability to train children and adults in this art approached genius. He could be forceful, even masterful, but he was not overbearing; he often got his way indirectly and by force of character. Visitors were struck by the handsome children and the warmth and affection of the family life, due no less to the quiet gentleness of the mother than to the versatile optimism of the father.

The friendship made with Desmond Chute at this time was lifelong, and the most influential and valued of all Eric's friendships. Yet when writing in his autobiography of friendships made at this period Gill says little about Desmond. But he gives the reason: "because my love for him is too intimate, too much a matter of daily companionship and discussion and argument, too close a sharing of life and work and ideas and doubts and difficulties—the only man and therefore the only priest with whom I have been able to talk without shame and without reserve". This companionship and sharing of daily life lasted in fact only four or five years, and thereafter physical contacts were but occasional. The friendship continued untouched. It appears in letter after published letter: Desmond must be told everything, no detail was unimportant, no idea must remain unshared.

Desmond Macready Chute, a collateral relative of the nineteenth-century actor, William Charles Macready, was born in 1895 and so was thirteen years younger than Eric Gill. He differed from most of the young men associated with the Gills at Ditchling in that he had been brought up a Roman Catholic; he went to school at Downside and from there to the Slade School of Art in London. Throughout his life he suffered from ill-health and in his later years his disabilities were chronic. During the war years he asked to be apprenticed to Eric Gill, whom he already regarded as his master, and he went to live at Ditchling, where he learned to carve and to engrave, wrote poetry, taught the children and exercised his talents generally. There he remained until the end of 1921.

In the summer of 1914 Gill had visited Edinburgh at the invitation of André Raffalovitch, a wealthy man and patron of the arts who was a very close friend of John Gray, parish priest of St Peter's church there. Raffalovitch helped Gill by commissioning work on very generous terms, and introduced him to Gray. As a young man in the 'nineties John Gray had belonged to the circle of Oscar Wilde. He was probably the original of the Gray in *The Picture of Dorian Gray*, and books of poems he published at that time are still not forgotten. Then he became a Roman Catholic, and in due course was ordained priest; by the end of his life he was a canon of the Edinburgh chapter. His church in Falcon Avenue was well known for the care taken in its building and decoration, its music and the conduct of the services; in one aspect of him, Father Gray was essentially a "cultured man of taste". To that extent, it would not be expected that he should be particularly friendly with Eric Gill. But this was not the whole man. I met Father Gray only once or twice, and exchanged a few letters with him, but he made an ineffaceable impression on me which is difficult to put into words. I remember his quiet courtesy, his interest in other people including those about whom he knew nothing, his combination of gentle deference with firm conviction. Gill saw less of him than of other priest friends; I did not often hear him talk about Gray and apparently no letters from Eric to him are extant. But I am convinced that John Gray's unobtrusive influence on Gill was deep and lasting; to a mention of his name in the *Autobiography* Gill adds the significant words "notable among saints". That too was the opinion of his parishioners; he was a father in God to the needy and the distressed with that singleminded selflessness and sensitive compassion which so often characterize priests and other people of aristocratic quality.

Nevertheless there was during this visit to Edinburgh an encounter with yet more far-reaching consequences. Eric Gill met Vincent McNabb, who was preaching at St Peter's church. Father McNabb was then forty-six years of age, a native-born Irishman and an experienced priest in the order of Dominican friars.* Gill said of him that he was "so very much our teacher and leader in our views on social reform and industrial-capitalism, on life and work, on

* The Order of Preachers, Black Friars or Dominicans. They were founded in southern France by the Spaniard St Dominic in 1215.

poverty and holiness, that it was natural that we should consult
with him . . ." For Gill had established himself on Ditchling
Common for the purpose of living with his family a certain kind of
life, producing as much of their food, clothing and other necessities
as was possible, and himself earning their living at his trade: a
daily life of prayer and praise and work, of fun and thanksgiving.
It was a life of baking and brewing and stone carving, of lessons
for the children and round games by candle-light after night prayers,
of careful study of ways and means and of trust in the Lord. It was
beginning to be, too, a life of discussion and argument and study;
there were enquirers, critical and otherwise: Hilary Pepler was
more than an inquirer, and he was established close to the Crank.
All this was in accord with Father Vincent's convictions and
aspirations. A few years later he wrote in a letter written on mendicant notepaper, a torn leaf from a discarded exercise-book:

> You ask "Is Ditchling practicable?" In true Irish fashion I
> answer by a further question, "Is anything else practicable?" Is
> not our modern industrialization of England a complete failure?
> England, the richest country in the world in natural wealth, is in
> the hands of the Official Receiver. (a) There are about 1,250,000
> unemployed; *people paid for not working!* (b) There are millions
> of acres not cultivated. (c) There are more millions of acres under-
> cultivated. (d) There are thousands of acres cultivated not for
> necessities but for leisure. (e) There are not houses for people to
> live in. (f) The system is so confessedly unable to give a family
> wage (demanded by the *Rerum Novarum*) that Englishmen are
> asked to lessen their families!
> There is no hope for England's salvation except on the land.
> But it must be the land cultivated on a land basis and not on an
> industrial basis. Nothing but religion will solve the land question.
> And nothing but a religious order seeking not wealth but God
> will pioneer the movement from town to land. O that I could
> make religious men and women see what I see!

This letter tells something about "Ditchling", as well as something about Vincent McNabb.

For a long time Gill and Pepler and Chute had been talking about
the desirability of forming themselves into the nucleus of a society
or guild of Catholic craftsmen, a fellowship not only in their work
but also in a general rule of living. But it was not until three years

after Gill's first meeting Father Vincent that the scheme took practical shape. In 1917 Father Vincent was prior of the Dominican house of studies at Hawkesyard in Staffordshire, and in March of that year Gill and Pepler visited him there. As a result of this meeting Hilary Pepler's uncertainty about becoming a Roman Catholic was dispelled, and in the following October he was received into the Church there. His wife Clare did not follow her husband at this time, but did so eventually, after considerable hesitation.

It was determined that the guild should be formed, but what rule of life was to be adopted had first to be decided. They could have devised one for themselves, but Father Vincent pointed out that something to meet their case had been in existence for centuries. The orders of mendicant friars founded in the middle ages had developed on a threefold pattern, a first order of friars, a second order of nuns, and a third order of lay people. The members of the third orders were men and women living "in the world" in the ordinary way, but associated actually or morally with the parent order and living in its spirit, taking on religious obligations over and above those incumbent on all Christians. These people are accounted true members of the particular order to which they are affiliated (Franciscan, Dominican and others); but they are specifically lay people, and are called tertiaries.* It seemed obvious that a tertiary rule was suitable for the Ditchling group; it was equally obvious that the particular one selected should be that of the Dominicans, and so it was settled. Pepler had furnished a small chapel at Halletts, and here on 29 July 1918 he, Eric and Mary Gill, and Desmond Chute were accepted on probation as tertiaries of the Order of Preachers; in due course they were "professed", that is they were ratified as permanent members.

Saint Dominic's Order of Preachers is what its name implies, a company of preachers and teachers and therefore an active order. Nevertheless, there is a strong monastic and contemplative element in it (for example, the daily celebration of the Divine Office of prayer in choir) to which fundamental importance is attached, as well as to study : the Dominican vocation has indeed been defined as "to

---

* Tertiaries living in community bound by temporary vows and engaged in the ministry and other good works are a later development, and irrelevant here. So far as the Dominicans are concerned, the most famous tertiary is no doubt St Katherine Benincasa (d. 1380), the dyer's daughter at Siena, who was on familiar, not to say admonitory terms with popes, princes and public sinners.

hand on the fruits of their contemplation to others". It is surely clear from this general statement that the association of Eric Gill with the Dominicans was providential. Gill had already met the monastic tradition in the person of Abbot Ford and the Benedictine house at Louvain, and he was later to have further contacts with the same order. With Pepler he was in touch with Carthusian monks at Parkminster in Sussex, and when he became a tertiary he was about to have an important correspondence with one of them. The monk assured him that the spiritual path he had been following was that of the monastic tradition of the middle ages (as distinct from that prevalent in post-Reformation Catholicism): "contemplation" open to all and not confined to an élite of specially favoured persons, the Christian patiently waiting and watching for God's power to come down on him, rather than striving and struggling to reach up to God by his own powers.

Father Vincent emphasized to Gill that there can be no mysticism without asceticism, and this was crucial for him. Gill was no ascetic by nature, but he tells us that he "yearned almost constantly for mysticism", and he realized the necessity for him to "discover an appropriate asceticism". Mysticism, he wrote, is living in a close union with God; "it does not mean living a life of vague and cloudy mysteriousness". Asceticism means training and discipline; it is a means to an end, and must be regulated according to the nature of that end. Quite apart from anything else, if a man is to keep his sanity his enthusiasms must be curbed in the interests of order and peace, "as music binds into a strict delight/the manifold random sounds that beat the air". St Dominic's Order showed him the way.

Mention has already been made of Gill's missionary forbears and relatives. He himself would often disclaim any missionary enterprise for his own convictions, but as the years passed he became in fact more and more of a missionary and publicist, and would sometimes with a wry smile refer to his family tradition in playful extenuation. And not only in speech or writing: the intention may not have been there, but in fact all his work had a missionary element: as he came to say himself, "All art is propaganda"; ". . . the special vocation of the Order of St Dominic, the very reason of its being, is devotion to Truth—and as that is so, it is and must be the Order of *Preachers*, because it is the truth that must be preached and it is truth which is the very substance of preaching. And it is clear that in the circumstances of our time it is the Truth which has been forgotten . . . That is the point, and it was the realization of that point which compelled us to become Dominicans." Thus Gill fulfilled his vocation and rule as a Dominican, and he continued to do so until the end of his days.

And to the end of his days he continued to reverence the memory of the man who first expounded to him the Dominican ideal, who opened up to him the ways of reasoning systematically and who introduced him to the mind of St Thomas Aquinas. Father Vincent McNabb was one of the best-known religious figures of his day, a giver of missions and retreats, a fiery debater, a versatile and moving preacher, known as such to the "Jews, Turks, infidels and heretics" who assemble in Hyde Park, as well as to the congregations of his own communion. The vigour and intransigence with which he held his devastating convictions on matters of public concern sometimes made him a difficult man to deal with, and a writer in the *Times Literary Supplement* (23 June 1966) remarks appositely that his "undoubted holiness did not exclude an undeviating, not to say cantankerous, conviction that the conclusions he drew from St Thomas Aquinas were invariably right". Later on this factor of temperament helped to bring about an estrangement between him and Eric Gill; but "through Father Vincent McNabb I learnt the truth and, through the truth, the good", and Father Vincent's rock-like integrity and goodness always had the last word with Eric.

But from Father O'Connor, Gill wrote, "I learnt the good, and through the good, the truth". John O'Connor, parish priest first of Heckmondwike and then of Bradford in Yorkshire, was described by his own bishop as "a unique parish priest". He was a man of wide interests, of extensive and sometimes esoteric knowledge, and of personal abilities which did not always equal the strength of his enthusiasms, for example in music and cricket. He used his instinct for good antiques and works of art to help find money for the building of two churches. In the words of Dom Ignatius Rice, he was "a humanist in the midst of industrial barbarism, ministering to his people, teaching the school children . . . Father John's real achievement was among men of all classes . . . understanding sympathy he had, and humour and wit . . . and withal a saintly simplicity and insight into the problems of men . . . He used all his gifts and graces to influence, guide and mould men in the Christian ways of life and learning". Among Father John's close friends were G. K. Chesterton and his wife Frances; when G.K.C. invented Father Brown, the priest-detective, it was Father John O'Connor he had in mind.

Desmond Chute apart, Father O'Connor was the closest of Eric Gill's priest friends. They were on very intimate and confidential terms, and in some respects Father O'Connor probably appreciated and understood Eric better than did anyone else. Gill continually consulted him at moments of doubt or difficulty, he delighted in his company, and the third longest series in the collected *Letters* is addressed to him.

Father Vincent's initiation of Gill into the thought and method of Aquinas (Thomism) was supplemented by several other people. There were in particular the Dominicans Father Austin Barker, a younger and more flexible character than McNabb, Dr John Mc-Quillan, professor in a Scottish seminary, and Dr Patrick Flood, at that time a parish priest in Glasgow. The last-named especially was devoted and of service to the Gill household, from Ditchling days onwards. With these mentors and others Gill talked endlessly. The systematization of ideas and the marshalling of arguments in logical form fascinated the tidy and mathematical bent of Gill's mind, and he gave his attention to metaphysics and arguments from reason rather than to revelation and theology. For most of his life he seemed unable to accept the idea that truth as apprehended by the human mind often has blurred edges.

Much could be written about Eric Gill in discussion, argument and controversy. For example, he did not realize that his insistence on the absolute necessity of definition of terms and sticking to the point, with which surely everybody agrees in theory, was for some people off-putting if not paralysing. His hearers did not realize that when he stated something with explosive force or in an exaggerated form, he was often simply trying to promote helpful discussion. Cross purposes of this sort are common enough, and the point need not be laboured. But there is one aspect of religious discussion Gill was continually coming up against, especially in these early days as a Catholic, which retains its importance at a time when relations between Christians of different communions are becoming more frank and open. He emphasized it years later in a letter to Mr George Horsfield, with whom he had stayed at Jerash in Palestine. He thanks his host for his hospitality, but then adds, "I wish we could have had or could have more talk about church and faith and what not. I'm upset, or, shall I say, scratched, by one or two of your remarks—little pebbles not too well rounded—thrown at me. Lack of charity, lack of humility, arrogance and so forth. What worries me, gnaws at me, is that it's not argument to drag those things in so soon; argument is stoppered at the start." These charges, he says, are no doubt true, "but it seems to me that these moral judgements ought not to be dragged in at all . . . We don't get any further, either morally or intellectually. The questions of right or wrong don't get touched. You sail off on a high horse of moral superiority and leave me grovelling in the mud of my sinfulness. You say I'm not humble. How can I not agree? Meanwhile the point of view I want to share with you is not shared, the things I want to say are not said. I am left miserable. I think we ought, as between more or less reasonable and friendly people, to assume charity and humility and freedom from prejudice (why, e.g., assume that I 'imbibed all the prejudices of English Catholics' when I was received into the Church?). However I'm only saying these things because you left me so jolly unsatisfied, in the lurch, and because it seems so unsatisfactory that discussions between your people and ours should always thus be frittered away in recrimination. Forgive me for dragging all this up, please. I can't tell you how much I enjoyed staying with you."

In the early spring of 1918 Eric Gill finished the Stations of the Cross in Westminster Cathedral, and on Good Friday they were publicly dedicated. He had not made the fourteen carvings, which were in low relief, in the order of the events represented, but arbitrarily according to convenience and personal inclination. In various stages of completeness or incompleteness they had long been available for public inspection, but their final inauguration let loose a flood of comment and controversy. Art critics, artists, architects, men and women in the street, all expressed their views with varying degrees of ability, cogency and relevance. There were complaints that the Stations were pseudo-primitive, Babylonian, or otherwise stylistically inappropriate to which Gill had one reply: that he carved them as they were because it was the only way he knew how to carve. They were said to be in unspecified ways an affront to the public or to Almighty God. There were also many defenders of the Stations by those interested in their differing ways, and their opinions were generally more moderately expressed. Roman Catholics, for whom the Stations had a practical and personal importance, were as divided as other people. It was not to be expected that those who had unprotestingly accepted the sort of Stations commonly to be seen in their churches—Stations which faithfully matched the naturalism and emotionalism of the meditations too often read before them—should have welcomed images which were designed, as the carver of them himself said, not to excite emotion but to promote religious devotion. Fifteen years later, an article appeared in *The Studio* in which the author's references to the Westminster Stations were another example of Gill's saying that "the artist does the work and the critic has the inspiration". *The Studio* critic praised certain qualities as evidences of the carver's independence of any authority outside himself; Gill replied that these, in fact, testified to his proper efforts as an artist to meet the Church's requirement that such images should be edifying to the faithful.

The Westminster Stations have stood the test of time. Whatever adverse criticisms specialists may still make, they are accepted, admired and used by ordinary people, who do not feel called on to consider whether or not they are great works of art. As to that, let David Jones have the last word. These Stations, he wrote, "remain appropriate, unworrying . . . They are adequate and right, and perhaps the only live things in the building . . . the workman succeeded where the artist might so easily have failed".

Over the past fifty years and more those responsible for the gradual completion of the interior of Westminster Cathedral have come in for many hard words; and their works are there to show the complaints were not unjustified. On the other hand it must be remembered that Gill's Stations of the Cross are also there, seen daily by hundreds of worshippers and visitors. In the course of an address to a distinguished gathering of Catholic clergy and lay people, Gill in parenthesis thanked heaven that the Roman Catholic clergy are not a cultured gang. When someone reminded him that Cardinal Bourne had commissioned his Stations, Gill replied that he would never have done so had he first seen a finished carving of any one of them. It is true that the Stations were accepted on the strength of a number of small drawings; but there were plenty of opportunities while the work was in progress for the expression to him of any official dissatisfaction that his work was arousing. It therefore seems clear that Cardinal Bourne and his advisers deserved the credit that has been given them.

Furthermore, appreciation of Gill's work in this line was not confined to the metropolis. The Westminster Stations were soon followed
by two other commissions to provide Stations, for Father John
O'Connor's church, St Cuthbert's at Bradford, and for the church
of our Lady and St Peter at Leatherhead in Surrey.

It could well be that the stereotyped description of Eric Gill, "the
sculptor of the Stations of the Cross at Westminster Cathedral",
would have been less common on people's lips and in the writings of
journalists and others if they had been more familiar with the West
Riding of Yorkshire. It certainly can be maintained that at least in
some respects the Bradford Stations are better than those in the
cathedral. Gill now profited by his experience in doing the Westminster work, and he had a further advantage in that most of the
first drawings from which he made his designs were the work of
Desmond Chute. At Bradford the Beer stone panels, 30" × 30", are
at the same time more austere and more alive; the cutting of the
figures has a sharp edge that immediately focuses the eye. There is
the same impact in the terseness of the English titles: "He is
stripped . . . He is nailed . . . He dies". In some of the Westminster
panels one may have a feeling of excess of detail, occasionally even a
suggestion of fussiness; there is none of this at Bradford. Objection
may be brought against the inscriptions in Greek capital letters,
and they sometimes do appear too large; but from the point of view
of language they are no more unintelligible to the average wor-
shipper than is the Latin of Westminster, and at least they have the
stimulus of novelty. For me to say the Bradford Stations as a whole
are better than those at Westminster would be merely an expression
of personal preference.

The Stations at Leatherhead are on a different footing from the
others; they are a product of Eric Gill's workshop, the drawings and
specifications were Gill's own work, but the carving itself was done
by Joseph Cribb, in 1924-25. They are small oblong panels of Caen
stone, carved in low relief, without any colour. Gill came to prefer
Stations of the Cross to be in their earliest medieval form, namely,
fourteen simple crosses with no attempt to depict the events com-
memorated.

The excitement over the Westminster Stations coincided with the
end of the 1914-1918 war, and the two things together helped to get
Gill many orders for war memorials, both personal and general. One
of the first was at Briantspuddle in Dorset; it was a complex design,

and the inscription below the crucified Christ may well be taken as an anticipation of the thought behind the Leeds war memorial, words from Julian of Norwich, "It is sooth that sin was cause of all this pain . . ." But the assurance of the conclusion of the quotation, "But all shall be well, and all shall be well, and all manner of thing shall be well", is not to be found in the Leeds work, of which there will be more to say later.

These memorials, whether monuments or simple inscriptions, comprised a variety of circumstances and locations, and a corresponding variety of invention. He made memorials, for instance, at Canterbury (for The Buffs), at Ditchling, South Harting and West Wittering in Sussex, Mells in Somerset (to Raymond Asquith), Dunmow in Essex, Bisham in Berkshire, Trumpington in Cambridgeshire, Chirk in North Wales, the Victoria and Albert Museum, Messrs Crosse & Blackwell's head office, Rugby School Chapel (to Rupert Brooke) and the wood altar-piece in Rossall School chapel at Fleetwood in Lancashire, which is mentioned again later. The memorial at New College has been called "perhaps the most beautiful of all post-medieval works in Oxford". From his supplying a small tablet for Chichester Cathedral in 1901 to his leaving Ditchling village for the Common at the end of 1913, Gill and his assistants executed over 250 commissions for lettering, memorials and other inscriptions; for his whole life, the published Inventory (1964) made by his brother Evan lists 762 such items.

In the issue of the *Burlington Magazine* for April 1919 there was a letter from Gill (Number 84 in the *Letters*) which is relevant to the subject of war memorials. This was prompted by the publication of Lieut.-Col. Sir Frederick Kenyon's report on war graves to the Imperial War Graves Commission. Gill's letter was very long and discursive. The gist of it was the impropriety of the mass-production by any means of half-a-million uniform headstones, and the desirability of having the inscriptions cut by local masons in any given place with consequent variety in wording, lettering and arrangement. In particular, Gill protested against a proposed use of some chemical process to bite the lettering into the stone. He clinched his argument by remarking drily that "a crowd in Trafalgar Square is very impressive; but if you were to replace it by an equal number of tailor's dummies it is not certain that the result, however architectural, would be equally impressive". It is not known whether Gill followed this letter up or had any correspondence or direct contact with the

War Graves Commission, many of whose files were accidentally destroyed in a fire before 1939; it is therefore impossible to say what, if any, influence his letter had on the deliberations of the Commission; but its eventual principles and practice in the matter were to a notable extent those that Gill had called for. In any case this is not surprising, because the standard headstone ultimately agreed on was in fact designed as to shape, size and lettering by Eric's brother MacDonald (Max) Gill, who was a member of the responsible committee of the War Graves Commission.

A later job associated with the war was the cutting of an inscription to the memory of Walter Hines Page, United States ambassador to Great Britain from 1913 to 1918, to be set up in the cloisters of Westminster Abbey. Gill quoted a price for the work, but was informed by the American committee in charge of the memorial that the sum was too low—if it did not cost more than this, the people back home would think the committee had failed to get a tablet worthy of its purpose (he was asking, I believe, about half of the sum allotted to the committee). The lowness of Gill's charges frequently occasioned comment. He costed each job with great care, basing his figures on what it cost per hour to keep himself and his family, plus allowances for materials, overheads and so on. On one occasion a business man, after Gill had had personal negotiations with his firm, complained bitterly that "This chap is not an artist, he's a business man". He was in fact an easy and pleasant man to do business with, for he was as orderly and conscientious in this as in everything else; he would often say "I am all for the cash nexus".

Throughout his life he was very careful of money, a legacy of the poverty of his childhood and youth, and there was always need for this thriftiness; in later life, when his annual earnings were considerable, his commitments were commensurately high. Though the "enough and no more" was less in evidence at Pigotts than on Ditchling Common he remained faithful to his ideal of decent poverty, especially as regards his own personal way of living. But this did not account for the fact that, in my experience, he always went into the public bar of a pub; this was because he preferred the company there to that of the saloon bar.

Gill's war-memorial work involved him in a lot of extra travelling about the country, and the making of new acquaintances in unfamiliar surroundings, which he usually took in his stride and enjoyed. Nor were amusing or embarrassing incidents wanting. At one mansion in which he was staying for the night he found that the man-servant had carefully unpacked his bag of tools, hammers, chisels, and so on, and laid them out neatly on the dressing-table in his bedroom. I believe it was in the same house that he found himself at dinner with a number of other guests and was feeling very much out of his element and rather miserable. But looking around he happened to meet the eye of an attractive and friendly-looking young parlourmaid who was waiting at table, and he at once cheered up, contrasting her favourably with his fellow-guests. When the girl came round to proffer vegetables, he put up his hand to steady the dish, his fingers met hers, and he could not resist giving them a squeeze. The pressure was returned by the parlourmaid. Eric's evening was made.

In the years after 1919 there was considerable development on Ditchling Common. Money for building was raised by borrowing in various ways and eventually there was a range of workshops round a grass plot, and a small simply-furnished chapel. These were on a corner of the land of Fragbarrow Farm, which had been acquired by Pepler. Some members paid for their own workshops, and each earned his living independently. Among the recruits in 1922 was George Maxwell, coach-builder and carpenter, who came from Birmingham with his family. He was a cradle Catholic and already a Dominican tertiary, a very intelligent man and a studious reader of philosophy, about which he was sometimes inclined to lay down the law. But fundamentally he was a modest man, and a considerable acquisition to the Guild; he undertook the building of several small dwelling-houses. Another recruit was Herbert Shove, a picturesque character who had been a submarine commander during the war and became a metal-worker at Ditchling. On a hillock called the Spoil Bank thrown up when the railway cutting was dug, a large crucifix was set up; the figure was cut from a board and painted by Gill, and was visible from a considerable distance, a daily reminder to the people of the neighbourhood not only of what it signified but also of the religious undertaking in their midst. "The community", as they called it, was well received locally; in due course, Hilary Pepler was appointed reeve of the Common, a job after his own heart, and he was zealous in his care of the commoners and their stock. Local people took part in some of the theatrical and other festivities, and a general atmosphere of goodwill was helped by the fact that at times beer of the community's brewing could be bought for tuppence a pint, licensing laws to the contrary notwithstanding.

The financial affairs of the Ditchling set-up were highly complicated, and an attempt to put them on a good business basis was made in 1921 by the formation of a private company, called the Spoil Bank Association, to own and administer the property of the guild. This guild had taken its final form earlier in the same year with the name of the Guild of St Joseph and St Dominic. Each member had to be a tertiary (and therefore a Catholic) and to ply a trade. Eric wrote in *The Game* that the love of God and neighbour required that the work they did should be good in itself and good for use, and that properly to exercise their responsibility, it was necessary that each should own "his tools, his workshop and the product of his work". The members met in the chapel four or five times a day, to recite or sing the Short, or Little Office; that consists mainly of psalms with a short hymn and collects, modelled on the daily Divine Office as celebrated in religious houses and read by the parochial clergy. Permission was eventually given for visiting clergy (of whom there were a good many) to celebrate Mass in the guild chapel, but ordinarily Catholics on the Common attended Mass at the institution called St George's Retreat, across the Common.

Gill wrote in his autobiography, "the chief influence at this time was our daily life as brethren of our guild . . . we endeavoured to unite the life of work with the life of prayer". He did not believe that those years were unsuccessful; there were difficulties, but they were mainly financial. "We were of course over-ambitious, and it was too readily assumed by us that our aims would be understood by our fellow Catholics. That was perhaps the chief or only unhappiness of those years."*

There had been a moment in a very early stage of these developments when it seemed possible that the enterprise of Gill and Pepler would not be carried on at Ditchling after all. In 1920 they were told that there was a small island, called Crappa, for sale off the Galway coast. In the previous October they had visited Ireland together on a tour of observation of this foreign country. They met

---

* This Guild still exists at Ditchling, though its constitutions have been modified. The last survivor of the original members, Gill's assistant, Joseph Cribb, died in 1967. Among the arts practised at Ditchling today are stone-carving, weaving and silversmithing.

many people, high and low, and were well received, but not understood. They wanted to talk about industrialism and responsibility
for one's work, and they did so; their Irish hosts wanted to talk
about political independence, and they did so. Gill kept a special
diary of this tour, which has been printed in several places, notably
in *Essays by Eric Gill* (1947). No doubt what they had learned on
this occasion was valuable in considering the opportunity offered by
Crappa, about which of course nothing was done. It is probable that
Pepler was more attracted by Ireland and Irish ways than Gill was,
for in 1922 he re-visited Ireland on his own account to inspect a
property not far from Lough Derg. The Irish tour was the principal
of several journeys together about this time, in which they did
"missionary work" in season and out, down to leaving propaganda
leaflets (printed at St Dominic's Press) in railway carriages and other
public places.

For some little time there had been much heart-searching on the
part of Desmond Chute as to his own future. His decision was to
seek ordination to the priesthood, and in the autumn of 1921 he
finally left Ditchling to make his ecclesiastical studies in Switzerland. It was a great personal loss to Eric, and to the Ditchling community as a whole; his quiet influence, the depth and sensibility of
his religion and his charm of character had been an important factor
in the early development of the community; we have already seen
that he remained in close touch with it through his correspondence
with Gill and others. He was ordained priest in 1927, but because
of his ill-health he lived in the warm climate of Italy, at Rapallo, as
a "priest at large" who was at the service of all and sundry of any
nationality.*

But in the same year there was a newcomer, who did not take
Desmond's place—that was impossible—but who came to do much
to compensate Eric for the loss of his personal presence. He was
quite a different sort of man from Chute, but he was to become one
of Gill's closest personal friends. This was David Jones.† After

---

* There is an excellent account of Desmond Chute by W. H. Shewring
in *Good Work* for Spring, 1963.

† David Jones is a not uncommon combination of names. This one will
not resent it if I identify him as the Welshman brought up in London
whose paintings and engravings are among the most valued of the post-
war years. He is a writer too: many esteem his *In Parenthesis* (1937) as
the most remarkable piece of writing that grew out of life as a soldier in
the first world war.

demobilization from the Welch Fusiliers he attended the West-minster Art School, but at the time he first met Gill he was very much at a loose end; so he left the art school and came to Ditchling as an apprentice in 1921, remaining there for nearly four years. But he was never a member of the Guild, for he was a disciple of Eric's mind and methods, not of all his ideas. In his work and other-wise David Jones was a man of lively and searching imagination, more so than Eric Gill, and his sympathetic and critical appreciation of his master's work is more understanding than any other.

Another newcomer was Reginald Lawson. He had been working in film production, and was a man of varied attainments; ability to become a craftsman was not among these, and eventually he became a lay brother in the Dominican Order. His talents and experience did not fit him for several of the jobs that came his way at Ditchling, but he was more successful in giving school lessons to the Gill girls. There was a farm-building which had been converted into a small cottage; it was here that Lawson lodged, with two or three others at various times. These young men tended to be rather serious-minded, and prone to be depressed at the prospect of human life, so that the cottage was derisively nick-named The Sorrowful Mysteries, a name taken from the second section of the prayer of the rosary. In a similar spirit, the girls called three of the young men The Three Graces.

One of the objects of the visit to Ireland in 1919 had been to encourage possible new customers for St Dominic's Press, whose printing and publications were now making a mark. It had a staff of some half-a-dozen, the father of the chapel was an old hand, and apprentices were recruited from various sources. It did commercial jobbing work as well as the production of books and pamphlets; fugitive pieces were a feature of its output, broadsides, rhyme-sheets, and so forth; type-setting was done by hand, and nearly everything, of whatever kind, was printed on hand-made paper on presses worked by hand.*

In 1916 Pepler had begun to print and publish at his press an occasional magazine; it was called *The Game* and it continued to appear until January, 1923. Copies of it are still in request, but by fanciers of print rather than for its contents. These included Gill's earliest writings (some of them unsigned) and many wood-engravings.

* *The Aylesford Review* for Spring, 1965, is wholly devoted to Hilary Pepler and the work of the St Dominic's Press.

Among these last was one called "Nuptials of God", in the issue of January 1923 (No. 68 in *The Engraved Work of Eric Gill*, H.M. Stationery Office, 1963). This engraving gave considerable offence to Father Vincent McNabb. He can hardly have failed to realize that its making was simply an application of principles which he had reinforced in Gill, but McNabb regarded it as an illegitimate application: his own words were much stronger. Gill promised to withdraw the offending picture. The incident seems to have been the starting-point of Father Vincent's wariness with regard to Eric which, at first imperceptibly, led to some estrangement between them.

In his article about Desmond Chute already referred to, Mr Shewring writes of *The Game*: "not least of the ironies that dogged the fortunes of Ditchling is that this small, unworldly and beautiful magazine, with its one-and-sixpenny sales to friends and neighbours, its practical aims of social reform, its pious intemperate utterances, should now be gloated over by cynical book-collectors or the puzzled librarians of institutions".

Mention is made in other places in this book of *The Philosophy of Art*, an English version of *Art et Scolastique* by the French philosopher Jacques Maritain. This was published by St Dominic's Press in 1923, translated by Father John O'Connor, with an introduction by Eric Gill. This book had a profound and lasting influence on all Gill's thinking about art, and it is unfortunate that the issue was limited to 400 copies, so that the book is now very hard to come by.*

St Dominic's Press is still in existence, no less solicitous for good work than before, but in an unrecognizable form. In 1935 it was separated from the Guild and took up new premises in Ditchling village, where it abandoned hand-printing and installed modern equipment. Even its name was changed, to the Ditchling Press.

* Maritain later produced a revised and enlarged edition of his work which was translated anew and published by Sheed & Ward under the title of *Art and Scholasticism*.

Chapter Six

DITCHLING COMMON

concluded

People at large were indifferent to and mystified by the goings-on at Ditchling, Roman Catholics no less than others, but there were some who understood and sympathized. For instance, it could be said that the Guild was trying to put into practice the principles advocated by the Distributist League of G. K. Chesterton and Hilaire Belloc. "Distributism" (a disagreeable word) was defined by G.K.C. simply as the doctrine that if people's liberty is to be maintained, the possession of property must be more widely distributed; Gill amplified this by adding, "distributists hold that large concentrations of wealth or property are bad, and they seek to promote the revival of ownership of land, workshops etc. by individuals, and are opposed to monopolies and amalgamations generally". At first sight it may appear surprising that Gill was not more intimate than he was with Chesterton and Belloc, but though they held so much in common the minds of the three men were too different. Gill respected Belloc, especially as the author of *The Servile State* and for his polemics against the money-power. But he did not share the importance Belloc gave to history or to the European (really West and Central European) cultural tradition as a sort of universal norm for Christians. Gill loved Chesterton (who did not?) for the goodness and sweetness of his character, his warm-heartedness and gaiety, and the wit which probed but did not cut. But Chesterton's methods were somewhat too untidy and his mind too elusive for Gill, who was no "wild knight", of Battersea or anywhere else.

Nevertheless, over the years Gill and Chesterton came more and more to appreciate one another, and Chesterton grasped and understood not only Gill's social ideas but his teaching on work and art.

This is made plain in the review of *Art Nonsense* written by Chesterton for *The Studio* in 1930, and included in the posthumous *A Handful of Authors* (1953). These half-dozen pages, entitled "Eric Gill and No Nonsense", are a condensation of much criticism and comment, and for penetrating understanding of what Gill was driving at could hardly be bettered. Gill himself was delighted with the review, and wrote to G.K.C., "I am most gratified and honoured by what you have written, and thank you very much"; the rest of the letter (No. 175) should be read in association with Chesterton's essay.

Hilary Pepler, critically, and Father Vincent, enthusiastically, were active supporters of the Distributist League; Gill attended and spoke at its London meetings, and contributed to G.K.'s *Weekly*, which was in some measure an organ of it. But I think he was never really at home in this movement, if only because the notions of most of its members about art and work by no means coincided with his own and were apt to be expressed with what could only seem to him to be improper levity. It has been said that "the disillusionment with socialism of ordinary men and women will be hastened. not by abstract moral objections, not so much by inefficiency and discomfort in practice, but by the sheer boringness of a socialist world". The Distributist League ideas were never boring, and Distributism might have become a valuable influence. Why it did not do so need not be gone into here, and its organization came to an end with the war of 1939. Years later Pepler wrote in a letter that distributism 'is still a fundamental conception, but so much so that it cannot be isolated. Like charity, stable society is not possible without it, but it is too universal to organize".

After the birth of her third daughter, Mary Gill had had more than one miscarriage. They learned that she could not have any more children, and accordingly in December 1917 they adopted a baby boy; he was christened Gordian. It was this adoption which six years later found expression in Gill's small carving in Bath stone The Foster Father. It is a work that has immediate appeal, and one does not need to be an art critic to recognize it as an excellent example of the stone-ness of Gill's carving.

One of the difficulties of living on Ditchling Common was the question of schooling for the children. It sometimes has been said that Eric Gill was opposed to schools; it would be more exact to say that he knew there were schools of which he could approve, but that they were not always easy to find and, when found, conveniently situated. There can be no doubt that if there had been a school adjacent to Ditchling Common, the children would have been sent there; in discussing the matter with Mrs Whitby Cox, he remarked, "if we were living in Hampstead, all their friends would be going to school, so we couldn't have refused to send them, now could we?" There was no school available on Ditchling Common, but there were lessons in plenty. At different times the girls were taught by their mother, their father, by Desmond Chute, by Hilary Pepler and by Reginald Lawson: from time to time there were governesses, three in all, one French. Then a small school was organized for the children of Guild members and some others; it was in the hands of a previous governess and another teacher, Ann Prichard, who became a lifelong friend. For the adopted son, Gordian Gill, the programme was rather different. After some very elementary lessons from an aged monk staying at Capel-y-ffin, he went for short periods when his parents were staying there to the parish school at Salies-de-Béarn, where he "learnt to talk French like a native . . . and to appreciate the fact that it is possible to describe the battle of Waterloo without mentioning the name of Wellington". This experiment was so satisfactory that he was subsequently sent as a boarder to the school run by Benedictine monks at the abbey of Saint-André near Bruges.

In 1921 the eldest daughter, Betty, was given the opportunity to go away to school, but she chose rather to go *au pair* to the proprietress of a small country hotel at Gruyère in Switzerland: this lady, Madame Rouffieux, became a permanent friend of the Gill family, and Betty too learned French and gained much other invaluable experience. Petra went for weaving lessons to Ethel Mairet who lived with her husband Philippe in Ditchling village, and she became an accomplished weaver. It goes without saying that all three daughters were encouraged and discreetly helped to draw and paint, even to engrave on wood. They were carefully trained in choral singing, Joanna began to play the harp, and all three of them were given more, and unusual, experience of foreign lands than fell to the lot of most English girls in those days. All this had a setting of traditional domestic life as lived in the country, so that forty years later one of them had to leave early from a pleasant supper-party after a recording at Broadcasting House because, as she said, "I've got a cow to milk before I go to bed."

Gill had no opportunity to work out and develop his ideas on the subject of schooling. Their foundation was that children should be given a good comprehensive view of the world in general, showing the growth and decay of peoples and nations in the light of man's spiritual nature and eternal destiny; and that the amount of formal learning to be done should be kept down to the lowest possible minimum, for we are educated, not by learning, but by *doing*— "that is, in my mind, the whole secret of education, whether in schools or in workshops or in life". In a letter to Denis Tegetmeier written on 7 November 1934 (No. 218 in the *Letters*) he points out that whereas most schools as they exist seek to teach intellectual discipline through books and moral discipline through games, they ignore *"things"*, and what he calls "poetic experience", which he equates with "grasping *things*". His thought here is far from clear, too vehement in expression, and the reader can but sympathize with Gill's doubt as to whether the schools can do anything about it. But one sentiment is perfectly plain: he says, not for the first or last time, "damn art and art schools as we know them".

Gill being so insistent on the proper discharge of parental duties, it is natural to expect that he would keep the formal religious instruction of his children in his own hands and those of his wife. In fact he did not do so. It was characteristic of him that he always disclaimed ability to expound his faith in any detail, he distrusted his own knowledge of it, and in those days when he was still a neophyte himself this reluctance was probably well-founded. (Indeed, if it came to a matter of apologetics as distinct from straight teaching, it was well-founded all his life.) So once a week for years his daughters trudged over a mile each way to St George's Retreat, to be taught their catechism by the nuns. It seemed to Gill unreasonable to burden the budding mind of a child with too much high intellectual stuff about duty and culture and all that sort of thing, and presumably the teaching given by the nuns would have satisfied him on that score. Nevertheless there must have been divergences between the teaching given at St George's and the precepts and practical example received at home, differing emphases, *nuances* of behaviour, and so on. In any tension of this sort, the influence of a good home is bound to prevail, which is as it should be, provided the parents are themselves competent and conscientious.

Eric Gill's children loved and respected their father as much as they did their mother. He was devoted to and solicitous for them from the moment of their birth; he always wanted to know what they had been doing, what they hoped or intended to do, and at any age if one was missing from the meal-table he would want to know the reason, this simply because the home circle was not complete without that presence. They were indeed a remarkably closely knit family, but significantly no visitor was ever, however unconsciously, made to feel he was an outsider. Eric regarded other people, even his own children, very objectively; he was not good at knowing what other people were thinking, or at seeing their hidden springs of action. How he would have handled a "problem child" is anybody's guess, but that is a trouble he was spared: the children in their well-marked different ways were natural and uncomplicated. Eric was essentially a gentle man, a kind man, a patient man, a sympathetic man—but not always an understanding man, and that because he did not readily see below the surface; one or two examples of this in relation to his family will be examined later on. Eric and Mary made a home where their children grew up in happiness and security, bringing all things to the test of "what we do at home" until the time when they were married and made homes of their own.

Between the world wars, and again after the second, the name of Eric Gill was associated in many people's minds with experiments in community living; especially in the United States, his name was constantly invoked as that of a sort of patron of such things. The Ditchling Common period of his life was the only one that gave any sort of justification for this. The group on the Common was indeed a self-contained community in a certain sense, and the heads of households were bound together yet more closely by membership of the Guild. But each family was an independent unit, living its own domestic life in the ordinary way, there was no attempt at communal living. It may be that one or two members would have supported proposals in that direction; as we shall see, Eric certainly thought this was so, but it never became a live issue. Gill did not believe in attempts at communal, inter-family, living; but he advocated like-minded families living independently, but near to one another in groups. This is what he meant by "communities" when, for example, he wrote to Graham Carey a few months before his death, "I am sure that all attempts to create cells of the good

life in the form of small communities are not only much to be
encouraged, but are the only hope".

There was of course a very close contact between the families,
much coming and going among them, and a lively social life, manifested particularly in parties. In a long life which has had its quota
of parties, I can remember few I enjoyed as much as one on Ditchling Common; men, women and children of all ages, singing and
dancing, home-brewed beer and strong tea, seemed infinitely more
civilized than sipping rot-gut drinks in an atmosphere of gossip and
cigarette-smoke.

It was a common notion that the Ditchling settlement was run by
a group of neo-medievalists and Merrie Englanders. But Gill was no
medievalist, in the common sense of an uncritical admirer who sees
in the middle ages an ideal of life and achievement which we should
in some mysterious way seek to restore, or at least approximate to.
He associated himself with a religious order medieval in its origin
and ethos—but it was also one of the most up-to-date; he sat at
the feet of Aquinas—but Aquinas was a man of universal and time-
less mind; he often referred to medieval conditions and practice for
illustration, contrast and commendation—but there was nothing
specifically medieval about his own dominating ideas. "I do not cite
the middle ages because they were good ages or because, in those
ages, a certain set of ideas were held to be just and seemly. I do not
'cite' them at all. I am merely describing . . ." Christianity teaches
that the enemies of peace and good order are self-seeking and
injustice, and for centuries that teaching bore fruit in the subordination of commerce, the outlawry of usury, the upholding of
law that defended persons and families as such and evolved the
noble concept of the *liber et legalis homo*, "free and lawful man"
(later to be superseded, as Richard O'Sullivan, K.C. pertinently
remarked, by that of the "insured, or insurable person"). Gill did
not say that that teaching never failed in its effect or that its fruit
was always plentiful; but it was with the end of the middle ages that
commerce and mercantile imperialism became insubordinate and the
results of money-lending were honoured, poverty became a disgrace
and the rich man as such was esteemed, the workman became on the
one hand the artisan and on the other the artist, men gave God's
glory to man. Nevertheless, "I am not advocating any indiscriminate
praise of pre-Renaissance or pre-industrial works. The seeds of our
worship of riches were sown long before Luther or James Watt. A

great deal of medieval cathedral-building was no more than human swank and aggrandizement", and the religion and law of the middle ages were disfigured by any amount of wickedness, superstition and violent tyranny.

Social relaxations on the Common were all the more whole-hearted for being well-earned; life there was essentially a life of work, for the most part led in accordance with Eric's saying that at work one should be doing what one *likes* to do, keeping what one *has* to do for spare time. Discussion and argument among the men at all hours of the day and night was commented on by everyone who made a stay there, sometimes with the criticism that men talked while women worked; they may have done so on occasions, but the output of the respective trades was so considerable as to refute that jibe. Each family had its own friends and acquaintances, local or visiting, and this greatly increased the number of people one was likely to meet there. There were also many visitors for professional reasons, artists and clergy for example, and increasingly the curious and inquisitive, notably press reporters. This last nuisance reached its height when national newspapers took up The Case of the Leeds University War Memorial.

In 1916 Sir Michael Sadler had seen the design made by Eric Gill for a war memorial, which had been unsuccessfully submitted in a London County Council competition. Sadler, who was a collector of works of art, admired the design, and wanted to have the monument executed for the University of Leeds, of which he was then Vice-Chancellor. The subject was Christ driving the money-changers from the temple, conceived as a very large group in bronze; the work was commissioned, to be done in stone on a somewhat smaller scale. Sadler had to use all his finesse to get the design approved by the university authorities, and criticism soon made itself heard; but it was not until May 1923, when Gill was finishing off the monument in position, that the storm really broke.

The monument showed Christ, dressed as a priest, driving before him with upraised whip half-a-dozen men in frock-coats with spats over their boots, and a woman carrying a vanity bag and a pawn-broker's sign : it was made clear that these people represented the world of money and business. The possible application of this allegory to the wealthy manufacturers of the West Riding was obvious. In the row that followed, Sir Michael Sadler was handling the situation with restraint and skill when, without a word of warning, Eric sent to the press a pamphlet which he had had printed at St Dominic's Press (later reprinted in *Art Nonsense*): it was called *War Memorial*, and in it he set out the meaning and symbolism of his work, with copious comment and some flippancy. The reports of the pamphlet in the press confirmed the opposition's worst fears, and stirred it to fresh protests, some of them measured and cogent. Sadler was nonplussed by Gill's intervention—the date of the dedication was only a couple of days off. He still behaved with tactful patience, sending Gill a courteous telegram urging silence. He continued to ride the storm, and the monument was duly dedicated by the Bishop of Ripon. It now stands in the entrance hall of the Arts building of the University.

It may well be that throughout this affair Gill was not spurred on by moral indignation alone, but almost as much by the sheer fun of showing the money-changers driven out dressed in the clothes of 1923; such indeed seems to have been the opinion of Desmond Chute, who ought to know. The result as a stone-carving is not among Gill's best works, and he was far from satisfied with what he had at one time thought might be his *magnum opus*.

Gill's precipitate manifesto was doubtless provoked by a sudden gust of exasperation at what seemed to him the obtuseness of the objectors, and their failure to see what to him was obvious. It is true that his was not a one-track mind. It had many tracks—and tracks is the operative word, highways defined and confined by rails: and he did not take into account that the outlook natural to Ditchling Common was not necessarily the outlook of Leeds or of Birmingham or Bristol. Nor was his, and Sadler's, chosen theme for the memorial above criticism even by those who shared their conviction about what Gill compendiously called "usury". It is an understandable idea that Christ driving the money-changers and traders from the temple they polluted should be made to stand for the wrath of God visited on those whose wickedness defiles the sacredness of his world. But it is difficult to see its relevance on a monument meant to honour and perpetuate the memory of those who lost their lives in a war.

This affair had a curious echo after the death of Sir Michael Sadler in 1943. It was disclosed that, when he heard the news of Gill's death, he had written some comments on him in his diary. In these he accused Gill of unreliability and bad faith, and of behaving "like a vain, wilful child"; he calls him a "vain poseur, a tiresome writer". If this was Sadler's considered opinion of Gill—and it looks as if it was—it says a great deal for Sadler's forebearance and patience with him during the time when they were associated. But it does not do any credit to his power of discernment. It would be difficult to find epithets more inappropriate to Gill than "vain" and "poseur".

Most important and most lasting of the things that happened to Eric Gill during the eleven years on Ditchling Common was his being brought into contact with the thought and method of St Thomas Aquinas,* in which he became immersed. This must not be misunderstood. He was never an accomplished Thomist, he was not even deeply read in St Thomas's works; he learned his teaching principally in the old way, by word of mouth, from the several Dominican friars who were his lifelong friends and admirers, and other clerical friends.

"The starting-point of human progress," says Christopher Dawson, "is to be found in the highest type of knowledge—the intuition of pure being . . . a man's development is not so much from the lower to the higher as from the confused to the distinct." The first need of our time, says Jacques Maritain, is an intellectual need, the need for clarity of understanding. "Good will is not so obviously wanting as good sense," glossed Gill, and agreed with Dawson and Maritain with passionate intensity.

St Thomas as the philosopher of being, as pre-eminently the philosopher of common sense, as a mind of almost unearthly clarity, with a method to match it—that was what first attracted Gill. And then he found in St Thomas, stated and argued clearly and succinctly as nowhere else, the principles of God and man which Eric used with devastating force (but not with corresponding effect) against the politico-industrial set-up of contemporary society. That, surely both in life and teaching, was the principal preoccupation of the Ditchling days, to show Catholics in particular that the material basis of what is called twentieth-century civilization is fundamentally incompatible not simply with Christianity but with man's natural

* Aquinas was a southern Italian, born about 1225, and a member of the Dominican Order. His relatively short life was spent in preaching, teaching and writing; his two most famous works, both translated into English, are the *Summa contra Gentiles* and the *Summa theologiae*, the classic systematic exposition of theology.

good. The ground work was laid of that social teaching which for the rest of his life he put tirelessly, not only before his co-religionists, but before all who were willing to listen.

And while Aquinas helped him with metaphysical and psychological principles, he found masterly statements of principles of practice and analyses of the evils of the day in the social pronouncements of two popes, Leo XIII and Pius XI, notably the encyclical letters *Rerum novarum* and *Quadragesimo anno*. These documents, translated into turgid Italianate English, explained and explained away time and again, used as slogans and stamping-ground for study clubs instead of springs of action, have lacked the influence they ought to have had in this country.

When his vigorous and systematic mind first came under the influence of that current presentation of Christianity which owed so much to Western medieval rationalism and counter-reformation juridicism, when he was first entranced by St Thomas's use of aristotelian logic and categories of thought, Gill ran some danger of becoming too exclusively engrossed in man's rational powers, of believing that truth can always be expressed in syllogistic terms,* and even of losing his way in the waste land of legalism, for in those days he was a stickler for the letter of ecclesiastical rules and regulations. He was in violent revolt from the confused thinking and emotional aesthetics of the art world, from the doctrinaire opportunism of socialist politics, from excessive dependence on religious experience that was not necessarily religious. And he was now coming into contact with people many of whom, with contempt for the supposed muddle-headedness, illogicality and compromise of their fellow Englishmen, continually lauded the fitful realism and logical consistency of Frenchmen and Italians and Roman Catholics in general. Gill was able to avoid these pitfalls, and he had too much good sense to confuse prejudice or arbitrary judgement, wishful thinking or emotion, with intuition. But most Roman Catholics consistently underrated the intuitive, the charismatic, the prophetic, and it was some time before Gill began to realize their one-sidedness.

At this time I was living with my family on Caldey Island off the Pembrokeshire coast, in the service of the Benedictine monastery

---

* But he used to point out that the use of reason is not the same thing as the process of formal reasoning.

there. A member of it, Father Joseph Woodford, had been given medical advice that he ought to be living at a higher altitude than nearly sea-level. It had therefore been arranged that he should go with a companion to a large empty house owned by the community at Capel-y-ffin in the Llanthony valley of the mountains of Brecknock, in Wales. We had agreed to go up there too, and my wife was to take charge of the monks' meals.

At the end of April 1923 I happened to be near Ditchling. I had been told that the community there was hospitable, but I had heard other and less attractive things about it; so I determined to go there and see for myself. I selected Eric Gill for my attention, his being the name best known to me. He knew nothing about me, but welcomed me warmly; and from the moment I set foot in the living-room at the Crank I was captivated. Mary Gill's welcoming smile and gentle manner (I guessed she could also be very determined), the self-possessed friendliness of the children, of whom the eldest was then eighteen, the solid serviceableness of the surroundings—the whole impression on me was one of human decency and happiness. I was invited to stay a couple of nights, and I well remember my first meal in the Gill household: the bare candle-lit table, the flickering logs upon the hearth, the plain and ample food cooked I think on that open fire, eaten from wooden platters and plates of pewter (scratchy material, liable to melt if overheated), the lively conversation in which everybody took part: these brought to my mind an old tag, "a modest and scholastical congratulation, and thereof neither insufficiency nor excess".

I took to Eric Gill at once, and we sat talking well into the night. He wanted to hear about Caldey—he was a good listener—and I found as I expected that he was a little prejudiced against the monastic community there because of some of the rumours that had been going about; this was easily cleared up. Other things were not so easily answered: he had been told that the monastery buildings were comic to look at (at least they were not imitation gothic), and he complained because one of the monks had written verses and things under the acknowledged influence of Rabindranath Tagore. He was afterwards very friendly with that monk, and in any case the criticism came curiously from one who did not disguise his own debt to Ananda Coomaraswamy, granted that the two Hindus were very different from one another.

The next day Gill showed me round and we went for a walk over the Common. I remarked that the settlement seemed well established, to which he replied that nevertheless he himself did not feel settled there. I made sympathetic noises to encourage him to say more if he wanted to, but all he did say then was something to the effect that he wouldn't have other people interfering in his family affairs. It did not appear that this had actually happened or who the possible offender might be; I did not pursue the subject, but asked why, if he wanted to go away, he didn't go. He then explained the difficulties of his requirements, a good-sized house, spacious workshops, an undisturbed neighbourhood, and so on. I at once told him about the house and buildings at Capel-y-ffin, saying that I thought the owners might well be disposed to let. He asked a number of questions, and was plainly interested. I left Ditchling convinced that Gill would pursue the matter further, and I was not mistaken. In September I visited Ditchling again, to have conversations with Gill, Pepler and other members of the Guild, which now included Philip Hagreen; he started as a painter but became a wood-engraver and carver of ivory, and in the event he was the only member to accompany Gill "into the wilderness".

In January of the new year, 1924, Gill and Maxwell visited Caldey; from there the prior, Dom Wilfred Upson, took them to inspect the buildings and their situation at Capel-y-ffin. Prior Upson returned the visit, being at Ditchling in the same month, and there were then other comings and goings between Ditchling, Caldey and Capel. By March, so far as he and his family were concerned, Gill had decided on the move to Capel.

For a short time there seemed a possibility that the whole Ditchling Community would be invited to settle on Caldey Island. Nothing came of this, but the negotiations about Capel at first envisaged that Gill's would not be the only family to go there. Pepler, indeed, was sufficiently keen on the move to take the first steps towards buying a farm at Capel-y-ffin for his son David. Not all the members of the Guild were equally enthusiastic and the guide and friend of the whole community, Father Vincent McNabb, was strongly opposed. However, the move to Capel was destined to remain as what it had begun: a private enterprise of Eric Gill and his family.

Early in June Gill made a working visit to Bradford, where he discussed Ditchling affairs with Father John O'Connor, and on his return to London he met Father Vincent, together with Pepler and Maxwell. At this meeting Gill put in a long itemized statement on the affairs of the Guild and its finances, a document which amounted to a serious indictment of Pepler's handling of money. This brought into the open certain latent but deep-seated divergences which already existed between Pepler and Gill.

The circumstances of this Ditchling split were very complicated and no complete records of it exist. In his *Life of Eric Gill* Mr Robert Speaight brings together all the evidence on the subject he could find; as he points out, it is incomplete and most of it depends on Gill's own statement, though there is one letter he quotes, ostensibly written by Mrs Pepler, which gives some of the other side. Any overall conclusion is impossible, and nearly fifty years later it is unnecessary. During the next four years I heard Gill talk about the subject from time to time, and he sometimes mentioned it to me, but I never discussed it with him, both because I did not want to be involved in any way, and because I was incapable of understanding some of his complaints: for instance, I did not know or care what a debenture might be.

One thing at least seems clear, after the event: namely, that given two such different characters as Hilary Pepler and Eric Gill a serious collision was bound to occur sooner or later about something or other. The contrast is plain between Eric's care and methodicalness in money matters and Hilary's no less sincere but far more flexible attitude. Eric had been influenced and marked by his upbringing no less than Hilary had been by his. Gill's ideas of how the evils of contemporary society could and should be remedied were very different from those which had formerly prompted Pepler's activities in social welfare; the latter were in the nature of first aid, Gill was for reform, revolution, root and branch. Eric seems to have underestimated the degree to which Hilary's attitude to social affairs had developed and changed, and come closer to his own. On another matter, however, Gill perhaps thought that Hilary had changed more than, in fact, he had. Pepler was still marked by the puritanism of his upbringing, and he was unable to come to terms with Gill's increasing freedom as expressed in some of his drawings and engravings.

Their differences were not only matters of method, but pointed to a fundamental cleavage between two minds and temperaments. Pepler's emerging desire to develop their association into a communal undertaking or into a "Catholic village" was another manifestation of the same divergence: to Eric it was obnoxious. From

hearing Gill himself talking about the situation, I feel sure that
fundamentally he looked on Pepler's aspirations and apparently
casual methods concerning money as a betrayal of what he, Eric,
believed to be a foundation element of the Ditchling set-up; and
Pepler may well have felt the same about Gill's rejection of any
pooling of family resources, however limited.

If on reflection this split is found to be not surprising, the same
cannot be said of Eric Gill's attitude to it. For some years afterwards
this "betrayal" seemed to be a sort of obsession with him; at times
he appeared even to nurse his grievances against Hilary Pepler, and
to allow them to warp his judgement or deflect his will in other
matters. Instances of this will be given later. That the whole business
should have made a wound was inevitable; but that Gill's sustained
attitude to Hilary Pepler should have prevented its healing for so
long, *that* is strange and surprising because it was completely out
of character.

Gill resigned from the Guild of St Joseph and St Dominic in July;
a final effort by the members, expressed in the most friendly terms,
to get him to withdraw his resignation, was fruitless. Of all the
people immediately involved, Gill was most unhappy at having to
differ from Father Vincent, to whom he owed so much. On 13
August 1924 the Gills left the Crank and the Common.

As has been said, Gill's decision to remove to Wales was reached
before the breach with Hilary Pepler was opened, it was not a result
of that breach. What then were Gill's reasons for leaving Ditchling?
The one which bulks most largely in his letters and correspondence,
and in what he said to me and others at various times, was the lack
of privacy and quiet on the Common. The length and vigour of the
discussions that went on persistently among members of the Guild,
both simply among themselves and also with visitors both critical
and enquiring, itself suggests a certain lack of repose in the general
atmosphere; while the frequency of interruptions of work must have
been enough to madden any man, especially one such as Gill who
appreciated the value of physical quiet for the doing of work, a contemplative spirit. It has been suggested already that the number of
visitors of various kinds was too large for comfort, and that one class
of caller was more and more of a nuisance. The impertinence of
reporters became unbearable: "the publicity was horrible," wrote
Gill in his autobiography. "This was partly our own fault, and partly
the fault of our Dominican friends—they told people about us and

made us a show place. What we had thought of as a rather secret enterprise, and essentially a company of craftsmen living by their work and earning such reputation as they had by the quality of their goods, our clerical friends thought of as a public spectacle of Christian family life". Nearly six years before the end, writing to Father Chute, Gill detailed some of the outside interruptions which were at that moment disturbing him, and added, "I wish my workshops were in the wilds of Central Africa and fifteen lions chained up outside".

As for the other reasons, the general unsatisfactoriness of the state of affairs on the Common, from Gill's point of view, has been sufficiently indicated above. He had hoped that a move of the other families, or most of them, to entirely new conditions in Wales would bring about the needed remedies. But they decided not to go.

Eric Gill had happy memories of Ditchling all his life; near the end of it he wrote:

> There were things about our life at Ditchling, when the children were children, which have the . . . quality of paradise . . . What ecstasy of memory could surpass that of the return in the evening through Poynings under the Downs, along past Newtimber and under the round hill of Woolstanbury to Clayton? How often we set out in the morning and climbed the hills by the mills at Clayton and went through Pyecombe and up the Devil's Dyke to drop into Fulking from above. And their mother would meet us at the Shepherd and Dog with the pony trap and the children and we would have tea with boiled eggs and bread and butter and jam and then, oh God, we elder ones would walk home in the balmy beneficent evening under the Downs.
>
> (*Autobiography*, p. 239)

Perhaps it was in the night after such an evening that Eric Gill had a dream in which "I was walking in heaven with Mary and the children. We came upon our Lord. And I said to him: 'This is Betty. And this is Petra. And this is Joanna. And this is Gordian.' And he shook hands with them all. And then I said: 'And this is Mary,' and he said, 'Oh, Mary and I are old friends'. It was a green open hillside with paths and bushes and a blowy sort of sky with Downland clouds."

Chapter Seven
CAPEL-Y-FFIN AND SALIES-DE-BÉARN
1924-1928

So Eric Gill and his family moved to the Black Mountains. These —not to be confused with the Black Mountain farther west—form a small compact mass in Monmouthshire and Brecknock, north of Abergavenny. Four parallel valleys run into it, roughly from south to north, gradually rising and flattening out into a sort of plateau whose steep northern face commands a magnificent vista across the middle Wye valley into central Wales. The second valley from the east, starting below the village of Llanfihangel Crucorney, is commonly called the Llanthony valley, but more properly takes its name from the Honddu rivulet, which runs down it to join the Monnow. Towards the upper end, the valley floor reaches a height of 1,000 feet above sea level, with the mountains on either side rising another 1,000 feet. It is sheep country; the upper slopes of the ridges are bare of trees and cultivation, but covered with coarse grass, heather or ling, bracken and bilberry. The lower slopes, culti-vated or enclosed for pasture, are broken by *cwms* or dingles, each with its permanent or intermittent stream and its coppices of thorn and birch and ash, alder and bird-cherry. The former considerable plantations of larch, fir and beech have been depleted by two wars, but are now in some measure being restored. On the lower slopes on either hand there is a succession of isolated farmsteads, con-nected to a road which in those days got progressively worse as it penetrated into the hills.

Four miles up this valley is the hamlet of Llanthony, grouped around the remains of a twelfth century priory of Augustinian canons, called locally The Abbey, one of the most beautifully situated monastic ruins in Great Britain. Four miles further on is Capel-y-ffin (End Chapel), which gets its name from a tiny chapel-of-ease. This building is still in use, but its importance is now exceeded by that of the adjoining Baptist chapel, which is of interest in the history of the Baptist cause on the Welsh border. Each has its own burying ground. At this spot a high ridge called The Tump drives in between the two main ridges, making a fork; one branch goes up to the cliff of Rhiw Wen, and the other to the pass over to The Hay. The word "End" in the name of this place rightly seems to the visitor to have a certain grim appropriateness; the nearest market town, Abergavenny, is fifteen miles behind, and in 1924 the station, telegraph and telephone were ten miles, the tiny post office nearly five miles away. Such was the place to which the Gill family migrated.

Descriptions of beautiful things are apt to be tiresome, and more often than not are inadequate; rhapsody is not a good substitute for report. But in South Wales there are valleys *and* valleys, and this one in the Black Mountains is certainly a place of extraordinary beauty at every season of the year. I can here particularize only two things. Within a very short time from the beginning of heavy rain, freshets break out all over the upper slopes of the enclosing mountains, splashes of shining white on the dun background, some remaining as small spurts, others gradually becoming threads, ribbons, streams of water which indeed seem to be living. And then, there is the low light of the early sun, streaming up the valley like a golden river and striking the bare cliff beyond the Monastery, seeming then to shoot upwards and be diffused throughout the blue of the sky.

In his account of the journey he had made through Wales in 1188 Gerald the Welshman wrote enthusiastically about the vale of Llanthony. He emphasizes its climatic disadvantages in winter; but he sums it up as "a place truly fitted for contemplation, a happy and delightful spot, amply able . . . to supply its own wants". And he adds a side kick at English luxury which might have been written by Eric Gill himself seven hundred years later. Gerald quotes Bishop Roger of Salisbury as telling King Henry I that all the wealth of his kingdom could not provide such lovely surroundings as the mountains which enclose this valley.

In addition to two places of worship and three or four farms, there is at Capel-y-ffin a large and unexpected building hidden from the road by trees. In the year 1870 there was a deacon of the Church of England, Joseph Leycester Lyne, who had been brought to loggerheads with the bishops by his flamboyant methods of evangelism. Father Ignatius, as he chose to be called, aspired to found a community of Benedictine monks and establish it at old Llanthony priory. The owners of these buildings, representatives of the former owner Walter Savage Landor, refused to let or sell, and as a next best Father Ignatius acquired a farmhouse and its land at Capel-y-ffin. Here he proceeded gradually to build a monastery, and in a measure to people it. The history of this community and its remarkable founder are no concern of ours here.* Father Ignatius died in 1908, and his bizarre experiment came to an end. The buildings eventually came into the possession of the Anglican Benedictines of Caldey Island, who in 1913 joined the Roman Catholic Church in a body. The new owners were unable to make any permanent use of them.

In 1923 the Monastery stood empty and dilapidated. The buildings were of local sandstone, built at various times round a small central grass garth, in an emphatic but elementary pseudo-gothic. Time and neglect made them look more uninhabitable than they in fact were. Diamond panes of windows had been pushed in by an exuberant growth of ivy (originating from a cutting taken at the grave in Margate of Father Ignatius's mother); overhanging branches of trees swept the western roof. Holes gaped in the roof of the low north side; all around was a mess of rusty metal fittings, tangled with nettles, brambles and fallen stones; a wooden outside stair sagged precariously. Inside, the rooms had been arranged with a masterly eye to inconvenience; they were dark and depressing, and a film of muddy dust lay everywhere. To crown all, in the garth near a broken iron fountain stood a decayed wooden cross, marking the burial place of a nun from the convent which once adjoined the main building. When Eric Gill first visited the place, he saw all this, and more—for example, that these buildings stood on the side of the valley that enjoyed the least sun. But he also saw further; he saw the possibilities of the place and the house.

On 14 August 1924 the Gill family, minus one daughter (Petra) and plus two unhappy goats and other livestock, arrived in a downpour of rain, to occupy premises which in some measure had been swept and garnished, and bedecked with masses of late foxgloves. The three Gill girls, Betty, Petra and Joanna were at this time aged

* Details may be found in D. Attwater, *Father Ignatius of Llanthony* (London, 1931) and A. Calder Marshall, *The Enthusiast* (London, 1962).

19, 18 and 14 respectively; the boy, Gordian, was seven. With the Gills came Philip and Aileen Hagreen and their two young children, and a farm worker from Ditchling, Dan Brennan, with his family. The Attwater household was already there, and also Father Joseph Woodford, the monk whose bad health was the occasion of our being gathered together in this particular place. He had a companion, Brother Michael Davies, and they were lodging in a house of an urban pattern inappropriate to its surroundings, which Father Ignatius had built for his mother; its original name Plas Genevieve was a reminder of this, but it had come to be called The Grange. Later on, the Attwaters moved into it.

The Gills took over most of the east and south wings of the monastery, with the Hagreens occupying the remainder, and the Attwaters were in the west wing. The fact that this last family possessed the only bathroom and the conveniences appurtenant thereto conferred on them no social superiority. The ground floor rooms were a collection of various shapes and sizes, mostly opening into one another, and with fireplaces which had to be very drastically dealt with. The distinguishing feature of the upper floors of the east and north wings was the two long rows of monastic "cells". These cubicles—or loose-boxes—were uniform, each just large enough to accommodate a narrow bed, a chair and a small table, and each lit by a tiny window. The wooden partitions of these apartments were only seven feet high, with a liberal space of open roof above them; the difficulties for domestic life presented by such an arrangement are obvious. But the partitions had the advantage of being easily moved and re-arranged to make rooms two or three times the size of one; and there were also on these upper floors several normal bedrooms.

Of these original settlers, the Hagreens and the Brennans did not remain long at Capel, but Joseph Cribb's brother Lawrence ("my noble pupil", as Gill wrote) came to help with the stone work in 1925, and remained. As time passed, there were others who joined the Gill household for extended periods, notably David Jones, and René Hague, who was eventually to marry the youngest daughter, Joanna. It may be said here, once and for all, that there was no attempt whatever to establish a Community at Capel; even the suggested formation of a branch, as it were, of the Guild of St Joseph and St Dominic at Ditchling was negatived. The primary bond of the families and individuals concerned was that of common religion.

They had a chaplain on the premises, and it was assumed—too hastily—that they had a place of worship all ready in Father Ignatius's church. This building was simply the choir of a large church that had never been completed. It was fitted up for monastic requirements with carved wooden stalls, and the east wall was filled by a hideous reredos (imported from Munich at great expense). The whole thing was badly built, and was found to have suffered from weather and neglect even more than the rest of the buildings. In particular, forty-five feet above the floor there were holes in the vaulting, stones from which littered the founder's grave in the centre of the choir. It was decided that nothing could be done with it. Instead, the partition walls and ceiling were removed from the passage that formed the upper floor of the north wing of the house, the roof was strengthened and tiled, and the whole turned into a very decent white-washed chapel with a plain stone altar. Here Father Joseph could celebrate Mass for us, and here those of us who were Dominican tertiaries could meet in the evenings and say Complin.

It was characteristic of the Gills that for them one of the first things to be done was to establish good relations with their neighbours. The life of the small farms, each of which had a sheep-walk on the mountain slopes, was in 1924 still much the same as it had been for a very long time. I myself have seen a steeply sloping field being sown broadcast by hand, I have heard the thump of flails on the floor of a barn : these and similar things were most certainly not general practice in the valley, but they still existed, and their persistence was an indication of the general position. At least from Llanthony upwards, it would have been difficult to find an internal combustion engine used for any purpose. The Abergavenny weekly market—a very lively institution—was reached simply by horse-drawn vehicles, notably the float, a more substantially built version of the milk-float familiar in towns. The "new people at the Monastery" used the same means of transport; the Gills had brought a pony from Ditchling, and soon acquired a second. The veterinary surgeon was itinerant, like the doctor of humans who rode over from Hay once a week on horseback, but this did not exclude the taking of sick animals to a mysterious person called "The Magician" over the hill. The farmers and their wives and children led a hard life, but, as Eric Gill wrote in another context, "The children of large families, especially when the parents are poor, do not complain with bitterness because they go short of clothes, firing or food. Unless their minds are poisoned by jealousy or covetousness, they regard all such hardships as being part of the game of life, and, as is well known, no people are happier than the children of the large families of poor parents when those parents are engaged in humane occupations, even under hard conditions, provided that the parents are examples of justice and charity". There was jealousy and covetousness in the valley, of course, and most of the other sins too. But our neighbours as a whole were simple, kindly, God-fearing people, self-respecting and dignified. At a National Farmers' Union supper at Llanthony, it was pleasant to hear speaker after speaker of these small hill-farmers get up and refer to themselves as "we land-owners". If life was hard, the weather often did little to help them, for it could be very hard too. But "the boy who helps his father in the cold nights of the lambing season does not curse the physical universe and refuse to attend church or chapel on Sunday".

It was largely through Mary Gill and the girls that good relations were soon established and maintained; and the local people were agreeably surprised that these newcomers knew something about farming, were doing a bit of it, worked as resolutely as they themselves did, and were as dignified and yet approachable as they were—and also were good customers when a pig was killed or there was a surplus of fowls for market. Eric saw less of his neighbours, had fewer contacts with them, than the rest of us, but he took a warm interest in them and their affairs, and they realized it and respected him very much, not with the respect sometimes accorded to people who are engaged in occupations esteemed superior, but as a man like themselves.

The farmer of Ty'r Onen, James Lewis senior, was as it were the patriarch of the upper valley: a man of seventy or more, a model of uprightness and goodwill whom everybody respected and of whom some stood in awe. I once saw him and Gill standing together, deep in conversation about something. They were physically in contrast: James tall, clean-shaven, grey; Eric short, bearded, dark-clothed; yet they looked curiously alike, sharing an air both of authority and benevolence.

Some of these people whom we lived near and knew for only a few years have a permanent place in our memories: such as George the Boxbush, who was reputed to wear a nightcap in bed; John Lewis, brother of James, who was bent double with disease and lived with his devoted sister Sarah at Ty Siors, a cottage almost straddling the Brecon-Monmouthshire border; the woman—her name was Howell—who lived at Llwyn On and who as a lady's maid had been halfway round the world, and was an accomplished needlewoman; William Nant-y-gwiddel, who was the valley's best pig-killer; yes, and Isaac Jones. This last had come into the valley years before from another part of Wales, and was, both metaphorically and in his life, a man apart. He was tall and dark, saturnine, with a caustic tongue fed by a sharp intelligence. He was, I suppose, concerned with sheep more than anything else, and was as happy to sleep under a hedge as under a roof at any time. It is one of my regrets that I did not write down some of the stories he told me of events in the valley.

But there was one man who stood in a quite special relation to the Gills. He was known as Charlie Baker (his surname was really Stones), a native of Lancashire and a carpenter by trade. In later life he had become an itinerant workman, and had been living more or less rough in the valley and doing all sorts of jobs on the farms. There was plenty of work for him at the Monastery, and he became practically a whole-time servant there. But he was more than that. He was guide, philosopher and tactful but sometimes very candid friend to all of us, starting with Mr Gill himself; and he was caretaker of the Monastery during the period when it was empty after we left. And so there is to be seen on its outside wall a stone tablet inscribed REMEMBER CHARLIE STONES FAITHFUL FRIEND AND GUARDIAN OF THIS HOUSE, 1928-1935. Charlie lies buried in the graveyard by Chapel Farm, next to Elizabeth Hawkins, another faithful helper of the family, and to Betty Gill who came back to the Monastery later on.

There was an exception to this state of neighbourliness and good feeling, which is worth mentioning only because it was connected with the origins of the Monastery. Across the dingle which bounds the eastern side of the property are the fields of Maes-y-ffin, a farm which was owned and occupied by David Lyne (born Pritchard), a valley boy who was the adopted son of Father Ignatius. He had married a devoted follower of Ignatius, and this lady took up a hostile attitude towards us. The root of her discontent seems to have been that the Monastery was now occupied by lay people, so that the peace of the cloister was being disturbed by worldly avocations and by unhallowed recreation, the embraces of lovers and the cries of children. Mrs Lyne was, I believe, a semi-invalid and house-bound : in five years I never saw her once. No male caller at the house was ever asked in, and even the girls had little success in their efforts to be friendly. David Lyne himself, though a little reserved and tending to be critical, did not wholly share his wife's attitude, and so far as I can remember relations with him and his daughter were always cordial.

On September 14 Eric was writing to Desmond Chute, "Well, we have been here a month and are now comfortable and in many respects settled . . . Everyone in this valley is most kind and friendly. We have been astonished at the welcome they have given us—and the place is marvellous". On the following day, Mary wrote to the same friend, more exuberantly and in more detail, not less satisfied, but detecting weak spots in the set-up. She ends by saying of Eric, "he is very busy and very well and happy. I am so thankful he is away from Ditchling—it made me furious to see his time and energy being wasted".

But his correspondence shows that during the early months at Capel Gill felt rather lonely in one particular. Philip Hagreen's health was bad, and he had not the energy for thought and discussion such as Gill was accustomed to. As for me, I had my own work and interests, and in any case was not wholly able to fill the gap: I could not remember what the Four Causes and their significances were, and have never been able to understand what Nominalism means or why it should be considered such an enormity by some. However, when visitors began to arrive—David Jones and Dr John McQuillan, for example—Eric had ample opportunity for making up for lost time. Meanwhile, almost from the day after his arrival, he got down to his daily work, finishing a stone carving, and doing engravings for a book of poems by his sister Enid Clay (*Sonnets and Verses*, 1925), and also some portraits. The stone was a low-relief carving in black marble, polished, of Christ's body taken down from the cross, a wholly unclothed headless torso; interest in this innovation, for or against, has tended to divert attention from the quality of the work itself, which Eric Gill regarded as the most satisfactory carving he ever did. Other people have accorded this pre-eminence to the one which immediately followed it, that of the head of the sleeping Christ. There is a faint irony in the fact that this first work is now at traditional Canterbury, in the King's School, and the more traditional second one in Manchester, in the Rothenstein Collection. This work was carried through with his usual energy and speed, and in very trying working conditions, because a regular workshop had yet to be set up. Eventually he settled down in the capacious but cold ground floor of the north wing (called by Father Ignatius the "Bible Cloister"), and further accommodation for stonework was provided by a temporary structure on the flat near the front door.

An early visitor to Capel was Theodore Baily, a monk of Caldey, a painter under strong Byzantine influence who had studied under Maurice Denis in Paris; Gill found that discussion with him was valuable, discussions in which a ruling part was played by that translation of Maritain's Art et Scolastique which had been published at Ditchling in 1923. Years later René Hague wrote, "Eric used that book as a sort of text book on which he hung an exposition covering religion, social affairs, the arts, the whole of human life, which amounted to an education in a very special university. Night after night we studied it and allied books* with David Jones and Theodore Baily, under Eric's sort of presidency, and the effect of that study, I believe, never ceased to show in Eric's thought and work, or in the minds of those who accompanied him". A particular fruit of these talks was Gill's essay entitled Id Quod Visum Placet (1926); the title, "That Which Pleases When Seen", is part of a saying of Aquinas which Eric discusses as "a practical test of the beautiful". Gill did a good deal of writing in 1927-28, and three long essays were published as small books, Christianity and Art, Art and Love, and Art and Prudence; the last two he illustrated by copper engravings.

Gill was now much occupied with wood engraving, especially for books published by Robert Gibbings at his Golden Cockerel Press at

---

* About 1914, an industrialist in Cornwall, Vivian Bickford, became a Roman Catholic, and wrote a long essay on the means by which truth can be arrived it. This work, called Certainty, was printed for private circulation, and a copy had come into my hands. It proved of interest not only to Eric Gill for these conversations, but also to Father Martin D'Arcy when writing his The Nature of Belief. Mr Hague records that Gill made much use of what Bickford called "the unity of indirect reference", as a criterion of certainty.

D

Waltham St Lawrence in Berkshire. When Gibbings had first invited his co-operation, along with that of other engravers, Gill had declined, on the extraordinary ground that Gibbings was not a Catholic, perhaps because of some complication introduced by his then membership of the Guild of St Joseph and St Dominic. But subsequently Gill became very friendly with Gibbings and his wife Moira, and in the event contributed a great deal to the success of the Golden Cockerel books. Gibbings was a tall, handsome Irishman, a good companion of lively disposition, and the friendship had a strong recreational element. More than once they visited Paris together, to make use of the facilities offered there for drawing from life, and incidentally exploring some of the less reputable by-ways of the city. Gill's boundless curiosity at times led him into some queer places, both literally and metaphorically. It is probable that more serious common interests were mainly confined to book production in its various aspects. After Enid Clay's *Sonnets and Verses*, the first fruit of the Gibbings-Gill partnership was an edition of *The Song of Songs*, for which he did eighteen engravings.

Already, writing in 1921 in *The Game*, Eric had set forth his views on this book of the Old Testament, and he welcomed the opportunity to make them more explicit in another way. The result was a mild commotion on the publication of the book, in the autumn of 1925. When he revised his essay for inclusion in *Art Nonsense* in 1929, Gill gave it the title "Songs without Clothes", a change for which the Golden Cockerel engravings amply prepared. Some of the pictures gave offence, and not to ecclesiastical persons alone. Father Austin Barker remonstrated gently with him by letter, and Eric replied quietly but vigorously and at length, pointing out among other things that his engravings had been approved by a responsible priest; the clergyman he had in mind when he wrote this was almost certainly Father John O'Connor at Bradford, though he was not the only one who raised no objection. Gill then received a letter from the prior provincial of the Dominican order in England, Father Bede Jarrett; it was a friendly and considerate letter, but he plainly invited Gill to have the book withdrawn. This Gill was in no position to do, even if willing: he was not the only person concerned, and in any case the book was sold out. But he replied to Father Bede at yet greater length than to Father Austin, respectfully, modestly, clearly and firmly. Another complaint about the book was concerned with the text and arrangement of The Song of Songs, which had been made by Father O'Connor and was said to rely too much on Ernest Renan's translation. However, the squall blew over, and Father Bede Jarrett took the opportunity for commissioning Gill to carve a statue for the Dominican house in Oxford. The edition of the book had been limited to 750 copies, and all that the opposition seems to have achieved was to stimulate public curiosity about it and drive copies to a premium.

This affair has sometimes been represented as an open confrontation of ecclesiastical authority and a member of the laity. It was not so. Father Austin Barker wrote to Gill privately, stating that the publication of the book in question was injudicious, even a scandal, and rebuking him in a perfectly friendly way. Neither the bishop in whose diocese Gill lived nor the bishop in whose diocese the book was published was involved. It is possible, of course, that a representative of the authorities of the Roman Catholic Church in England intimated to Father Bede Jarrett that it might be desirable for him to have a word with Mr Gill who had so long associated himself with the Dominican order; but if so, nothing is known about it: the whole thing was private. Moreover, certain protests were made which were obviously expressions of purely personal reactions, and this perhaps more from clergy than from laity. Gill protested, now as at other times, not merely his willingness but his eagerness to obey the directions of the Church's authorities; but when he had addressed himself to those persons to whom a layman usually goes in questions of this sort, he had received conflicting answers. He therefore pursued his own course, and gave detailed reasons for his decisions, repeating them patiently, consistently and forcibly, and never getting equally reasoned answers. But inevitably people attributed his behaviour to defiance, so that on the one hand he became regarded as a contumacious and perhaps immoral fellow, and on the other he was acclaimed as a brave man who stood up to an obscurantist authority in the sacred name of freedom. Both ideas were mistaken.

It seemed to me at the time that this unfortunate business was a storm in a teacup, and I still think so. But it brings up the whole question of what is often called Gill's "eroticism". The word "erotic" is defined in the dictionary in quite neutral terms, pertaining to the love of man and woman. But in latter years obsessive interest in sexuality and the psychological and pseudo-scientific probings and labellings which are such a wearisome bore have loaded the word with hostile overtones that imply disorder, morbidity and even

pathological states. None of this was true of Gill. "To the pure all
things are pure": this word of St Paul, accommodated to a sexual
context, has often been misused, even made "a cloak for malice". It
was really true of Eric Gill. He could not understand why people
should take offence at, or misinterpret, the engravings in *The Song
of Songs*, or that one which had upset Father Vincent McNabb
earlier, or some of his carvings, or his own speech and conversation.
He thought of and treated the sexual aspect of life with the most
perfect naturalness, he talked or wrote of it in just the same way as
any other topic of conversation or writing; in a word, he did not
treat sexuality as something different and apart from everything
else—a mistake which is still made by apparently large numbers of
people. So he was bound to be misunderstood.

And he was light-hearted about it all, "candid and gay", as Sir
William Rothenstein said. This certainly accounted for some of the
misapprehension, for the atmosphere in which these things are considered is so often one of ponderous solemnity, and here was a man
who was as far away from that as from the sniggering of the bar
and the smoking-room. Incidentally, it is a strange reflection that
there are people who utter the name of God as an expletive without
a tremor and without rebuke, but regard it as a serious transgression
to refer to bodily actions and organs in words which have been
debased and ostracized through just such thoughtless and vulgar
treatment. Or are people supposed not to talk or write about such
things unless it be in stilted conventions or in Latin? And if so,
why? Gill had no qualms on this score, and did not hesitate to use
proscribed terms for convenience in conversation or when he wanted
to make his meaning clear to the man and woman in the street: as
he wrote to Graham Carey, "There is no such thing as impropriety
when it comes to saving souls—such souls, our souls, the souls of
our fellow-men, brothers, sisters, lovers".

The engravings in the Golden Cockerel *Song of Songs* were of
course not the only works of the kind that aroused unfavourable
notice; the number and nature of his drawings and engravings of
what are technically called "nudes" were bound to excite comment,
and there were many more, which were not intended for publication or sale. Gill's engravings, drawings and carvings of naked men
and women are characterized by a marked detachment, an objective
vision sometimes almost amounting to coldness: even in the most
circumstantial and unusual of them, the beholder is never moved

to say this man is "kissing and telling". It has been said of Gill by several people who knew him well that their self-respect was enhanced by his presence, they felt almost ennobled; and this ability to bring out the noble quality in everything he touched came out in the works under consideration. In his writings, there are numerous references to the general subject of drawing from life as an exercise of skill, and drawings from life as the products of that skill. In his short introduction to 25 Nudes (1938) he gives a summary account of the subject, emphasizing that it must be taken seriously but not solemnly; hair on the belly is as amusing as hair on the head, and "the funny is certainly a part of the good. The human body is in fact a good joke—let us take it so. The only serious and solemn part of drawing from the life is the technique itself".

Critics have often commented on the detached, objective quality of Gill's drawing, which some find praiseworthy and others a defect. He discusses the matter himself on pages 155 ff. of the Autobiography, where he explains quite clearly that what he aimed at, whether he was drawing a transept of Chartres cathedral or a wildflower or a man and woman embracing, was to make not a picture but a record of structure, free from what he regarded as irrelevancies, light and shade, colour, and so forth. He sought to draw things, things as they are, not the effects of things on the beholder. The unconcern with emotions that might be aroused in those who looked at his drawings was where he fell out with the moralists. For convenience, he distinguished such drawing as heraldic as opposed to naturalistic, and in doing so he was pointing to its ultimate significance: heraldry is an art of symbols, and "heraldic" drawing is an art of signs, signs of the Creator and Giver, a sacrament of God. Human emotions and reactions are no part of the thing drawn.

It is putting it mildly to say that Gill delighted in the human body; he exulted in it, and every part of it, as something seen and touched, but also as revealing the shining beauty of its Creator. I say human body: for it was one of Gill's regrets that he did not take more opportunities to draw and carve male bodies. He wrote to Graham Carey in 1939, when sending him such a drawing, "I wish I could do more drawings from boys and men. I'm sure one's men friends wouldn't refuse. I really must put it to them before it's too late. I really truly must". Six months later he told Father Chute the reasons why you cannot sell drawings of nude men in London Art

Galleries: "(a) Because men are so modest; (b) because ordinary men only want pictures of girls; (c) because both sellers and buyers are suspected of perverse intentions". Reasons (a) and (c) sound almost like a joke—but they are not.

On the other hand, Eric Gill was a champion of clothes as well as of nakedness. He wrote a whole book on the subject, published by Jonathan Cape in 1931; it was called simply *Clothes*, a title which he amplified as "an Essay upon the Nature and Significance of the Natural and Artificial Integuments Worn by Men and Women". For anyone who wants a more manageable account of his views on the subject, I recommend No. 239 in the collected *Letters*. This was addressed to *The Sun-Bathing Review*, and was provoked by an article in that publication by Professor C. E. M. Joad, in which Joad "makes fun of the Papal edicts regarding bare arms and bare knees in churches, and contrasts this narrow-mindedness with the enlightened behaviour of the Russians, 'lying in hundreds in the hot sunlight on the banks of the Dnieper at Kiev without a stitch of clothing!' "* In this letter Gill had some cheerful fun at Joad's expense, but in fact the two men had a number of ideas in common. For example, Joad's famous signature-tune, "it depends what you mean by . . ." might well have been Eric's; but Gill knew more about philosophy than the philosopher knew about Catholicism. The letter, however, had a serious intention, and he makes his standpoint clear: "clothes are not natural in the sense that they grow on man without his conscious effort; they require his intelligent contrivance. But I hold that it is natural to man to use his intelligence. I hold that clothes are primarily for dignity and adornment and secondarily for convenience and modesty (and modesty is a kind of convenience)".†

There was one priest who remarked that Gill stood for "baptized animality", and this was certainly intended as a hostile verdict. Such an ill-considered judgement suggests a failure to control the emotion

---

* Presumably this spectacle was to be seen only in the summer months, for though the peculiar qualities of citizens of the Soviet Union have been well publicized in the West, it has never been suggested that they are actually seals.

† In his biography, Mr Speaight gives a hilarious account of how the then Dominican prior provincial Bernard Delaney visited Pigotts to remonstrate with Eric for his latest unintentional provocation of the ever-watchful Vincent McNabb. What Father Bernard saw, heard and experienced there caused him to leave with his mission unfulfilled.

excited by one's moral indignation. The human being is indeed in one aspect an animal; by controlling that animality and drawing out its transcendant significance, Christianity does indeed restore it to a higher level, "baptizes" it. The struggling Christian—or any other man or woman—who abuses sexual functions does not reduce himself to the level of the beasts of the field : he falls below that level. Such loosely-worded accusations as the above were only too common, and Gill met them patiently and with amused tolerance, for he appreciated the good motives that prompted them, and understood how it came about that they were so clumsy.

"Man is matter and spirit, both real and both good"; that was Eric Gill's invariable text in these matters, and he reiterated it in season and out. Yet throughout Christian history there has been a tendency to belittle, or worse, the material side of human life. This tendency varies in strength from formal heresies to the hardly less mischievous exaggerations of those orthodox people—of all communions—who seek to keep themselves or others from sin, or to answer the question of evil, or to ensure a godly detachment from this world, by an attitude that seems to imply the essential evil of created matter, especially of the human body. So widespread and continuing is this attitude (by no means confined to Christians) with its accompanying mistake of seeing asceticism as an end and not simply as a means, that it looks as if it is a specific result of that spoiling of human nature which Christians call The Fall. Against this Gill struck hard and often, directly or indirectly, sometimes so regardlessly of contemporary convention that some were shocked to silence, and others provoked to calling him names, from "pelagian" and "antinomian" to much less polite expressions.

But Gill went deeper than his critics. He saw the ultimate term of the false mysticism that would have us behave as pure spirits while yet inhabiting bodies. He wrote, "The 'degradation' of making anything useful, the 'sordidness' of child-bearing, the 'mere animality' of digestion : such are the phrases of Sodom and Gomorrah . . ." This is as much as to say that matter is not good enough for man. He was far from being unconscious of the disorders that so properly alarm the moralist, but he did not trust for their remedy, humanly speaking, to simple negation. God is the source of enjoyment, and when we share his creation in the way he intends, we share his enjoyment. Adam sinned "when he saw himself as self-satisfactory, when, like Herod, 'he gave not God the honour'. There is indeed this danger. It is of course and obviously man's besetting sin. It is pride, the root of all sin. But the remedy is not the denial of enjoyment but the giving of thanks. The remedy is not the denial of material goods, but the recognition of material goods as gifts, and not only as gifts, but as gifts which signify the Giver." And if Gill emphasized the goodness of material things strongly and often, he emphasized the primacy of spirit more strongly and more often.

Naturally enough, what are called progressive people looked approvingly on Eric Gill as a champion of human rights, which he was, and as an advocate of what amounted to a lowering of certain social standards, and of all-round permissiveness, which he was not. But they were disappointed when it came to the question of the practices known as birth-control, otherwise than by abstention from sexual relations. There is no extended treatment of this matter in Gill's writings, and his references to it are generally incidental to the discussion of other things. But there can be no misunderstanding of his attitude towards birth-control: he opposed it inexorably.

The Roman Catholic Church bases her forbiddance of the practices referred to on an argument drawn from natural law, an argument the force of which simple people are unable to understand. I never knew Gill make use of it. Instead, he based his opposition to these methods of birth control on the fact that they "spoiled a good thing", a thing ordained by God. This, he would point out, is certainly true, and the consideration most likely to influence ordinary men and women. He declared that the Church's endeavour to discourage artificial birth-control among her members could not have much success unless her ministers and other spokesmen made the most of this consideration, in pulpit and lecture-hall as well as in the confessional and round the fireside. Husbands and wives are not interested in the vital statistics of their country, or in implementing the conclusions of a philosophical argument; or, many of them, in just being obedient: they are interested in one another.

Gill sometimes expressed himself surprisingly loosely as regards this matter. For instance, writing of his parents' large number of boys and girls, he says, "Those were the days before children were regarded as disasters". But not all children in 1939 were looked on as disasters by their parents; and in 1889 many babies must have been so regarded, because of the indigence of the home or the effect on the mother's health. Gill probably meant by the words quoted that there are nowadays, in proportion to births, many more babies who are unwanted (for whatever reason) than there were half a century ago, and it is a pity he did not say so. But it may be questioned whether in fact he ever really faced the birth-control problem; even before 1939 it was, in its purely personal aspects, as acute for individuals as it is today—and often with more reason than now.

Another Golden Cockerel book that disturbed Eric's friends was *Procreant Hymn* (1926), a poem by E. Powys Mathers, but here the trouble was with the poem rather than with Gill's copper engravings. Mathers, who was the original "Torquemada" of the *Observer* cross-word puzzles, was a man of considerable charm and literary ability; but his personal appetites were as strong as his literary interests were varied. In *Procreant Hymn* he let himself go, with insufficient literary judgement and without respect for the possible susceptibilities of his readers. To make matters worse, the publisher's "blurb" was shameless—Gill himself was disgusted with it. The publication of this book was the more unfortunate in that it followed by a few months the *Passio Domini*, the account of the crucifixion and death of Jesus Christ taken from St Matthew's gospel in the Latin Vulgate text, with five full-page wood engravings by Gill. He also began at Capel the engravings for the Golden Cockerel *Canterbury Tales*, Chaucer's text in Skeat's edition, in four volumes which were published in 1929-31.

At Pigotts Gill was to illustrate or decorate several more books for the Golden Cockerel Press, including another volume of his sister Enid Clay's poems, *The Constant Mistress* (1934), and *The Travels and Sufferings of Father Jean de Brébeuf* (1938), written by himself. Brébeuf was a Jesuit who was martyred by the Hurons in 1649. Gill was busy on work for this press during the last weeks of his life, finishing drawings for *Glue and Lacquer*, tales translated from the Chinese; these were subsequently engraved on copper by Denis Tegetmeier, his son-in-law, (1941).

Eric and Mary Gill, his temporary secretary Elizabeth Bill (Ansted) and myself spent the Christmas of 1925 in Rome, most unexpectedly. It was what is called by Roman Catholics a "holy year", which occurs every twenty-five years, and during which special encouragement is given to the faithful to visit Rome on pilgrimage. The Catholic Association of Great Britain had organized, among other pilgrimages, one at a specially reduced rate in which the pilgrims would travel third class. This was a bold innovation. A pilgrimage is not in essence penitential; the participants undertake it to give honour to God, directly or through his saints, and that is an occasion for high spirits. So pilgrims from England were accustomed to travel in some comfort and to be accommodated in hotels. Obviously most people couldn't afford this, and all four of us were glad to take advantage of the new opportunity. We received horrid warnings of the discomforts we should suffer, but in fact we did not experience any that were worth noticing.

We reached Rome about midnight, and were lodged at the hostel of St Martha, immediately adjoining St Peter's. This was the very sort of place to appeal to Eric: high airy rooms, bare wooden tables, white-curtained beds, such things spoke to him of decency and holiness. And there were other good things which no hotel could have given us: mingling with other pilgrims, Austrian, Italian, French; the gaiety of the nuns who were in charge; the meals in big dining halls, where the food was put at the end of the tables and we waited on one another.

We were up again by half past six, to join in the pope's Mass in a large hall above the portico of St Peter's. It was a glorious experience: the Mysteries celebrated by the parish priest of Christendom, the Roman Mass in its simplest form, every word audible in the common language of the Western church. The pope was Pius XI, that very great man; when I first saw this sturdy, muscular figure, I reflected how fortunate we were to have a father in God who had been a mountaineer. Our stay in Rome lasted four clear days, and our visits extended from the great basilicas to the forum of Trajan, the Coliseum to the Pantheon. Perhaps more than anything else, Gill was delighted by the upper church of St Clement (nobody told us about St Sabina's) and moved by the Catacomb of St Callistus. All this was mixed up with glimpses of the daily life in the city, such as the naked baby rolling on the sanded floor of the pub we went into on Christmas morning, and the murderousness of the street traffic. We did not try to do too much, but let the City speak to us; the general atmosphere, especially its timelessness, was probably its most lasting impression on Gill. We saw the outside of St Peter's for the first time in daylight with a shock of surprise because of its unexpected colour, and the dome looking like a soap-bubble. Inside was another matter. Gill was prepared to regret it, and he did: "swank and aggrandizement", as he said of certain examples of medieval building. He wrote in *Clothes*: "If some future pope would have the courage and the power to carve off all the carvings in the Vatican basilica and remove all the mosaics and paintings, we should have a building so stupendously beautiful that even the lilies of the field, who can quite easily hold up their heads before a rather gaudy potentate, would agree that art improves upon nature, and that that is what art is for".

The English pilgrims were given a general audience of the pope in the Sala Regia. We were marshalled into two groups, of men and of women, by officials of fine manners and in finer attire. It is characteristic of the mixture of formality and easy-goingness that seems to prevail in the Vatican that nobody was overawed by all this. We chattered away for an hour without any feeling of constraint. Then the pope came in with a few attendants, and walked down the line blessing us in turn, each as if he or she were the only one. Some time before, apropos a visit to Rome by Father Chute, Gill had written, "I feel that I and the Pope are pals," and the words that he uttered then more or less as a joke were made real for him. He had a particular respect for Pius XI, and after 1931 he made continual use in controversy and otherwise of the encyclical letter *Quadragesimo anno*, issued by the pope on the fortieth anniversary of the publication by Leo XIII of his encyclical on social affairs, *Rerum novarum*. But now Gill was more concerned for his wife than he was for himself, and as he watched the pope approach her he gripped my arm and murmured happily in my ear.

Having thus seen the pope as the father at home, the next day we were present in St Peter's when he brought the holy year to its formal close before a huge concourse. The people there were drawn from all parts of the world, and the processions before and after were no less representative. Of the fifty or so patriarchs and bishops, and half as many cardinals who passed before us, Gill remarked to me how encouraging it was to see so many fine human faces.

We got back to Wales after nightfall, and on our way up the valley several of our people from Capel-y-ffin met us near the Half Moon. Recollections were vivid, but already Rome seemed a long way away. It had been Gill's first contact as a Catholic with one of the two places in the world whose memories of the earliest days of the Christian Church are still living, conscious and all-pervading. Jerusalem was yet to come.

By this time, the once monastic buildings had been got into more reasonable shape for domestic use, and the Hagreens having left, the Gills had more space at their disposal. Much of the necessary work was done by Charlie Baker, and the job of renovating windows fell to me. The original glazing was of course all in diamond panes; many of these had been smashed, and others were decayed, and here and there an entirely new window was necessary. It was decided to use leaded lights throughout, but rectangular in shape as being the most convenient and reasonable way of meeting the actual requirements. There was some disagreement as to what windows are for. Eric maintained that their primary purpose was to let in light, and surely he was right; but there were some who emphasized that windows are to be looked out of, which Eric did not deny, but pointed out that in that case there should never be a vertical strip of lead in the middle of the window, because people going to look out inevitably looked first through the middle. I remember that on one occasion I was using up odd squares of glass to fill in a small opening above a door, and was puzzled how to keep the pattern symmetrical. Eric came along, and I told him my difficulty. "Have you ever seen a cow?" he asked; I admitted that I had. "Well," he said, "haven't you noticed that a cow may have a body of one colour, three legs with an irregular pattern of another colour, and the fourth leg of the body colour?" "Yes?" said I, interrogatively; and he went on, "Very well, then. A cow is a beautiful animal; we may learn from her that symmetry is not all that important. Don't worry about it."

The domestic economy of the Gills at that time may be summed up in Eric's own words. "The eldest daughter managed the animals and the farm. Their mother did the baking, and the two younger ones did the house and the cooking; but of course they all helped with everything." The last sentence is not to be overlooked, for "everything" included a great deal more, and here one perhaps thinks first of the eldest daughter, the indefatigable Betty. But then they were all indefatigable, their mother Mary as much as any. In conditions in which variety of food was necessarily somewhat curtailed, bread was of even more importance than it is in any well-fed household, and many people when they speak of Capel in those days recall the Gills' bread with pleasure and longing. There was a small woodstore and bakehouse just outside the house, and bread was baked in a brick oven; that is, a cupboard-like recess very carefully constructed in the thickness of the wall, closed with an iron door, which had to be sealed when baking was in progress; a fire of twigs and small wood, constantly replenished, was lit inside the oven, and when it had reached the required heat, the embers were raked out and the loaves of dough put in—and not dough only, but anything that needed to be baked, cakes, pies, and so on. It sounds a primitive and messy business, but it is an unsurpassed way of making good bread in the hands of those who know how, and the Gills knew how.* The trees planted by Father Ignatius on the steep slope behind the house provided plenty of wood for firing of all kinds; there was coal in the mines a few miles away over the hills, and this we used too when convenience dictated it. But the casual visitor who found himself at a loose end and asked for a job was more likely than not to be given an axe, a beetle and wedge, and a saw, and invited to get on with it. At the altitude of Capel seasons were late, and hay-making might not come before September. This was one of the occasions when everybody, whether Gills or not, turned out to make and to cart.

Every visitor commented on the meals in the Gill household, some with more perspicacity than others. The evening meal was certainly leisurely, and sometimes memorable. Apart from the phy-sical setting, a long narrow table, scrubbed and candle-lit, with Eric presiding at one end and Mary at the other, it was the readings that aroused interest. While the food was being served and eaten, Eric would read the day's entries from the Roman Martyrology, and then one or other of the girls—or a suitable visitor might be asked—read the epistle and gospel from the day's Mass. This often gave rise to good conversation, though I used to ask myself whether the reading from the martyrology really served any good purpose; some of its entries tended to promote hilarity, even ribaldry, rather than the intended edification.†

These and other religious observances were quite unaffected, with no sign of self-consciousness or flavour of mere pietism; they struck

---

* While she lived in Ditchling village Mary Gill jumped at the oppor-tunity to learn from her neighbours how to bake in a wall-oven, and other traditional domestic arts.

† The Roman Martyrology is a catalogue of martyrs and other saints from the earliest times, compiled in its present form in the sixteenth century. It has long been in need of drastic historical revision and correc-tion.

me as just natural and right. But then the life of the household was all of a piece.

The conversation, in which the youngest and least well-informed were encouraged to take part, did not depend simply on what had been read. Almost any subject under the sun was liable to come up; and as well as the martyrology and the missal, there was kept close at hand a copy of the Concise Oxford Dictionary, to help keep disputants on the rails. It was after one of these meals that I heard Eric read Keats's "Grecian Urn", which I remember because it was then that I realized for the first time why such a fuss is made about Keats's poetry.

Gill was never the man to monopolize a conversation; he wanted to hear every bit as much as to speak. But his talk was sometimes heard at its best when it arose spontaneously at a meal. It was punctuated by his characteristic chuckle; that chuckle was more characteristic of him than a laugh, but a smile was more characteristic than either.

We joined our neighbours in their weekly expeditions to Abergavenny market, and we necessarily had to make the journey pretty frequently at other times to visit a doctor or dentist, to do extra shopping, to meet a visitor or to catch a train at Llanfihangel. After Brother Davies had returned to his monastery taking his parents' discarded Daimler with him, pony and float or individual expeditions on foot, pony or push-bike were all that we had, and all that most of us wanted. Towards the end of our time, an enterprising man decided to run a weekly bus to Capel-y-ffin. Its first journey was its last, for its steering failed, and it came to rest with its front wheels already over the edge of a ravine; any local confidence there may have been in the innovation was thus destroyed. In those days, the farmers and others who came to market in Abergavenny from miles around in every direction practically all came in horse-drawn vehicles; every bit of accommodation for horses in the town was taken up, and floats, traps and the rest were parked down the middle of the main streets. Somewhere about half way between the two wars all this seems to have given way to the internal combustion engine overnight.

Of the life at Capel, not only his own but that of others as well, Gill wrote in his autobiography: "It was a good life and it was a marvellous training for the girls. For the great thing about it was that we were compelled by mere geographical circumstances to live in a way which would have been fantastically heroic and unnatural and pedantic in any place less remote from industrial civilization. We *had* to do our own transport by pony and cart. We *had* to bake our own bread—we couldn't have bought enough loaves and got them from the shop. All our neighbours were doing the same. We were not, as we should have been at, say, Wimbledon, living according to some theory, however excellent."

If there was one question which was asked us more than another in those days, it was, "But what do you do in the long winter evenings?" The question always made us laugh, and became a byword. It often seemed that the evenings were not long enough. They were certainly given up chiefly to recreation of one sort or another. There at once springs to mind a picture of grown-ups and children giving themselves up wholeheartedly to various round games, but this may be a recollection of Christmas or other special occasions. During the later time at Capel, the Gills had a good deal of reading aloud in the evening, with a very assorted collection of books; I remember myself taking my turn at *Dombey and Son* with a discreet skipping of its more arid tracts of verbiage, and also, with no discretion at all and no skipping, Powys Mathers's translation of the Mardrus *Arabian Nights.* But the most continuing and regular occasion of evening gatherings at the Gills' was singing. Here there was first of all the requirements of the chapel for the sung Mass every Sunday. For this purpose we sang, and wanted to sing, nothing but the plainsong of the Roman church, from the editions of the Solesmes monks. The girls had been brought up to it, and there could not have been better teachers for them than Desmond Chute and their father. And so every week we had to have a sing-through of the following Sunday's music. Father Joseph Woodford was a monk and he was gratified by this enthusiasm for church chant, and gave us every encouragement. One of the very few occasions which I recall of his expressing displeasure about something was on one Whit Sunday when, without asking his approval, we had sung the hymn "Veni Sancte Spiritus" to Webbe's tune instead of the plainsong melody. We had a specially good repertory of carols for Christmas—real carols, not simply Christmas hymns, good though some of them are —carols in Latin and French as well as English. One Christmas at least, a group of us set out with a portable crib and a hurricane lamp, and, led by Eric with his whistle-pipe, sang carols outside the farms down to Llanthony, where we ended up about midnight with a hymn in the ruins of the priory church. The real carol was a new form of singing to those who welcomed us, and they asked for more.

But singing was by no means confined to religious songs. The number of folk songs we knew between us was also large; we sang some of these over and over again, in season and out, and again we chose to sing them not because it was the thing to do in certain circles at that time (as it became the thing to do in certain very different circles and in very different conditions forty years later), but because we liked them; we thought they were a peculiarly good sort of song, having an immediate relation to life and to things that we knew. Nor did we expect other people to sing them, as if there were some moral duty about it; as Eric said, speaking of clothes to his niece Evelyn Cox, "It would be frightful if everyone went about wearing home-spun". A good deal of nonsense is sometimes talked about the pleasure and utility of singing together informally, but the nonsense is an embroidery and exaggeration of the truth; and one person who took part in these occasions was led, perhaps with an unconscious reminiscence of "Jerusalem, my happy home", to conceive Heaven as a company of people sitting under the trees on the side of a hill in the evening of a sunny day, just singing.

The idea would have appealed to Eric, for he had a quiet, inward passion for music, perhaps rather inarticulate, for there is little reference to it either in the *Autobiography* or the *Letters*. He does say that "We all know that music is the one thing which can hold us in pure, disinterested enjoyment", and after all, a phrase of plain-chant in the abbey church at Louvain had its part in his recovery of Christian faith. In his reminiscences of Ditchling days, in *Black-friars* (February, 1941) Hilary Pepler speaks of this interest of Gill's and what an important element it was in his life at that time. Eric's own voice was of little volume, very true and sweet, and Pepler says of his singing of a certain Latin chant in the chapel at Ditchling that it was "the most beautiful sound I have ever heard". That is high praise for any man's singing, but it might well have been repeated by those who have heard him singing at the fireside, such songs as "Must I go bound and you go free", "Down by the salley gardens" and the Sussex Blacksmith Song. He had, too, several favourites among those English songs compendiously called Elizabethan. A visit to Dolmetsch at Haslemere introduced him to the clavichord, and he learned to play a few simple pieces with the same quietness, delicacy and accuracy that characterized his singing. Walter Shew-

ring, in a valuable note on this subject in the introduction to the
Letters, mentions his playing a piece by Frescobaldi, and he was certainly particularly fond of the work of the English and Italian composers of the sixteenth and seventeenth centuries. Later on, at
Pigotts, the Gills were to acquire a gramophone, and it was from
this and from some of his friends that he chose to enlarge his
experience and knowledge of music, rather than by assiduous attendance at concerts : he did not really like the concert hall.

As for reading, Eric Gill was hardly what is called a great reader,
and, though he did read widely, he did so enthusiastically or critically rather than studiously.* One wall of the long office workroom
at Pigotts was filled by rows of very varied books (and among the
diverse objects on the top shelf was a small stone carving which was
turned to the wall "when the parish priest called"). Mr Speaight in
his biography provides a list of some contrasted books which caught
Gill's attention, and this list gives a good idea of the unsystematic
variousness of what he read. Enumerating some works of art which
are a source of pleasure to most people, Gill included four works of
fiction : *Moby Dick*, Joyce's *Ulysses* (Stephen Dedalus seemed to
him a very decent young man), *The Tale of Genji*, and *Love and
Mr Lewisham*; and among the books which he shared and discussed
with the members of his family were *The Constant Nymph*, the
several instalments of *The Forsyte Saga*, and *The Prisoner of Zenda*.
He read *Lady Chatterley's Lover* on its first appearance abroad; about
this book he expressed to me considerable reserves, but he was
interested in and sympathetic towards D. H. Lawrence, and the day
after Lawrence's death Mass was offered for him in Pigotts chapel.
The assertion that Gill illustrated the Chatterley book is mistaken,
but he did make two engravings suggested by it.

Historical works did not figure in Gill's preferred reading. It is
true that he greatly valued the historical writings of Christopher
Dawson, and he assiduously read the four volumes of Belloc's *A
History of England*, an extended exercise in advocacy which Gill
remarked was "too good to be true". (Belloc's *The Servile State* made

* The two things are unconnected, but Eric was not able to read before
he was eight years old. A propos this, he writes in the *Autobiography* a
few lines on the vexed question of English spelling which seem inept if
not perverse.

a great impression on him.) But in a letter to Dr G. G. Coulton (who was as unrelenting a controversialist as Gill himself) he wrote that history seemed to him no more than "a sort of highly interesting hobby": so it did, and this was a source of weakness in his thinking. In the same letter, he goes on to say explicitly that he tries to avoid the historical bases as much as possible in all that he writes and thinks; he implies that historical research is pointless, and that, since the knowledge and love of God are infinitely more important than being a student of history, it doesn't matter whether things are historically true or false. This is surely an odd line of thought for a Christian, whose religion depends on the truth of certain historical events. It is an example of Gill's tendency—a tendency which lies in wait for us all—to dismiss as unimportant those things which did not particularly interest him.

Among the philosophical, theological and ascetical books which he read with care were Adler's work on *St Thomas* [Aquinas] *and the Gentiles*, Maurice de La Taille's *Mysterium Fidei* and the writings of Abbot Vonier. These were the days when Father C. C. Martindale was pioneering in English a more adequate way of writing the biographies of holy men and women, but in fact biography did not seem to figure much in Eric's reading. But in his *Sacred and Secular* (1940) he himself wrote a discerning and manly appreciation of St Teresa of Lisieux, and it was a book about that young nun which provoked him to a review which was perhaps as near plain abuse as he ever got: he was merciless towards any prettifying of religion and religious themes, and writing about "The Little Flower" had been responsible for a lot of it. Maritain's *Philosophy of Art* became an armoury of weapons rather than a book, but I must mention Julien Benda's *La trahison des clercs*, called in English *The Great Betrayal*, which he very highly approved and frequently recommended to others.

Probably the greater part of Gill's reading, especially in later life, was for recreation. I remember a very long row of novels at Pigotts which began with the English translation in eight volumes of Proust's *À la recherche du temps perdu*; I never heard him refer to this work: it would have been interesting to hear what he had to say about it. There followed on the shelf volume after volume of detective stories, especially those of Dorothy Sayers, and this was one of the favourite areas of his reading. Characteristically, he read these stories, not just for the tale as so many of us do, but watching for the following up clues, and trying to find the answer before the author told him. This characteristic, with the mathematical bent of his mind and his appetite for brain work, is a reminder that he was very fond of puzzles and problems. He used to exchange these with Graham Carey in the United States, and there are several references to them in his correspondence. He writes about the solution to a "spider and fly" problem that it was "very good and painstaking but lacking just that flick of perfection which the true solution has". Eric was always looking for perfection, everywhere, from Heaven to the hippopotamus.

There were of course many kinds of printed matter that he never, or almost never, looked at. The daily newspaper was one of them, but for all that, he appeared usually to be as well-informed as any ordinary man need be about what was going on in the world. Later on, he regularly studied the correspondence page of the *Catholic Herald*, and more cursorily that of the *Tablet* to see if there was anything there which required his attention and intervention—and there often was. For the rest, he agreed with what Baron Friedrich von Hügel wrote to his niece in a well-known letter about abstaining from ecclesiastical newspapers and magazines.

Chapter Eight

CAPEL-Y-FFIN AND
SALIES-DE-BÉARN

concluded

Eric, with Mary and Gordian and the girls in turn, spent the winter of 1926/27 at Salies-de-Béarn. Salies is a small country town in the foothills of the Pyrenees on the French side, not far from Lourdes. It is the market for the country round about, with industries of salt-distilling and sandal-making, and an inconspicuous spa; there seems nothing to distinguish it from many other French towns of the kind. The Gills' friend Elizabeth Bill, who had been on the Rome pilgrimage, had bought a small house just outside Salies, and it was arranged that the Gills should share it. They supplied the furniture and other necessaries, and Eric rented a workroom for himself in the town; over the years several lengthy stays were made here. On this first occasion the work in hand was the set of engravings for the Golden Cockerel edition of Chaucer's *Troilus and Criseyde* illustrations, borders and other decorations, over sixty in all.

It is unquestionable that these visits to Salies formed one of Gill's "revelations". In the *Autobiography* he deals with them and the impressions they made on him at length, writing with a fervour and conviction that leave no doubt in the reader's mind that here was something of the first importance in his life—indeed, he says so almost in so many words. Gill was happy at Capel, in some respects it fully met his ideals of a place to work in; but at Salies he found something more. He writes: "The experience was of course perfectly in harmony with our life at Capel. The great difference was that the French life was vastly more cultured. It was as though Capel were our kitchen and Salies our salon. And we had the experience, nowhere obtainable in England, of living not only in a civilized town but a civilized life also". There was no trace of the highbrow or the esoteric in this culture: Salies had its small-town politicians, its shoddy "development", its hideous monuments, its hotel which had failed and was falling down, its shabby church full of knick-knacks. But, as he wrote in the essay *Sacred and Secular*, "the only culture worth having is that which is the natural and inevitable product of an honourable life of honourable work", and this is what he found at Salies, in a superlative degree diffused over a whole community. Gill saw the result of this as being holy: "hale and hearty and whole and healthy with a mind set heavenwards". At last he had found a human "city" that was in its degree holy, where he could live a "city life" which was holy too.

Day after day Gill followed the same programme: Mass at 8, breakfast at a café in the *place*, work till 12.30, home for lunch, and work again from 2 to 6; evening prayers and benediction in the church at 6.15 and so home to supper, reading and music till bed-time at 10, "and that's that, and one day follows another. I call it an earthly paradise".

For more extended recreation, there were expeditions to neigh-bouring places on high days and holidays, including one across the Spanish border to Fuenterrabia, where one Palm Sunday they found the church full of green branches with children's faces peeping through the leaves. In speaking of these expeditions, Gill makes one of his rare references to music; coming home through the dusk with the girls, they would sing, and he comments on the number of songs they knew: "Songs of England and Scotland, the Highlands, the Hebrides, of Ireland and France, a never-ending succession, one reminding of and leading to another, and what one didn't remember another would". And he sums the matter up, "Did anyone ever before have three such daughters?"

At Capel-y-ffin the cell of good living for which Eric and Mary Gill were always striving was achieved in its degree, but had about it something personal, circumscribed and in a measure cut off from its immediate surroundings. At Salies, their cell was simply one integrated into a honeycomb of cells, and so they were much nearer their goal. Whether a complete expatriation, a final exodus from England to Salies or some similar place would have been a good next step, whether it would have continued to work, is a question that could usefully be discussed only by those with a taste for that kind of speculation.

The return to Capel after this first sojourn at Salies could have had an element of anti-climax, of regret for a lost paradise. After all, some of the contrasts between the Salies district and the Llanthony valley were pretty stark. For example, the religious and social life of one was dominated by a Catholicism which Eric shared, the life of the other was strongly coloured by Baptist Protestantism, and the contrast between these two interpretations of Christianity, both in theory and in practice, needs no emphasis. Again, whatever dangers may have been threatening it from afar, the life and society of the Lower Pyrenees was a living and thriving whole, while the Llanthony valley represented a decaying survival, one of many, of a state of affairs that was past. In his autobiography Gill gives a whole page to being taken by Elizabeth Bill to a large farm at Castanniède nearby, where they were entertained to dinner. There was a big gathering at table, representing four generations; there was "a most sumptuous and tremendous feed", all of it, including the cognac, produced on the farm, and a spontaneous welcome for the visitors; everything spoke of a patriarchal home and of hard, self-sufficing labour. There was nothing like that in the Black Mountains, or indeed anywhere else in this island; and Castanniède was not an isolated show-place, it was representative and typical of a whole countryside. The reader with specialized interests may be tempted to discount the descriptions of Salies and its life by Gill's obvious enthusiasm and his personal involvement; but he was looking at it all simply in terms of human daily life and happiness. He was not an economist, he was not a sociologist, he was no advocate of a welfare state; "Politics is one of the things I can't do". He did not want "to go to the south of France to find a human life. But I want to find a human life. And if I can't find it nearer than a thousand miles away, a thousand miles I'll have to go. And it's not merely for myself. I'm burning with desire that my children shall know and desire the good . . . And thank goodness, it worked—you have only to ask them."

The year 1927 marked a point in the last phase of Eric Gill's disagreement with Hilary Pepler, and its occasion was the marriage of Gill's eldest daughter Elizabeth, Betty, with Pepler's eldest son David. In their childhood Betty and David were inseparable playmates, they grew up together, and it appears that everybody took it for granted that one day they would marry. Gill had refused to recognize an engagement between them before Betty was twenty-one, and she was now twenty-two. Her determination to marry David brought about a certain state of tension between her and her father. On one occasion Gill, in my presence, reproached Betty for allying herself with his "enemy"; he even turned to me and asked me to side with him on this matter, and when I refused, he reproached me—"And you call yourself my friend". It was all done quietly enough, but it was a painful scene: this was the only time in all the eighteen years that I knew him that I saw him behave really badly to a member of his family, or to anyone else.

The wedding eventually took place on June 3 in the Catholic church at Brecon; it was a double wedding, for at the same time Gill's assistant Laurie Cribb married Teslin O'Donnell. The mere journey from Capel-y-ffin to Brecon was in those days something of an undertaking. On the afternoon before, a group of the younger ones among us, friends and relatives, set off on foot up the valley to Rhiw Wen, down the steep slope and across the flat to Talgarth; there we took a bus and, singing all the way, we arrived in Brecon. At the last moment the next day it was discovered that the clearance certificate, or whatever it is called, from David Pepler's registrar, had not arrived (it was learned later that a postal sorter had confused Brecon in Wales with Brechin in Scotland). Betty took this check in her stride, but her bridegroom looked very miserable indeed. The difficulty was solved by proceeding with the marriage of Laurie and Teslin, and then having the wedding breakfast; after which, the difficulty having meanwhile been cleared up by telephone, Betty's marriage took place just within the legal hours.

It was as cheerful a wedding as anyone could wish. The only person who was not completely happy was Eric himself. He was eaten up with nervousness of meeting Hilary Pepler, for the first time since the break. He even asked me to come and sit beside him if at any time during the reception it looked as if he and Hilary would be left alone together. I don't know what he thought might happen; nobody likes being embarrassed, but there was in Eric a curious sort of resentful fear of it which at times amounted to a weakness.*

* This characteristic went back to Eric's childhood. The children found their father's sentimentality, his emotional manner when reading aloud, preaching and so on, what is today called "shy-making"; there was an element of sentimentality in the grown-up Eric, and he was continually on his guard against it.

It shows how worked-up he was that he must have written to Father John O'Connor telling him all about his fears; for when it was all over, he asked me to write for him to Father John reassuring him that everything had gone off well, or as Eric put it, "without bloodshed". I did so, and that was the last I heard of the Gill-Pepler controversy. But in spite of Father Bede Jarrett's efforts to bring the two together, it was still some time before there was a reconciliation. Meanwhile, having seen the brides and bridegrooms off, we all returned to Capel, those of us who did so by way of Rhiw Wen wet to the skin.

René Hague, himself a printer, wrote in the article in *Blackfriars* which has already been quoted that by giving the world a form of letter that was demonstrably based on the needs of the machine and a mechanized world, Gill "made a revolution in lettering greater than any Englishman had made since Charlemagne employed Alcuin. In that was his greatest work as a master, and his most important and enduring success". Many people who are competent to judge are in agreement with that verdict; others who have some acquaintance with Gill's work and who use their eyes realize what an effect he has had on English printing; yet others, who are not in the habit of noticing print at all and say they can see no difference between one type face and another, when meeting a notice in Gill Sans, or a title-page in Perpetua capitals and its italic, will at once comment on the legibility of the one and the solid elegance of the other. The epitaph on Eric's tombstone describes him as stone-carver, but it may well be that posterity will judge that while stone carving was his love, lettering and printing types were indeed his great work.

Apart from the experience gained in lettering on stone and in book decoration, the remote origin of the famous Gill Sans type face was a series of notice boards which he and Laurie Cribb painted freely to be put up at strategic points round the monastery at Capel-y-ffin. One way and another, there was a considerable number of casual visitors who wanted to see Father Ignatius's grave and the monastery, or even to "see a monk"; the good manners of some of these were less than their curiosity, and on occasions they could be found wandering about inside the house and premises.

One of these notices was in the house chapel and read MEN and

WOMEN, to indicate their places on either side of the gangway. Something must be said about this, because it has led to a misapprehension expressed in the preposterous statement that "Gill thought it indecent that husband and wife should kneel together". The fact is that the segregation of the sexes at public worship is a custom going back to antiquity, and in some parts of the world it is still carefully observed by Christians. The custom is obviously one that would appeal to Eric's tidy mind.

The lettering on the notice boards at Capel was more or less derived from the sans-serif* lettering designed by Edward Johnston for the station names on the London Underground. A further development of the sans-serif lettering was the painting of the name over a bookseller's shop in Charlotte Street, Bristol. This young bookseller was Douglas Cleverdon, who became very friendly with Gill and was a frequent visitor at his home. The board was seen by Stanley Morison, who was typographical adviser to the Lanston Monotype Corporation, makers of mechanical type-composing machines; and in 1927 Mr Morison asked Gill to draw an alphabet of sans-serif letters for the corporation. The work was eventually completed, the designs were accepted by the Monotype Corporation, and thus the Gill Sans type-face came into being. Unlike Johnston's sans-serif, which was designed originally for public display purposes, Gill's was designed from the first for printing-types and for punch-cutting by machine (that was the theory; in fact, he did not at that time know enough about what a machine could do and could not do). He wrote, "It therefore seemed desirable to me that the forms of the letters should be as much as possible mathematically measurable, and that as little reliance as possible be placed upon the sensibility of the draughtsmen and others concerned in its machine facture". As has been said, Johnston's letters were designed for display and were afterwards adapted for printing; with Gill Sans the process was reversed, and the resulting letters have become familiar to everybody, even if they can't put a name to them. Gill made explicit acknowledgement of his great indebtedness to Edward Johnston when he wrote to him, "I hope you realize that I take every opportunity of proclaiming the fact that what the Monotype people call *Gill Sans* owes all its goodness to your Underground letter."

* Sans-serif letters do not have serifs, that is, cross-lines finishing the strokes, thus : **A**, not A.

SOME GILL PRINTING TYPES

ALPHA

PERPETUA

abcdefghijklmnopqrstuvwxyz

ABCDEFGHIJKLMNOPQRSTUVWXYZ

1234567890

Look after truth and goodness,
and beauty will look after herself.

abcdefghijklmnopqrstuvwxyz

ABCDEFGHIJKLMNOPQRSTUVWXYZ

First I think, and then I draw my think.

JOANNA

abcdefghijklmnopqrstuvwxyz

ABCDEFGHIJKLMNOPQRSTUVWXYZ

Man is matter and spirit,
both real and both good.

abcdefghijklmnopqrstuvwxyz

ABCDEFGHIJKLMNOPQRSTUVWXYZ

Artists are no more immoral than stockbrokers.

GILL SANS

abcdefghijklmnopqrstuvwxyz

ABCDEFGHIJKLMNOPQRSTUVWXYZ

We are to be children in heart, not in intellect.

abcdefghijklmnopqrstuvwxyz

ABCDEFGHIJKLMNOPQRSTUVWXYZ

Magnificat anima mea Dominum

OMEGA

This, then, was the beginning of Gill's work as a designer of printing-types, but it was also the beginning of something else of personal importance, namely his close association (indeed, co-operation) with that business world he so often attacked. It was, in fact, his relations with the Monotype Corporation* which in the *Autobiography* are the occasion of his saying, "few associations can have been more honourable or more pleasant—or, from my point of view, more helpful". And he goes on to disclaim any intention in his attacks of imputing malice or wickedness to any individual man of business; so many of those whom he had met were "more than nice", men with inherited traditions of honesty and good service, trying to maintain those traditions within a system that must prove fatal to them sooner or later. His meeting with Stanley Morison was the beginning of a long friendship, and of a considerable and valuable correspondence, which unfortunately was destroyed during the 1939-45 war.†

Through Morison he met Beatrice Warde, a faithful friend whose writings on typography in general and Gill's work in particular were always read with respect. The men with whom he worked were as attracted by him as he was happy to meet them; the technical staff learned to regard him as one of themselves, and years later in *The Monotype Recorder* of autumn 1958, a mechanical engineer is quoted as recalling that "you never would have put him down as a famous artist. You'd sooner have said he was a good mechanic, or anyway some good workman who knew his job". No verdict from a fellow worker could have given Gill more pleasure.

Some people who were sympathetic towards, even enthusiastically in favour of, Gill's ideas on the subject of industrialism and massproduction were sharply critical of his increasing association with the industrial world. But they had been insufficiently attentive to what he used to say about "teetotalism", and did not understand

* Not necessarily his first contact with big business. Gill was asked by Gordon Selfridge to submit drawings of letters for notices in his emporium. When he called with them at the office, Selfridge greeted him with the words, "Well, Mr Gill, I hope you've got something good to show me"; to which Gill replied in his usual modest way, "I've done my best, Mr Selfridge". And Mr Selfridge said, "Oh come, Mr Gill, we want something better than that".

† Together with the whole of Morison's library. Among his many distinctions he was designer of the Times New Roman type face. He refused knighthood three times.

what he really thought about machines and all that goes with them. He repeated time and again that the primary objection to industrialism is its effects on the people concerned, both employers and employed, not the quality of its products, bad as so many of these are. Industrialism is perfectly capable of producing things good of their kind, but so often fails to do so because machines are owned and controlled not by those who design or use them but by persons whose one concern is profits. The Monotype Corporation offered him, a designer and user, a workman, an opportunity to take a hand in the game, to show so far as one man could that for the workman to develop his proper responsibility to the full is good for industry as well as for the workman. Moreover, he had his living to earn; a man's first duty is to himself and his family, and he has to meet that responsibility within the conditions imposed by the society in which he lives, however wrong and bad these conditions may be. The attitude of his critics in accusing him of inconsistency was an understandable mistake, but in fact he was being quite consistent with himself. The situation was recurrent.

Looking forward a little, towards the end of 1928 Gill's book face Perpetua made its first public appearance in the seventh issue of *The Fleuron*.* This type originated in letters drawn with brush and ink, without reference to printing; but the skill of the Monotype workers produced a fount which had those characteristics which Gill looked for in a good book-type, "commonplaceness and normality"; the success of Perpetua was immediate and lasting. The first book in which it was used was published in the following year, by Cassell and Francis Waterson. It was called *Art Nonsense*, and consisted of reprints, revised, of twenty-four of Eric's own shorter writings, beginning with the first of them, a couple of pages on Slavery and Freedom in 1918. They included *Songs without Clothes*; *Id Quod Visum Placet*; *Art and Love*; *Architecture and Sculpture*; *Christianity and Art*; and *The Future of Sculpture*. A peculiarity of this first edition which at once catches the eye is that words and phrases which would have been printed in italic are all in roman, but underlined. This was because the italic type corresponding to Perpetua, which was to have been called Felicity, was not yet available.

* It was in the form of an inset (dated 1929) consisting of a translation by W. H. Shewring of the contemporary account of the martyrdom, at Carthage in 203, of SS. Perpetua and Felicity. Hence the name of the type face.

Looking forward yet further, Gill designed eleven type faces in all, only one of which, the Arabic, was never cut; in addition to Perpetua and Gill Sans, they were Golden Cockerel, Solus, Perpetua Greek, Joanna, Aries, Jubilee, Bunyan, Hebrew and Arabic. Of these, five were cut by the Monotype Corporation, four by Caslon, and one by Stephenson Blake and Co. Ltd.

Apart from tombstones and other inscriptions, the demand for which was steadily increasing, there was not a great deal of sculpture done at Capel, after the Deposition and the Sleeping Christ which have already been mentioned. As an example of the sometimes almost casual way in which he appeared to work, I remember one day at this time going through the workshop in which Eric was busy on a crucifix, when he called me over to him. I stood by his side to see what he wanted, when he rolled up my trouser leg and took a glance at my knee: "All right, thank you", he said, "I only wanted to remind myself what a knee looks like". In 1925 there was one of those controversies which break out from time to time about some public monument or a picture and so on: it concerned the monument in Hyde Park to the memory of W. H. Hudson which represented the character in *The Purple Land*, Rima, and was the work of Jacob Epstein. However, Gill was in the thick of it because he was in London cutting the inscription on this monument. He was careful what he said in public about Epstein's carving, because he did not wish to be too outspoken about the work of a man with whom he had formerly been closely associated; my own impression was that he thought the design acceptable, but its execution discreditable. Anyway, young Gordian Gill at Capel found a suitably shaped slab of stone on the hill behind the house; he got help to drag it down to the workshop, and on it Gill produced a characteristic piece of carving in relief of a girl holding up her flowing hair, a theme clearly suggested by the Hyde Park Rima. This work in Capel-y-ffin stone became the property of Sir Francis Meynell, who years before with the help of Stanley Morison had brought about a revolution in the printing and production of the books of the Roman Catholic publishing firm of Burns and Oates.

It was during the Capel period that Gill carved his monumental "Mankind", but the work had to be done at a studio lent to him in Chelsea. It became the principal exhibit in a show including Gill's

Reproduced from engravings for "The Song of the Soul"
by St John-of-the-Cross (translation, 1927)

work held at the Goupil Gallery in March 1928: a more than life-size figure of a woman, from below the neck to just below the knees, in polished Hoptonwood stone, whose calm dignity and classic beauty made the name of Mankind appropriate. This work is now in the Tate Gallery. At the other end of the scale, both in size and conception, was a carving called "Head-dress", a rather exotic piece which Gill himself was specially fond of. Among the other exhibits was the cartoon by Gill for a war memorial in the chapel at Rossall School; it was an oaken altar-piece, showing the crucified Christ with attendant figures, and at the ends St John baptizing Jesus and the Baptist's own execution. This venture into wood-carving received warm commendation from the critics of the day, who were loud in their praise of the works which Gill had shown.

The shrewdness of the judgement of those who saw in this exhibition Gill's return from what they perhaps regarded as the wilderness of craftsmanship to the garden enclosed of fine art can hardly be disputed. For those who cannot accept that the distinction between craftsmanship and art is a proper one, the exhibition simply confirmed that Gill was a magnificent workman. Gill did not care either way. In a letter to Desmond Chute he showed a certain incredulity at the enthusiasm of the professional critics and was full of jubilation at the financial success of the show—"We can breathe freely for a bit and really pay our debts".

But the official art world had the last word. Even before the Goupil exhibition was closed Eric received a letter from the sculptor Reid Dick, asking for permission to enter Gill's name in the nomination book of the Royal Academy. Gill replied at some length. He took the line that he was an outsider, without any of the appropriate academic qualifications, and in support of this he gives an account of what training he had received, beginning with certificates in perspective drawing and geometry earned at evening classes at Chichester, and ending with evening classes in lettering and picture-frame making. Finally he says ". . . it is one thing to *receive* this honour, and quite another to ask for it. In brief, I should regard my acceptance by the R.A. as an honour conferred. I do not regard it as a thing for which I have a natural right to be nominated". He was in fact made an Associate of the Royal Academy ten years later.

It is clear from what has been said that during the years of his residence at Capel-y-ffin, Gill was often away from home, sometimes for lengthy periods. As one of the other residents there I find that, looking back after forty years, these absences do not obtrude in my recollections: Eric seems always to have been there, I do not ever picture the Capel of those days without him. And there is plenty of evidence that when he was away, the Llanthony valley was continually in his heart and his mind, even at Salies, where comparison and contrast of the two places were always present with him. One of his reasons for leaving Ditchling was that it was so easy there for people to make casual calls, for reporters to come scouting for "stories" for their newspapers, and so on. He complained to me that, once a Catholic gets into the news, he is never again allowed to have a private life; but he had experienced something of the sort before ever he was a Catholic. Capel was remote enough; apart from holiday-makers and the like during the summer months, the only people who penetrated there were those who had a good reason for coming. This does not mean that there were not a fair number of visitors, but they were generally friends who made a short stay.

Two whose visits were frequent and always welcome were David Jones and Denis Tegetmeier, and each left his mark on the building as it stands today. On the wall of the "Bible cloister" there is a painting of a young Jesus on the cross, made by David; on the opposite wall at the other end there is a painting light-heartedly depicting the practice of lettering through the ages, done by Denis much later. This was at a time when Eric had a passing fad for the system of shorthand called Phonography, which he proposed should be taught in the school started at Capel by his daughter Betty and Miss May Reeves.

From time to time individual monks from Caldey came on short visits, including the prior, Dom Wilfred Upson, whom we were always glad to see; he was a man of attractive presence and varied accomplishments which included a remarkable skill in fireside conjuring.* Eric always remained faithful to the Dominican connexion and influence, though actually this was largely a matter of a limited circle of friars, and exercised in part through diocesan priests, Canon Gray, Dr P. J. Flood, and others. But the Benedictine tradition (e.g. as set out in Abbot Cuthbert Butler's *Benedictine Monachism*) influenced him in some degree especially as he grew older; had he been under this influence from the first, his development would doubtless have been rather different.

* Like Eric, Father Wilfrid had been brought up religiously as a child in the Countess of Huntingdon's Connexion.

Eric Gill

Arthur Tidman Gill

Rose Gill

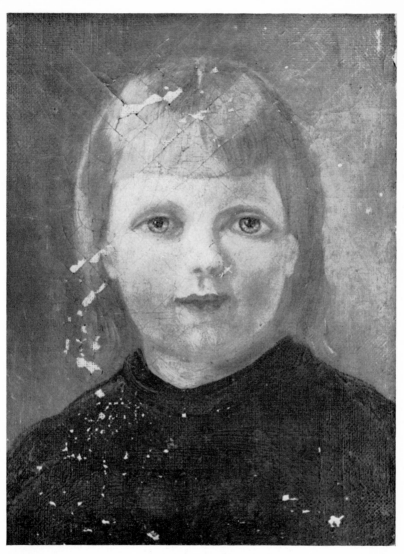

Eric as a child
from a portrait painted by his father

Mary Ethel Gill
from a drawing by her husband, 1940

Ditchling Common
Top: Hopkin's Crank
Below: Workshops and Chapel

Top: in St Cuthbert's Church, Bradford. Size, 2 ft 6 ins by
2 ft 6 ins

Below: in Westminster Cathedral. Size, 5 ft 8 ins by 5 ft 8 ins

War Memorial at the University of Leeds, 1923

Capel-y-ffin

The Monastery and Grange in the middle distance

Incised Alphabet, 1932

The Sleeping Christ, 1925

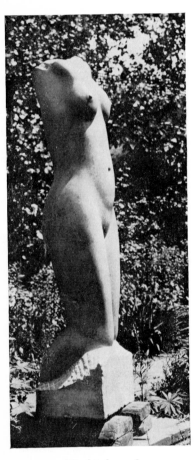

Mankind, 1928
in the Tate Gallery, London

The Sower, 1931
in Broadcasting House, London

Deposition, 1925
Christ's body taken down
from the cross

Christ the King
with the Virgin Mary and Mary Magda
on headstone at Clovelly, Devon (1930

Pigotts from the air

Workshop at Pigotts

Child-bed

Marriage-bed

Death-bed

Head-board of Bedstead
carved in oak for Mr Graham Carey, 1929

The Re-creation of Man

One visitor to Capel must be specially mentioned, Gill's former patron Count Harry Kessler, who arrived after dark one evening in January 1925. It was their first meeting since before the war of 1914-18, and something of an event for both of them. In his diary Kessler records that Gill remarked that since the war art had lost its first place with him, which had been taken by a search for the renewal of life, and this had brought him and his family away from the narrowness of Ditchling into the wilderness. Kessler judged that the venture had so far been successful, and that those involved in it were enjoying themselves.

Some of Kessler's impressions were amusingly common form: he seems to have been one of those people who have rather romantic notions of monks and monasteries, and tend to see evidences of monasticism where these do not exist, a mistake made more easy on this occasion by the fact that Prior Wilfred of Caldey was staying with the Gills.* With his particular continental background it was natural enough for Kessler to see in Eric Gill a Tolstoyan figure; but the working smock of a stonemason took on in his eyes the amplitude and dignity of a monk's habit; a little later he referred to Eric as looking like a mendicant friar, and turned his smock into a cowl.

Kessler had come to Capel in the hope of enlisting Gill's help in the decoration of an edition of Virgil's *Georgics*; he examined examples of recent work done by Gill, and they finally agreed that he should do initial letters for the projected book. By the time their talk and business were completed it was getting on for the middle of the night. Kessler had come out from Abergavenny in a taxi, whose driver had had considerable difficulty in finding the way. This man had now spent several hours contemplating the problem of the return journey, and getting more and more impatient to be home. At length he sent in a polite enquiry to his fare, asking when he would be ready to go back, pointing out the lateness of the hour and the dangers of the road. To which Count Kessler replied haughtily, "Tell him to go to hell". The message was not delivered in that form. It may be added that Kessler remarked in his diary in, as it were, a surprised tone of voice that the Gills were living without any servants whatever.

* Misunderstandings of this sort were a perennial nuisance at Capel, as at Ditchling. Very early on we tried to discourage them by giving The Monastery a more non-committal name, but local usage was too strong for us: a monastery it had been, and The Monastery it remained.

There were further meetings between Gill and Kessler in London a few weeks later, in Paris in 1927, and at Weimar in 1930, and the first two of these are referred to in Kessler's diary.* Kessler was not the man to be shocked by any manifestations of the sexual aspect of human beings; but Gill was obviously a religious man, a Christian at that, and the perfect naturalness and plain speaking of his attitude to these things seems to have startled Kessler. Doubtless the combination was unfamiliar to him, though it must be supposed that he knew of the long Christian tradition of signifying divine love by human love—indeed, he was going to commission Gill again to illustrate The Song of Songs. He answered the problem for himself by lumping together a number of disparate characteristics in Gill, or which he thought he saw in Gill, and calling the result "pantheistic lasciviousness", dragging in references to Van Gogh and the hermits of the Egyptian desert. On the other hand, in the diary he attributes to Gill certain declarations and sentiments which on the face of it do appear startling enough, as for example that "it was high time for one to create works of art that would shake the morals that have poisoned us all to their foundations". But it does not appear that Kessler tried to get from Gill exactly what he meant by such statements, and had he known him better, the question would have been unnecessary, for the answers were to be found time and again in Gill's speech and writing.

In Weimar Gill met for the second time the sculptor and engraver Aristide Maillol, then at the height of his reputation. His verdict to Count Kessler on Gill's engravings had been "not bad, but too facile". Nevertheless, Gill engraved initial letters and eleven illustrations for Kessler's Cranach Press edition of The Song of Songs; the text was that of the Latin Vulgate, and the book was published in 1931.

"I did not ever intend to leave Capel, I did not anticipate any reason for doing so. The distance . . . was no hardship and made no

---

* This was a work of considerable interest, for the range of his friendships extended from André Gide to George Bernard Shaw, from Einstein to Isadora Duncan, from Brecht to Diaghilev. It was published in Germany in 1961, Tagebücher 1918-37. The passages relating to Gill are printed in Speaight's biography. They also appear in Encounter (July and August 1967) with a number of other extracts, but there they are in an abbreviated form.

serious difficulties to my work, so from my point of view there was no reason for moving." Those are Eric Gill's own considered words (*Autobiography*, p. 227).

For some time life for the Gills there had been getting increasingly difficult. In the same letter which tells Father Chute about the success of the Goupil exhibition, Eric said, "C-y-ff is v. heavenly—but . . . whether we stay here or not when P[etra] gets married remains to be seen. V. difficult for Mary with only Joanna". This was written on 25 March 1928. Moreover, it became known that Father Joseph Woodford's health required that he should go away for long treatment elsewhere, and that the Prior of Caldey could not spare anybody to take his place. It was because of Father Joseph that the Gills had been able to come to Capel, and his departure was weighty among the reasons for their leaving. He was a gentle, simple man, who for most of the time lived in a sort of hermitage constructed near the south wall of the ruined church; he must have been very puzzled by the curious and assorted gang of which he found himself in pastoral charge. Eric was much attached to him, seeing in him a good monk "who knows that contemplation is the secret key to all things".

And so it was decided that another move must be made. In his autobiography, Gill makes it quite clear what the reasons were. The first was Betty's marriage, which had deprived household and farm of one of its chief workers; more work still in the house was put upon those who remained by the Attwaters moving from their wing of the monastery to The Grange, and eventually away altogether; and then the loss of Father Joseph left them without a chaplain and the nearest Catholic church impossibly distant. "It was not my work," Gill says, "or my wish." The inconveniences of Capel's remoteness were doubtless felt more by Gill's customers than by himself.

In the *Autobiography* he dilates at some length on why the domestic situation was the really decisive factor (after all, the chaplain difficulty might well have been got over), and this passage is of much interest and importance—it is a whole-hearted and vehement vindication of the position of women in the home, and that position is paramount. Home and family are fundamental in society, and on the man devolves the responsibility of seeing that the woman's position and interests in them are respected and safeguarded. It is in the nature of things that the partners in the family must both be satisfied and content—but not equally: it is more important for the woman than for the man. "If you take a little place in the country and man and woman like it equally well, that's all right. If the woman likes it more than the man, that's all right too. But if the man likes it more than the woman, it won't work; it will be a misery and a wreck. Because a contented woman is a better thing than any other of God's creatures and will make the most disgruntled man see the bright side of things." This is not merely a bit of domestic social policy; it is the enunciation of what Eric believed to be a law of nature. That was why it was decided to leave Capel, for the sake of the women; if things were still manageable, they might not long remain so. It has been said of the Roman Catholic church that it is anti-feminist, but pro-feminine; the same can be said of Eric Gill.

In his last years, Gill expressed a wish that he had been able to write a special book about the four years in the Black Mountains. Clearly he did not look back on them as simply an interlude between Ditchling and Pigotts, much less as a mistake, but rather as something attained, for which the preceding years had been a preparation. For a brief space, the cell of good living which he was always striving to maintain in the chaos of the contemporary world was realized in appropriate surroundings—I do not mean only surroundings of natural beauty, but a neighbourhood in which a fundamentally natural daily life was still being lived, in however attenuated a form. Not that the cell did not continue to live on at Pigotts; there too the natural situation was beautiful enough, but the life of the district was fragmented, decayed and alien. The waves of the great city already lapped round it.

Like other people who live in the country when it would be more convenient for their work and their friends not to do so, Eric was often asked why, not being a farmer, he chose it. People from the towns seem to find it hard to believe, much less to understand, that there are those who live in this way simply because they like and are able to do so; in particular they like to feel the life of the earth and its seasons going on around them, that their environment is one of quiet and security. It stabilizes them; if they will let it, it stabilizes their work; it keeps them in touch with the rock from which they were hewn, the pit from which they were digged. And so it was that Gill took his home to Capel.

"Home" was one of Gill's sacred words, the highest commendation he could give to any place or situation in which he found himself

was that it was a "home from Home". His own home was the
centre, the pivot, of his existence, made even stronger by the fact
that so much of his work was done there. Many of his friends, when
recalling him to memory, must spontaneously picture him in that
setting, at some moment of daily life: at a meal, with Mary and
the children; later with those children's children; or, at the end of
the day's work, coming slowly into the soft light of the sitting-room,
rolling a cigarette, greeting a group round the fire with "Hullo, boys
and girls !" In his autobiography and letters so many happy moments,
so many delightful recollections are recorded as having taken place
at home or in connexion with home, often expressed in terms of an
almost ecstatic joy. Eric loved gaiety in people and things—it comes
out clearly in many of his decorative engravings for books—and he
was himself never gayer than when at home. The great League of
Nations carving at Geneva, done at home, was the work of a man
whose life and interests were in a real sense bounded by that home.
For him, one of the most horrible things he ever heard was the
reply of a child, when asked who his father was: "Daddy is the
man who carves the joint on Sunday"—it summed up a situation
which he knew was all too common.

Though he appeared to move easily in it, Gill was not at home in
any sense in the world of industry, of money, of official art, of
cultured leisure. His world was his domestic home and workshop,
not as a refuge from "the world", but as the place in the world
where all his love and sympathies were engaged. Incidentally, this
helps to account for the apparent anomaly that this man, who with
all his emphatic convictions was so noticeably quiet and patient in
argument with others, was apt to be impatient and resentful when
he was contradicted or challenged in discussion by a member of his
family. The fact was that this really hurt him, it was worse than
being physically set upon in the house of a friend. The arguments
which, sometimes, had convinced others had failed with those who
were part of himself; and when he had as it were spent the day in
combating the perversities of others, he now found the same perversities at home. This surely is how it seemed to him. His unfair-
ness in this matter need not be extenuated, but the reasons for it
should be understood. Moreover, he took very seriously his duty as
a father for ensuring so far as he could that his children should
not grow up with any ideas that their parents were convinced were
false: as St Augustine declared fifteen hundred years ago, a father

in relation to his family is a sort of bishop, and a bishop as such is guardian of the faith of his flock. But he ought not to be rough about it.

There is a significance here in Eric's love for the idea of the heavenly Jerusalem; it was not only the idea of the blessed City which is above, of "Jerusalem the golden", the place of endless rest in God—it was "Jerusalem, my happy home".

For four years the concentration-point of home was at Capel-y-ffin. By this time he was reaching maturity, he had come of age (he was in fact forty-two years old when he went to Capel). Discarding irrelevances and superfluities, he was "proceeding confidently" in mind and in life and work. This process is indicated in his letters of the period. They are still high-spirited and colloquial; but the familiar phrases and slang of the earlier letters—already sounding a bit old-fashioned even when they were written—are gone; and with them are going the little religious flourishes and pious phrases, and the touches of facetiousness and sentimentality.

Looking back during the last months of his life to the days at Capel, Eric saw them as a time for himself of what he called "spiritual puberty". From his adolescence he had always been wrestling with the psycho-physical problems which beset mankind, and he now began to see the answer. It came to him in the setting of the age-long monastic tradition.

I do not know whether he ever read through the Rule of St Benedict, that epoch-making sixth-century charter for monks in the West, whose spirit and general principles can be of great service also to lay people in the world of the twentieth century. But Gill certainly came under its influence, particularly as mediated to him through a monk of Caldey, Ambrose Holly, a New Englander from Connecticut, whose memory is held in benediction by all who knew him. Eric came to see that the key, the answer, to his difficulties was to be found—at any rate for him—in St Benedict's injunction "to cast all things on the rock which is Christ" :* all things. To cast on that impregnable rock the burden of temptations and sins and worries, is good, but there is more to it than that. If you "place at his feet . . . as offerings which his love will purify and redeem . . .

* The biblical source is 1 Peter 5, 7 : "casting all your care upon him, for he careth for you". A Jesuit preacher told his congregation that the above quotation from Eric Gill's *Autobiography* (p. 224) was the best commentary on this passage in St Peter's epistle which he had ever seen.

all the wayward sensualisms of thought and secret action which otherwise burden or torment you, is not that also good? . . . There can be no movement of the flesh or the imagination which cannot thus be turned to sweetness."

Thus the questions that first begin to present themselves to every thoughtful man at adolescence began to receive their final answer at Capel. And here, too, Gill learned for himself that there is a real connexion between physical quiet and contemplation. Life at Capel had its troubles, and Gill learned, what so many other men learn, that the inevitable bustle of domestic life is the "most disturbing of all hectic disturbances". But such things are not incompatible with that core of inner quiet which is sometimes a necessary adjunct to the most strenuous physical labour. At Capel there was that wider and diffused physical quietness which is so powerful an aid as to be almost a necessity for the attainment of a life, a state of contemplation at any level. "Be still and know that I am God" : this is possible in a tube train in the rush hour—but that is not the best place for it.

And so Eric's final verdict on the years at Capel was, "It was a good life". He underlined it : "I say it was a good life, and it was, and it was a natural life". In holiday mood he recalls how we bathed naked together in running streams, had picnics in groves and by little waterfalls, climbed mountains and "smelt the smell of a world untouched by men of business". Only man can ignore and disfigure the manifold beauties of nature; but also "man alone can give thanks . . ."

APPENDIX

to Chapter Eight

A conversation between Eric Gill and a member of the British Public

The following interview took place about the time that Gill left Capel-y-ffin in 1928; but for some reason now forgotten it was never published. It is of interest as an informal statement of some of his thoughts and feelings at that time. Looking back, the interviewer remembers vividly the good-humoured kindness and earnest attention with which Gill listened to the reporter's importunities and fatuities.

MEMBER OF THE BRITISH PUBLIC: I'm sorry you've had such a bad press lately, Mr Gill.

MR GILL: It's very kind of you—but I hadn't noticed it. What notices struck you as being unfriendly?

M.B.P.: Oh, the Roman Catholic ones principally. For example *The Catholic Times* was very superior over the engraving for "The Passion"* and the same paper blackguarded you twice in one issue over the reproductions in Benn's book.†

E.G.: Oh, was that blackguarding? I thought it was meant to be complimentary.

M.B.P.: You did, did you? Listen to this then:

". . . the collection of photographs of his sculptures in this volume devoted to his work shows him defying not only convention, but human anatomy, more recklessly than ever Mr Epstein in his most bolshevistic moods. We find it hard to believe that any but the most sophisticated connoisseurs can really admire some of the

---

* *Passio Domini Nostri Iesu Christi* (The Golden Cockerel Press, 1925).
† *Eric Gill* in the "Contemporary British Artists Series" (Benn, 1927).

grotesquely distorted figures which are included in this collection. To most people they will be thoroughly repellent."

That's *The Catholic Times*, of London and Liverpool, and I'm afraid it fairly represents the attitude of the average Catholic in this country, whether English or Irish, who takes any interest in the matter.

E.G.: You take it too seriously. It only means that they do not like my work.

M.B.P.: But why don't they? It can't be said that your work is unappreciated in England, among critics, connoisseurs, collectors, authorities, and even ordinary people like myself. But not among most Catholics. Third-rate artists like—well, you know the people I mean—get plenty of commissions and *kudos* from the faithful; but how many of your customers are Catholics?

E.G.: Very few, I admit. But I fear I *seem* to flout their notions of orthodoxy, of anatomy, of art. They think it's deliberate, but it isn't.

M.B.P.: Yes, and worse than that *The Catholic Times* reviewer also said that, "Mr Gill tends to emphasize sex in his sculpture in a way that the ordinary mind finds extremely repugnant". You appear to flout their notions of morality, and Catholics in England won't stand that.

E.G.: I don't do it on purpose. But you can't expect me to bother about one small section of uninstructed critics any more than another.

M.B.P.: You mean that Catholics are uninstructed in morals?

E.G.: No, not specially. But it is certainly true that regarding sexual morality Catholics in England suffer not only from the general post-reformation puritanism, but also from the influence of Ireland, which in this matter has apparently gone quite off the rails.

M.B.P.: It is certainly disturbing to think that there may be Christian maidens who blush, even metaphorically, at Luke, 1, 31-34, and men for whom Lot and his daughters are matter for nervousness.

E.G.: What can you expect? I know a doctor of theology who maintained that boys and girls should be preserved in complete ignorance of sex until they came to be married. True, it was only his own private and impious opinion, which he may have since discarded, but . . . I contend that if the things to which your critic refers are repugnant to the ordinary mind, then to that extent and on that matter the ordinary mind is de-christianized.

M.B.P.: It seems that Roman Catholics in certain countries are suffering from crypto-manichaeanism.

E.G.: Yes, and not so "crypto" either. It is quite usual for people to pick up the idea, both from press and pulpit, not merely that things forbidden to celibates are allowed to the married only because of the hardness of their hearts, but even that they are unpleasant, if not positively sinful, *in se*. We shall never get this sex business right until we treat it as frankly as does the Bible or Shakespeare—as printed, not as acted. Moreover, at present we play into the hands of the sex-confusionists. Boys are boys, and girls are girls. Sex distinction is a good thing in itself, not a bad, as feminists and fashionists teach; it's one of the basic things in God's order. Indeed, I think it is tenable that the admirable papal attitude towards contemporary "civilized" female dress is prompted fundamentally by a concern to check the movement which tends to merge woman's activities into man's, rather than by any prudish objection to the display of female arms and legs. Many a "modern young woman" is conspicuously unwomanly and conspicuously able to take care of her chastity—when she thinks it is worth doing. After all, the civilized white races and their problems are still only a minority upon earth, and that's all the more reason why we must try and see the problems whole. Sex is not a matter concerning only folk in industrial countries—nor is Catholicism. Every one of us has to be continually re-converted, and so we are in the position of unbelievers to whom missionaries are sent; we should present the Faith to ourselves at least as intelligently as we hope it is presented to Jews, Turks, infidels and heretics. No intelligent Hindu, for example, will ever be converted to the Catholicism of Tooting or of Babbitville. Yet it is that sort of Christianity we Catholics are apparently trying to foist on ourselves—as if the radical disorder of industrialism were not enough!

M.B.P.: Your views are somewhat borne out by the eruption of certain Catholic groups, colonies, and so on, whose members *ex professo* are seeking something better and further removed from industrialism than what they see around them. Your name has been connected with a venture of that sort.

E.G.: I am sorry to say that it has. I owe it to the virtual impossibility for a Catholic to maintain his privacy in England, and
the well-meaning but precipitate enthusiasm common to all rebels
and reformers, who see in every private society an opportunity
for advertising their own ethical preoccupations.

M.B.P.: Then you think these Catholic stunts (to one of which
Father Martindale referred as a "self-sacrificing application of the
Church's principles") are not good at all?

E.G.: I don't say that; but assuming industrialism to be an enemy,
if not *the* enemy (the Catholic Social Guild to the contrary notwithstanding), it can't be destroyed or even attacked *by laymen*
on ethical grounds, for a man can be a good Catholic in a factory.
The ethics of industrialism are the business of theologians, not of
those who work in it. From the workers' point of view, the real
trouble is that the system provides us with things that can be
made better under conditions wherein individual workers are not
only concerned with the quality of their work but are *responsible*
for it. A group rebelling on ethical grounds is going outside the
boundaries of lay powers.

M.B.P.: But do you suppose for a minute that people care a damn
whether things are good or not? Or even know a good thing
when they see it?

E.G.: I might be able to answer that question, but I'm not at the
moment concerned with it. All I know is that I care, and to some
extent I know. And man's business in this world being "to know
God, to love God, and to serve God", that is all that any one of us
need worry about. Even a professional missionary is, like any
other workman, chiefly concerned with the well-doing of his job,
and if he does it properly he need not be concerned about results.
Watching the effects is of no concern to the workman or artist
(another name for workman). That's one reason why I don't
collect press-cuttings.

M.B.P.: And that's why you are unmoved if your stations of the
cross in Westminster Cathedral make Bishop Smith sick or Lady
Jones tired?

E.G.: Yes. But nevertheless one has carefully to consider the effect
on one's own customers! And that's another advantage of what
may be called individual, as opposed to industrial, methods—that
the workman and his customer meet one another face to face.
And whatever your Bishop Smith may think, the Cardinal Arch-

bishop of Westminster was apparently satisfied, and that was enough for *me*.

M.B.P.: Should then the expert artist defer to the views of the in-expert not-artist, even a cardinal?

E.G.: Both are expert and inexpert in their several spheres, and it is always a matter of annoyance when the customer takes that line and expects the artist to do the customer's part as well as his own. If a man wants a house built, for example, he ought to know the number and sizes of the rooms he wants; just as the builder knows, or should know, the best way of meeting the customer's require-ments. When a painter or sculptor is asked to make a set of stations of the cross, he should be instructed exactly as to what each panel is to signify, the number of figures, how they are to be dressed, and so on. In actual practice, as things are, he is expected to supply not only the carving, but also the ideas.

M.B.P.: I notice that you speak of your clients as customers. This is in accordance with "business" rather than with that dignity of art of which many artists seem so conscious.

E.G.: It's only a matter of words. "Client" is a snobbish name for a "customer". I prefer "customer" because it suggests the cash nexus, i.e. the relation of justice which exists between the one and the other; for the workman or artist requires food and clothing and however much he might work to please himself, he will only work for another on account of that need.

M.B.P.: But what of the service of the community?

E.G.: That brings me back to my main contention; that the com-munity is best served when the workman is in a position most completely to please himself, that is, to do his work as he really thinks it ought to be done, or, as they say St Augustine said, when he "loves and does what he likes". I wish someone would give me the reference; it seems too good to be true. I can't find it in the *Confessions*.* But talking of confessions, wouldn't it have been much better had Mr Henry Ford written his autobiography as a thing addressed to God, as St Augustine did?

M.B.P.: Are we not continually exhorted to address *all* our actions and work to God?

* St Augustine did say it, not in the *Confessions* but in his commen-tary on St John's First Epistle: *dilige et quod vis fac*; Love, and do what you will. The learned can find the whole passage in Migne, P.L. vol XXXV, c. 2003.

E.G.: Actions, certainly, but not work; preachers are always careful not to particularize about that.

M.B.P.: The distinction seems a rather fine one.

E.G.: No. They say that an Ingersoll watch employé can do his duty as one serving God, but they do not suggest that God has any use for Ingersoll watches—nor has He.

M.B.P.: But for what human works *has* God any use?

E.G.: Now you're fairly asking for it. He has the same kind of use for human works that He has for His own material creation, i.e. as something which gives glory to Him. But the whole point of human work is that, whereas the flowers and works glorify God, and, not having free-will, can do nothing else, man, having free-will, can do so consciously, and thus a work of art (i.e. simply anything made as well as a man knows how) does indeed improve on nature. But industrial products, admirable as they *may* be and useful (as is the pencil with which you are writing), at their very best glorify only man. This sounds very fine and grand, but it is none the less true. We are forced into the high-falutin' attitude as much by our teachers as by our "natural enemies", the men of commerce and captains of industry. In a decent society a man would be able to work without talking about the glory of God, just as the good monk or nun (i.e. a professional prayer) prays "without noticing that he is praying". St Anthony the Abbot said that.

Chapter Nine

PIGOTTS
1928-1940

It was one thing to decide that they must leave Capel-y-ffin, but quite another to decide where to go. Eric's personal requirements were simply manageable premises in reasonable condition, the precise neighbourhood was more or less a matter of indifference to him, provided it wasn't a suburb; the place must be, he said, right in or right out. The only city or town that appears to have been considered was London itself, and Mary was not wholly averse to living there; but she much preferred her bit of land and her bit of farming, and, when just the right thing turned up, this tipped the scale in her favour. Pimlico was explored; there was a house and garden in Kilburn that was nearly taken; an un-built-on site in St John's Wood was considered possible; there was talk about older residences, good and solid but run down, in Whitechapel or Stepney. Then suddenly Denis Tegetmeier, who had got to know the Gills on Ditchling Common, reported a likely property for sale near his parents' home in Buckinghamshire. It proved to be the very sort of thing, down to details, which Gill would have asked an estate agent to find for him if he had supposed for a moment that such a place could be found. This property was not as expensive as it would have been had it been in a better state of repair and fitted throughout with modern encumbrances, but even so it was expensive enough: the Gills bought it for "five hundred down and the rest on the bank". The exodus from Capel-y-ffin early in October 1928 was an even more impressive exercise in household removal than the arrival there four years previously. The whole thing was tackled with the usual high spirits, and on their arrival at the new home van-drivers and removal men all sat down to a meal of bacon and eggs with the family, which included Laurie Cribb and his wife and their baby—they must have numbered about fifteen persons. The house, Pigotts, was four miles north of High Wycombe, beyond Hughenden. At The Harrow the road forked, the left-hand branch going on through North Dean to Speen, the other continuing on through Bryant's Bottom. In the angle between these roads a spur of the Chilterns thrust out, and Pigotts stood on the brow of this hill, approached by a steep lane—1 in 6—through the beech woods, leading only to Pigotts and one other house.

From the time that he lived in Lincoln's Inn Gill was persuaded that in a quadrangle is "the only decent place to live", and his pre-dilection was well satisfied by what he found at Pigotts. The farm-house itself was of medium size, built of local red brick on two floors, and very pleasant to look at. Behind it a large brick-built stable was destined to provide the workshop in which Gill engraved, drew, and wrote, with two rooms above it, and its timber extension, once a threshing-barn, became his stone-working shop. On the opposite side of the large grass quadrangle were two cottages (even-tually occupied by the two girls when they married) and the storage barn which became workshops for Gill's stone-carving assistants, and for Denis Tegetmeier. On the third side at the back was a range of miscellaneous low buildings, the fourth side was open but for a low wall and a projection of the house. An elegant red brick pigsty stood in the middle of the quadrangle, and it did not remain empty for long.

Between the back of the house and the engraving workshop there was a small space on two levels, with an open staircase in one wall by which the rooms above the workshop were reached; it had three doors, into the house, into the workshop and into the open air. It was this unpromising area that soon became the chapel—the lower space being partitioned off by an open screen, and the small stone altar built in the middle. Six months later, it was licensed for Mass. From time to time there was a temporary resident chaplain, notably either Dom Bernard McElligott, a monk of Ampleforth, or that old friend Dr Flood; at other times a priest would come over on Sunday from Heythrop or elsewhere. In front of the house was a small garden enclosed by a low brick wall, adjoined by an orchard. The other dozen or so acres of land were meadow, with a small plot of arable on which for a time wheat was grown for bread. The whole property was surrounded on three sides by beechwoods.

It was here that Gill lived the last twelve years of his life, twelve full and fruitful years in which, by unflagging work and perfect orderliness in the conduct of his affairs, his thought, writing and lecturing were enabled to keep pace with his stone carving and typography, his life with his work.

Eric Gill did not remove from Wales to the Home Counties in order to escape the isolation of Capel-y-ffin, or to renew his connections with the world of art and affairs which he had known before the Ditchling days (though this in fact happened): his simple purpose was to make life easier for Mary and the girls. And so it came about that anyone who, having known Capel, visited Pigotts after a year or two, was startled by the innovations he found there. There was a telephone, there was a small car, there was up-to-date cooking apparatus, and a typewriter; the pewter plates and the open log fires were still there, but there was now a real bathroom, even if you did have to pump the tank full when you wanted to use it. Many appeared to be genuinely surprised by such things, yet they need not have caused surprise. When, as often happened, someone said to Gill that to do this or use that did not seem "consistent with your principles", he would reply, "Why? I am not a teetotaller". His family wanted to get around and see their friends, at Pigotts a car was more convenient than a pony and trap; Mary was not able to do all the work she had formerly done, telephones and the rest were available, and it would be perverse not to use them in the circumstances. Eric himself used them very little, and then as handy conveniences in abnormal circumstances. His criticism was not directed at motor-cars and telephones and flying machines as such, but at a social and industrial set-up which made the use of such things imperative in ordinary everyday life, made them conditions of living instead of merely aids to living for those who wanted them.

On one occasion he was shown over a sham-gothic residence by its proud owner, a scientist. When asked what he thought of the building, Gill replied that he liked the electrical switchboard in the hall. His questioner expressed surprise; "Oh, I like anything reasonable," explained Eric, to which his host replied, "That's too abstruse for me".

Gill's refusal to be merely doctrinaire, to be a "teetotaller", is important for any understanding of him. He was essentially a practical man, and he believed that any course of action was open to rational consideration provided it was not something sinful. Many have assumed that he thought that anything he disapproved of was sinful, but in fact he protested that it was not for himself to decide what was in itself sinful and what was not—he was not a Christian for nothing. In 1934 he received a letter from a woman librarian in South Africa, in which she asks how it is that if industrialism is bad we can get benefits from its products e.g. Medici prints, gramophone records. In his reply (Letter 212) Eric set out some of the evils of industrialism as such, and went on to point out that it does not follow that all industrial products are bad THINGS: "A machine-made nail is not necessarily a bad NAIL. A photograph of a picture isn't necessarily a bad PHOTOGRAPH. But it is a bad civilization which makes men and women more and more dependent upon such things". Gill was keenly aware of the tensions that exist for those who share his way of thinking, and he wrote to this correspondent, Miss Hall: "The only real advice I can give (at this great distance of miles away) is that you, by 'prayer and fasting', perfect your mind—by reading, writing, talking, loving, thinking, probing, criticizing—referring all things to their sources . . . Thus, in spite of all the misery which you must necessarily suffer, you will have an interior peace of mind . . . In this welter of today the most and the best we can hope for is peace of MIND".

Gill mixed freely and sympathetically with cranks and highbrows and *exaltés* of all kinds, and it is not surprising that he has been labelled (sometimes mutually exclusively) with some of their enthusiasms. But it is all nonsense to think of Eric Gill as a crank, a "medievalist", a man out of touch with his own time, who approved of nothing invented since the Industrial Revolution, a freak who wanted to live on nuts and to have his stockings knitted with fingers to put his toes in as if they were gloves, and a lot more rubbish of the same sort. When in 1934 there was an outcry against running electrical pylons across the South Downs, he came to their defence in *The Times*. "I write," he says, "not only as an artist, but as a Sussex man born and bred, to whom love of the South Downs is as natural as it is enthusiastic. Anyone who has seen the aqueducts striding, almost galloping, across the Roman Campagna, must have been struck by the inexorable majesty of them, and the need of Rome for water is analagous to the modern world's need for power. In France I have seen these great electric standards striding across the country, delayed by nothing, hindered by nothing . . . An attachment to 'Nature', which goes with a refusal to see beauty in engineering while making use of engineering and making money by it, is fundamentally sentimental and romantic and hypocritical. Let the modern world abandon such an attachment, or let it abandon its use of electric power."* He never lost his boyhood enthusiasm for steam locomotives, but that did not make him decry air travel, when during his lifetime it was invented and developed into a normal alternative. Indeed, it was for him a form of transport in both possible senses; I met him soon after his first flight, and asked him how he liked it. "Donald," he exclaimed, "I can't tell you how nice it is—it is nice enough to be a temptation." But all his appreciation of the beauty and convenience of the gadgets that what is indiscriminately called progress confers on us never made him forget the evils of the set-up that produced them. To the solemn young man who groaned that something or other he wanted could be bought satisfactorily only at Woolworths, Gill said, "Very well then, get it at Woolworths. But whenever you do so, make an inward act of repudiation of all that Woolworths stands for".

In his reiteration of the principle that designing and making should be the work of one and the same person, Gill made constant use of the profession and practice of architecture as an illustration. It says much for the good temper and good sense of architects that they took his criticisms in good part and were ready to listen to what he had to say. He was invited to address architectural bodies in various parts of the country, and three of these addresses were printed in *Beauty Looks After Herself* (1933), namely "Architecture as Sculpture", "Architecture and Machines", "Art and the People"; there are other of his architectural communications in the same book. However destructive some of his ideas must have seemed to the profession, his deep concern about buildings and his own work on some of them were appreciated, so much so that in 1935 he was made an Associate of the Royal Institute of British Architects.

Gill was convinced that the nature of modern building—that is, buildings constructed of new materials by the latest methods—precluded decoration, such as that which could be supplied by stone

* It was another story when concrete lamp-posts tried to look artistic. Confronted by one of these when walking in a street, he stopped before it and said to me, "The surprising thing is not that this has been put here, but that someone *chose* it".

carvers. In spite of this he was in 1929 and 1930 engaged on just such work on the offices of London Underground railways at St James's Park station, and later on Broadcasting House. This may appear inconsistent; but Gill did not see it like that. For him it was just another case of not being a "teetotaller", and as a workman he accepted the customer's instructions; what was done with the work was the customer's affair. (In any case, it has been acutely remarked that consistency is a good reason only where there is no better one.) It may even be hazarded that one of Gill's reasons for accepting these commissions was that, when they had been carried out, the truth of his conviction of the superfluousness of decoration on modern buildings would be made plain to all. In any case, stone carving was Gill's job, he enjoyed doing it, and here was a chance to do some more.

The decorations of St James's Park station were entrusted to a number of sculptors, and Gill himself was responsible for figures representing three of the Winds; much of the work is no doubt excellent and skilfully integrated into the building, but it does strike an observer as extraneous. At Broadcasting House the problem was not quite the same. The Governors of the B.B.C. seem to have wanted external carving which would announce the building to the passer-by and impress him with what it stood for. These governors were very conscious of the powers and possibilities of broadcasting, and had a lofty conception of the undertaking which had been entrusted to them. Eric Gill hardly shared such views : to him the radio was an ingenious toy, and he was more conscious of the possibilities of its misuse than of its potentialities for good. He never broadcast (except once in Palestine), and listened but rarely, and never willingly.

The Governors of the B.B.C. wanted allegorical and symbolic carvings, and chose for their principal figures over the entrance Prospero and Ariel, from *The Tempest*; the theme of the wide-ranging messenger was carried out in supplementary low-relief panels alluding to the B.B.C.'s varied activities. Gill could not enter whole heartedly into all this, and though he succeeded in satisfying his employers, he did not satisfy himself by his work. He carved with other interpretations of Prospero and Ariel in mind, interpretations which are equally open to question, refusing to be overawed by Shakespeare's text (like George Robey in the First Part of *King Henry IV*, though less amusingly). "I took it upon me to portray God the Father and God the Son," he wrote. "For even if that were not

Shakespeare's meaning it ought to be the B.B.C.'s." Given the high
ideals of the Governors of the B.B.C., it is arguable that their purposes would have been better served if Gill's work for them in the
entrance hall had appeared outside the door : it represents The
Sower.

Just before the Underground job, Gill finished the second of his
notable pieces of wood carving, the first being the Rossall School
altarpiece. It was a bed-head for Graham Carey, representing Child-
bed, Marriage-bed, Death-bed, with Latin inscriptions which Gill laid
out but did not himself carve. Gill wrote to Carey that he was "a
very inexpert wood carver", but he was satisfied with certain parts
of what he had done; less exacting critics find considerable satisfaction in the whole thing.

On 25 May 1929, just before the birth of his second grandson,
Eric wrote to his mother about the death in New Guinea of his
brother Cecil's little daughter : "We've got to see life whole—none
knows that better than you who have borne so many and borne so
much in life—a new baby in Sussex and a new baby in Heaven—
and flowers blooming and dying all the time and everywhere. In
any individual case life is either too tragic or absurdly lovely and
successful, but the whole thing is neither tragedy nor comedy. We
can only say 'Thy will be done' and endeavour to mean what we
say and rejoice . . . I hope you will soon stop doing over much and
will have a rest". On the following August 6 Mrs Gill died, thinking
of her children to the last as Eric testified. Their father, who for
some years had been vicar of West Wittering in Sussex, retired
shortly after his wife's death, and himself died four years later.
"There has never been a time," wrote Eric, "when I have not known,
or even when I have forgotten, that the main lines of my parents'
teaching and example were the main lines of the road to heaven."

There was a wedding in January 1930, when the second Gill girl,
Petra, married Denis Tegetmeier.* After the war he had attended
the Central School of Arts and Crafts and had helped Eric from

* For those interested in religio-social customs, it may be noted that
on this same day, in Pigott's Chapel, Joanna Gill and René Hague were
solemnly betrothed. This custom is still provided for in the Roman
Catholic Church, though in practice it is virtually unknown, at any rate
in these islands.

time to time on various jobs; now, after settling in at Pigotts with
his wife, he went on with his free-lance work. He was a painter,
letterer and engraver, and his father-in-law continued to make use
of his talents as occasion offered. In addition to his other abilities,
Tegetmeier was a cartoonist; he ought to be more widely known as
such, but it is probable that editors were shy of him—he made no
concessions. He was merciless in his satire, his eye was unerring and
his line of the greatest delicacy. In 1934 his *Seven Deadly Virtues*
was published in a limited edition by Lovat Dickson. It consisted
of forty-odd drawings, demy-quarto in size, each provoked by a short
sentiment or similar item taken from newspapers or other periodicals;
they were all mordant and some of them were murderous; as we
look at them we see not only other people—we see ourselves. For
those who knew Tegetmeier, piquancy is added to his cartooning by
the knowledge that it is the product of a quiet and self-effacing
character.

Another publication by Tegetmeier, one intended for wider circulation, was produced in immediate collaboration with Gill; it was
a sort of pamphlet, printed by Hague & Gill and published by Dent
in 1937. This was called *Unholy Trinity*, and consisted of eleven
satirical drawings by Tegetmeier, each with a miniature essay in
comment by Gill. Some of these essays and the pictures that went
with them were of the sort that helped to encourage the idea that
Gill the Catholic was anti-clerical. In the continental sense of the
expression, which implies opposition to a given church or even to
Christianity itself, obviously he was not: in the English sense,
which seems ultimately to convey the idea that clergymen necessarily know less about true religion than anybody else, his words
sometimes appear to be imbued with it. I do not refer to such good-
humoured digs as that "[the problem of evil is such that] even
theologians have been humble before it", but to harder sayings. "The
clergy are in the position of men standing on the brink of a frozen
pool and shouting to men drowning under the ice that they should
take good deep breaths if they want to be healthy." "The clergy
are everywhere acknowledged to be custodians of faith and morals
—the faith is what you more or less blindly believe because your
schoolteachers taught it during 'religious instruction', and morals
are little more than a list of things you mustn't do. Man as an
intelligent and intellectual being is hardly mentioned, and never
expected to function." "It must be a commonplace of our experience

that the wide-spread scepticism of our time is as much the consequence of loss of respect for the preachers of Christ as it is of
the writings and teachings of unbelievers, and that that loss of
respect is a necessary preliminary."

For the teaching office of the Church, for the priestly office of its
ministers, Gill had the profoundest reverence and respect, because it
is a special participation in the one true universal priesthood of
Jesus Christ (and he was very alive to the truth that every Christian
shares in that priesthood). But this is not to say that the mistakes,
exaggerations, deficiencies of persons exercising authority in holy
orders should be extenuated or ignored, or that as a matter of
discipline it is good to treat clergy as outside criticism: that is
obscurantism, weakness, laziness, and produces that "clericalism"
of which Archbishop Saliège declared, "the Church disapproves of
it and we don't want any of it at any price".

Gill visited Count Kessler and met Maillol and others at Weimar
in the summer of 1930, and returned home via Salies-de-Béarn. Two
months later, he became gravely ill and it was another two months
before he was well again. His life was in danger for a time, and
among the people who came to see him in hospital was Father Vincent McNabb with whom he had not had any contact for so long.
Hilary Pepler, whose real affection for Eric never wavered, called too,
but Gill was too ill to see him. From now onwards, Eric's life was
punctuated by illness; in marvelling at his astonishing output of
work during his last ten years, it is often overlooked that it was
interrupted and made more difficult by serious ill-health.

He was about again in time for the wedding of his daughter
Joanna to René Hague, on 19 November 1930. Mr Hague had been
in close touch with the family ever since his sojourn at Capel-y-ffin,
and in the previous year 1929 Gill had taken him into partnership
in a printing business which they established at Pigotts. In doing
this Gill did not intend to set up a private press, that is, one that
prints solely what it chooses to print, but an ordinary business that
would undertake any work within its capacity, from bottle-labels to
books. In 1937 their workshop was removed to High Wycombe, and
a couple of years later a third partner joined them, the firm becoming Hague, Gill and Davey. The business closed temporarily during
the war, in 1941, and re-opened in 1946 at Pigotts again; there it

continued for another ten years, until it ceased to be a paying pro-
position in 1956. Gill's son Gordian was among those employed in
the press for some years before 1940, and again for a time after the
war.

No doubt the best known production of this press was a study
written by Gill himself on *Typography*, which was published by
Sheed & Ward. The first edition, in 1931, was printed on specially
made hand-made paper, and was limited to 500 copies. This book
ran to three more editions, ordinary and unlimited. Hague and Gill
also printed two short works by Canon John Gray, a book of poems
and a fictional essay set in a problematical future, called *Park*. They
also printed the first edition of David Jones's *In Parenthesis* for
Faber & Faber; a number of publications for J. M. Dent & Son,
including René Hague's translation of the *Song of Roland*; and
collections of engraved nudes and drawings from life by Gill. The
reputation of their printing crossed the Atlantic, and they did two
books for the Limited Editions Club of New York, *Hamlet* and *A
Sentimental Journey*.

Reference has already been made to the book called *Clothes*; this
was published by Jonathan Cape in 1931. On the strength of its
title, it has doubtless come into the hands of more general readers
than any other of Gill's books except the *Autobiography*. Possibly
it has been productive of more disappointment than any of them,
for though there is a lot about clothes in it, the reader has to work
hard if clothes are at the moment his only interest; Gill contrives
to touch on many subjects the reader may (wrongly) think irrelevant,
and the first section, called "Preliminary Considerations and Asser-
tions", is considerably more wide-ranging than the subject of the
book would suggest. His well-directed broadsides against the idea
that trousers are essentially for males, and skirts for females, sound,
at any rate as regards the first part, quite unnecessary in these days;
but his final prophecy of the clothes of the future seems to be
farther away from realization than ever, despite some of the efforts
of Carnaby Street.

Gill argues that the normal garment for both men and women
should be and will be the girdled tunic, mini-length in childhood and
gradually lengthening to the calf for grown-ups. It was this that he
adopted for his own dress. After about the year 1922 he was always
dressed in a collarless tunic or smock which reached to his shins,
confined by a leather belt, woollen stockings, and shoes. Those who

hoped for some amelioration in male attire and had heard Gill had made a move in this direction were apt to be disappointed when confronted by what he had made of it; the material was always a homespun varying in weight and texture according to the time of year, brown or dark grey in colour, and no difference was made in material or colour whether the particular tunic was to be worn on formal occasions or when at work with hammer and chisel. Some people so got it into their heads that Gill was playing at being a monk "in the world" that, presumably having never seen a monk or friar in his ankle-length tunic, scapular and the rest, they saw something monastic in this costume of Gill's. It was in fact simply derived from the sort of smock that he found convenient for stone-carving. The same sort of tendentious misinterpretation was made about his headgear. Out of doors, he wore a beret and often an ordinary overcoat; at work he covered his head and kept out the stonedust with a square cap made of stiff paper. This was the thing that newspaper reporters and others called a biretta. Probably Gill when a boy had seen one of these caps in use in carpenter's shop or mason's yard (does Mr Chips the Carpenter still wear one in a pack of "Happy Family" cards?); he was determined to make one for himself without help, and spent hours folding and re-folding paper to find the right way to do it without cutting.

Gill gave up shaving in early manhood, and in middle life his neat full beard was reddish brown. He used to relate that, walking one day down Fetter Lane in London, a boy shot out of a door "as if propelled by somebody's foot" and fell at his feet. As the urchin scrambled up, his eye lighted on the bearded man looking down on him, and he exclaimed, "Coo-er! 'Oo says we can't grow terbaccer in Hingland?"

It seemed to me that Gill's sensitiveness to embarrassment did not extend to his own clothes; had it done so, I do not believe he could have gone on wearing them. They were sometimes an occasion of embarrassment to other people, and even of displays of snobbishness and bad manners; but here the interesting thing is the number of people who declared that when they were with him they were never bothered by his peculiarities of dress. For those of us who knew him well, this was understandable, we were used to them; as regards others, it resulted from the appropriateness to Gill of his own idiosyncrasies.

Towards the end of 1897 young Eric Gill gave up the drawing of

steam locomotives which had absorbed him throughout his boyhood. Towards the end of 1932 he one day climbed into the cab of
the "Flying Scotsman" at King's Cross; he did not leave the foot-
plate until the train arrived at Grantham. It is safe to say that the
man of fifty was as thrilled by this experience as he would have
been at fifteen, more so, for his capacity for enjoyment had grown
with the years, as had his probing curiosity about every new thing
that was presented to him. Objectively, it was a small event in his
life, but to him it was an occasion he never forgot, and it so
impressed him at the time that he wrote an account of it for *The
London and North Eastern Railway Magazine*, in which it was
printed in the January issue of 1933 (and reprinted in the *Letters*,
No. 197). It was one of the best pieces of writing he ever did. His
approach was severely practical : he was there to see what happened,
not to experience aesthetic emotion; but the human being cannot
experience without reflecting, and in his account there is reflection
too. He was particularly impressed by the primitiveness and simplicity (sometimes deceptive) of the operations entailed : the colossal
labour of the fireman, who almost without a pause shovelled coal
from tender into fire mile after mile, hour after hour; at the other
end of human energy, the need to catch the dangling, jiggling ring
at the end of the whistle wire. He was fascinated by the combination
of physical strength, mental alertness and technical skill required of
human beings to control five hundred tons of moving metal, a
weight of which the living passengers were but a fraction : "there is
no sensation of travelling *in* a train—you are travelling *on* an
engine. You are on top of an extremely heavy sort of cart horse
which is discharging its terrific pent-up energy by the innumerable
outbursts of its breath"—yet man is in control, and can stop the
whole thing by the movement of a lever no bigger than a bicycle
brake handle. "All the luxury and culture of the world," he wrote,
"depends ultimately upon the efforts of the labourer. This fact has
often been described in books. It has often been the subject of car-
toons and pictures—the sweating labourer groaning beneath the
weight of all the arts and sciences, the pomps and prides of the
world—but here it was in plain daily life."

Within a few weeks of this adventure Gill received a commission
from the London, Midland and Scottish Railway to decorate the
lounge of their hotel at Morecombe. He was to carve low-relief
panels illustrating the story—believe it or not—of Nausicaa befriend-

ing Ulysses, embellished with a quotation from Homer which in
plain English means "There is still hope that you will see your
friends". It is not recorded whether the person responsible for this
theme was moved by admiration for classical literature or by an
elusive sense of humour; perhaps both. But one may hazard a guess
that Gill must have been tempted to be a "teetotaller" for once.

During the early thirties there was a continental enterprise which
engaged Gill's attention for a short time. A Dutchman named Weij-
develd was planning an organization which was known as the
European Mediterranean Academy, that is an academy of the arts.
Its representatives in London were Erich Mendelsohn and Serge
Chermayeff. At this academy Mendelsohn was to teach architecture,
Chermayeff interior decoration, Hindemith music, Zadkin sculpture, and Gill lettering and typography. A property had been
acquired for this purpose at Le Lavandou on the French Riviera.
This scheme was promoted in England with some enthusiasm, and
its French prospectus was translated and printed by Hague and Gill
for distribution, but it all came to nothing because of insufficient
funds. Gill co-operated with Mendelsohn and Chermayeff in their
deliberations, and they all got on very well together; but it was not
Eric's world, there was a flavour about it of what he called "art
nonsense", though of an exalted kind, and it is just as well that he
did not have to add this to his other activities. How he would have
managed to commute between Pigotts and the south of France has
not been divulged.

Palestine, the Holy Land, and in particular Jerusalem, the Holy
City *par excellence*, was the last of Eric Gill's "revelations". He
went there first in 1934, the occasion being the carving of ten panels
on the outside wall of the Archaeological Museum at the Hebrew
University on Mount Scopus; these tablets represented in various
symbolic ways ten of the nations which have most strongly influenced the history of Palestine, from the Canaanites to the crusad-
ing Franks. He sailed from Tilbury in March with his assistant
Lawrence Cribb; they landed at Port Said, journeyed up the way of
the land of the Philistines to Lydda by the railway first built by
British military engineers during the 1914-18 war, and then on by
rail to Jerusalem. Gill stayed at first in the Dominican priory of St
Stephen outside the Damascus Gate; here there is a famous School

of Biblical Studies, and he was fortunate enough to make the acquaintance of two of the leading authorities on Palestinian topography and archaeology, Father Hugues Vincent and Father Marius Abel. Later he moved to the Austrian hospice outside the city walls where he was joined by Mary and his youngest daughter, and by David Jones.

Palestine was at this time half-way through the period that elapsed between the turmoil and destruction of the 1914-18 war, with the expulsion of the Turks, and the fighting and disturbances that attended the setting up of the state of Israel in 1948. Consequently Gill saw Palestine as it was before the many developments and changes, whether good or deplorable, of the past twenty years. Certainly the administration of the Mandatory Power had done a lot of cleaning up, and instituted desirable improvements, parts of Jerusalem were probably tidier than they had ever been in the whole course of their history, but on the whole the country and its life were not yet radically changed. Gill was at home at once. He soon found that the most comfortable and inconspicuous clothes to wear were those of any Palestinian workman, and adopted them accordingly. Gill had been brought to Palestine at the instance of the government architect, Austen Harrison, and he was well received by officials from the High Commissioner downwards, and was welcomed also by Jewish and Moslem scholars. But as usual, he was happiest among the men and women literally in the street; it was David Jones who happened, unknown to Gill, to see him kiss the diseased hand of a beggar woman at a street corner.

Gill saw a good deal of the country and of its people outside Jerusalem, from Tiberias to Hebron, and he had the inestimable advantage of experiencing it not simply as a pilgrim, not at all as a tourist or sightseer, but as a temporary resident with a job of work to do.

Many people have been to Palestine and come back having apparently seen nothing but flies and touts, dirt and "backwardness", the rivalries of religions and the quarrels, emulations and meannesses of their sects. All these things were there and in good measure, and Eric saw them, but there were other things to be seen, and he saw them too. "In the Holy Land I saw a holy land indeed; I also saw, as it were eye to eye, the sweating face of Christ . . . To me it was like living with the Apostles. It was like living in the Bible." And the beauty he saw was of people, of the Palestinian Arabs living without pride and with dignity in their poverty, sinful but humanly sinful; of places, Galilee and the Jordan wilderness; of the work of men's hands, above all of that Moslem shrine, the Haram as-Sharif* at Jerusalem, which he declared to be the most beautiful place he had ever seen, the most spiritually pervaded. "Tell me where there is another. Is it in London, in Trafalgar Square? Is it the Place de la Concorde? Is it on the Acropolis at Athens? They tell me that is very lovely, but at Jerusalem living men worship the living God: at Athens there is but a memory of what was. Is it even in the piazza of St Peter's? No, not there . . ."

As for the shrines of Christendom, the basilica of Bethlehem, reminder also of the pride and glory of blood-stained Byzantium, the church of the Holy Sepulchre, reminder also of the brutalities and arrogance of Western Europe breaking in on Asia—these he would rather have as they were, half-ruinous, cluttered with the ecclesiastical junk of half a dozen churches, dirty and profaned, than restored and polished by Caesar's building-contractors. "By the inscrutable decree of God the sweat is not thus to be wiped from His face"; the squabblings of Catholics and Orthodox, Armenians and Greeks, do less dishonour to Christ than if they should abandon his cross entirely and "hand the whole notion of salvation to the sanitary authority", as our civilization seeks to do. Jerusalem has "not yet rendered to Caesar the things that are God's".

Blessed are the poor, for theirs is the Kingdom of God: that truth was first taught in the Holy Land and Gill found that it could still be learned there, and he came back with his mind made up. "Henceforward I must take up a position even more antagonistic to my contemporaries than that of a mere critic of the mechanistic system. I must take a position antagonistic to the very basis of their civilization. And I must appear antagonistic even to the Church itself. Of course that is all nonsense but that is how it must appear. For the Christians everywhere have committed themselves to the support of capitalist industrialism and therefore to the wars in its defence, mechanized war to preserve mechanized living, while I believe that capitalism is robbery, industrialism is blasphemy and war is murder." It was with these convictions, more or less clearly envisaged, that Eric Gill had lived most of his life; and with them thus reinforced, seen as it were from a Pisgah height between the

* Generally called in English the Temple Area, with the Dome of the Rock in the midst.

hill of redemptive Death and the tomb of bodily and spiritual Resurrection—the spot in which Palestinian folk-wisdom so aptly recognizes the centre of the world—he worked out his few remaining earthly years.

When Gill determined that he had to present a yet more radical opposition to the contemporary western set-up, he was not envisaging any political activity. As Bernard Kelly wrote in the issue of *Blackfriars* of February 1941, "The categories in which Gill lived, worked and wrote were absolute: religious, moral, metaphysical. They were not the categories of political expediency. Thus he was eminently qualified in the critique of social programmes, Catholic or not, put forward to restore a tolerably Christian social structure: but he was not qualified to judge them precisely as politically feasible", or, as Eric put it, "politics are not my line of business". If he agreed with Canon F. H. Drinkwater that "the economic problem fills the whole sky", yet the only socio-economic reform he put forward (apart from his insistence on production for use and not for profit, and with one notable exception to be mentioned later) was the abolition of the middleman and the financier.

Way back as an architect's pupil in London he had realized that "it was not so much the working *class* that concerned me as the working man—not so much what he *got* from working as what he *did* by working", and he had got firm hold of the notion that "a good life wasn't only a matter of good politics and good buildings and well-ordered towns and justice in economic relations". Social reform is the business of those who know the nature and destiny of man, he declared, and "the trouble with the present age is that it is just the knowledge of those things which it is most uncertain about, and consequently politics and social guidance are left to a crowd of amateurs—novelists, multiple-storekeepers, manufacturers of motor-cars or chemicals—whose profession of disinterestedness is only slightly more credible than that of thieves and robbers".

As for the professional politicians—"Liberals and Conservatives—Labour! All these parties wish to preserve the *status quo*. But it is just the *status quo* which is in question". People of all kinds toy with communism both because it seems better politics than *that* and because it seems to offer an approximation to absolutes in a world wherein religion has grown cold: afraid to face Love, too

tired to rebuild his house, they "fall back on an 'economic interpre-
tation of history', and are satisfied to live by bread alone". It was in
Palestine that Gill fully realized in all their beastliness the
materialism, exploiting imperialism and mechanized labour in which
England has been a pathfinder and pioneer, and he came back
determined to keep clear of all politics and politicians.

> "For . . . politics is beyond me. Politics is . . . outside my scope,
> something I can't do. Moreover I do not believe political arrange-
> ments and rearrangements are real. It is all a confused business
> of ramps and rackets—pretended quarrels and dishonest schem-
> ings, having no relation to the real interests of peoples . . . The
> prestige of Parliament is an empty fraud. It is not too much to
> say that [parliamentarians] are not and never have been any-
> thing but agents for the defence of monetary interests. Such was
> the origin of parliamentary representation, such is its very soul . . .
> And, particularly, do not believe politicians. By the nature of
> their trade they have no professional pride and can have none.
> The phrase 'professional politician' has brought the very notion
> of professionalism to dirt."
>
> (*Autobiography* pp. 259, 148.)

Again there is a lot of exaggeration, but it would be pharisaical to
stress it. Years before, Eric had been strongly impressed by Julien
Benda's book, *La Trahison des Clercs* (called in the English version
The Great Betrayal); he came to see ever more clearly that the poet,
the artist, the scholar, the "clerk", who should be a disinterested*
man, is indeed a traitor if he puts himself almost unreservedly at
the service of the relative and contingent: and if it be a question of
professional politics, he will be buried under a mountain of mud,
"whereas it is necessary that he should keep his feet on the earth
and his head above ground". In the words of The Preacher, without
the craftsmen and the husbandmen the city cannot be built or
flourish, "but they shall not dwell or go up and down therein; nor
shall they go up into the assembly or sit among the judges". In
other words, let them keep out of politics. "Nevertheless they shall
strengthen the state of the world, and their prayer shall be in the
work of their craft . . ."

---

* In view of an increasing misuse of this word it seems desirable to
point out that it is *not* a synonym for "uninterested". I think it was
Eric himself who defined the saint as "the wholly disinterested man".

The increasing "politicization" of people was very grievous to Gill; for himself he hardly ever adverted of his own accord to such concepts as democracy, dictatorship and the like. A man who was about to address a meeting of war-resisters asked him for a message to them. "Tell them to keep clear of politics," was the reply.

Politics even at its best is quite insignificant beside Christian doctrine and its implications. The Magnificat is irrelevant in our dirty struggles between interests and classes and nations and political programmes—so it must be the struggles themselves that are really irrelevant. "Religion is politics, and politics is brotherhood," said William Blake—"and brotherhood is poverty," added Eric Gill.

"All our politics," he wrote in a publication of the Cotswold Bruderhof which existed at that time near Cheltenham, "are based on a denial of the Gospels. Our capitalist society is founded solely upon the notion that those who have money have the duty to get more, and that those who have none must be enslaved or exploited or 'employed'—until machines make their existence unnecessary. The fascist societies want to create empires and become as rich and great as the others. The communist societies want to make the rich poor in order that the poor may become rich. But the Church of God wants to make the rich poor and the poor holy.

"This is the circle of human politics: When we have accepted poverty there will be peace among men. Only when we make peace shall we become the children of God. Only when we love God shall we love our fellow men. Only when we love our fellow men shall we have peace. When we have peace we shall have poverty, and when we have poverty we shall have the kingdom of Heaven."

After over four months in Palestine, Gill arrived home, prostrated by an abcess in the jaw. During the voyage he had heard of the birth of a son to the Tegetmeiers, christened Adam "because he was the first man"; but he had also had news that Betty's husband, David Pepler, was very ill indeed. David, a man of noble and patient character, as his father-in-law wrote, died four weeks later. His funeral was the occasion of Gill's first visit to Ditchling since he left it ten years before.

David Pepler's death eventually led to the re-occupation of the Monastery at Capel-y-ffin. Some three years previously a legacy had enabled Mary Gill to buy this property as a holiday place for the family. After David's death Betty and her children lived for a time with her parents at Pigotts; but plans were made for her with the help of May Reeves, sister of Father John-Baptist, to run a small girls' boarding school at the Monastery. Extensive changes and improvements were made in the buildings, and a prospectus was issued; but the number of parents who would consider sending their children to a place still inaccessible by ordinary standards was few, and the undertaking never got off the ground. Betty married again, her husband being Harley Williams, of Abergavenny, and they continued to live at the Monastery until Betty's death in 1956.

So it comes abcut that the property at Capel-y-ffin is now occupied by two of Betty's daughters and their husbands and children. Thus representatives of the third and fourth generations of the two families, Gill and Pepler, whose names are associated with the re-peopling of this place in 1924, are continuing to live in it; and it is gratifying to know that they live there because they like it.

Gill's biggest work, which many consider the best of all his carvings, was commissioned in the spring of 1935, his formal customer being King Edward VIII. This was a gift from Great Britain to the League of Nations, and took the form of a long frieze panel for the entrance hall of their new building in Geneva. It brought Gill into contact with such unaccustomed persons as British and foreign ministers of state and other exalted officials, most of whom as usual confirmed his worst fears while surprising him by their pleasantness as persons. He seems to have got on best with Anthony Eden, with whom he exchanged long letters. He made two exploratory visits to Geneva, in the course of which the project was discussed at a meeting of people concerned, and there is in the *Autobiography* an entertaining account of what took place. It is an example of Gill's extraordinary simplicity that he actually suggested to these gentlemen that the most suitable subject for the carving, meant to represent the aim and object of the League of Nations, should be the destruction of usury or financial power, after which peace would reign among nations: this destruction would of course be symbolized by Christ driving the money-changers from the Temple. He notes with some surprise that the reception given to this modest proposal was cold. An outraged financial delegate from the United States exploded that if such a sculpture were put up, it would be "the last and greatest hypocrisy of the British Empire" (Gill saw the point of that). The ostensible reason for rejecting the suggestion—and here diplomacy could be seen at work—was that the illustration proposed was so specifically Christian that it might give offence to Jews and Moslems; but such an objection, they ruled, did not lie against some illustration taken from the Old Testament. Some of the alternative suggestions were peculiarly calculated to excite Gill's derision : for example, a French proposal, made with scant regard for Gallic taste for novelty, was that the nations of the earth should be represented as men in a rowing boat all pulling together. The design that was eventually chosen was, as we shall see, Gill's own. He was engaged on this work off and on from 1936 to 1938.

The great work at Geneva was not the first occasion on which Gill had been approached by a Government office. As early as 1913 the Lord Chancellor's office asked him to submit a design for the new Great Seal of the Realm; he did so, but war interrupted the project, and Gill heard nothing more about it. In reply to an inquiry from Graham Carey in 1936, asking whether he had ever made designs for coins, he wrote, "Yes, I have several times done designs for the Mint people but they have never actually used any . . . I did these a long time ago and I don't suppose they are very much good". He was also concerned with postage stamps, and supplied some of his own designs to the Post Office in 1924. These were not used, but they perhaps influenced the design of the stamps issued under King Edward VIII, which met with Gill's emphatic approval. In a letter to The Times on 22 September 1936 he commended the quality of the photograph of the King's head and its reproduction, the plain lettering, the absence of meaningless ornament, and con-gratulates the Post Office on "releasing us from the banalities of imitation hand-engravings and stupid ornamentation". With the accession of King George VI and another new issue of stamps, there was a reaction, and the irony of it was that Gill himself had a hand in it by supplying the lettering for the nine values from ½d to 6d, together with the frame design to enclose a fancy portrait of the King by Edmund Dulac. Gill wrote to his brother Evan (himself an expert philatelist) that "the responsibility for the design is more the Post Office's than mine. I only drew the stuff as instructed".

F

But if Gill capitulated in deference to the demands of the customer in 1937, his ideas were destined to triumph at the hands of another man thirty years later with the issue of new stamps which began in the summer of 1967: these stamps would surely have pleased him as examples of reasonable mechanical reproduction, consisting simply of the head of the Sovereign on a monochrome ground, with the denomination numeral and no other lettering or decoration whatever.

During the second half of 1935, Gill was writing *The Necessity of Belief*, a full-length book which he wanted to call simply *Believe It or Not*. Messrs Faber & Faber overruled him about this, but he had his own way with the sub-title, which reads: "an enquiry into the nature of human certainty, the causes of scepticism and the grounds of morality, and a justification of the doctrine that the end is the beginning". In spite of this sub-title, Gill said in a letter that it is a book for ordinary people, and hastened to add he was not writing down to the level of the unlearned "because I am on the low level to start with"; it does not follow from this "that the learned are therefore of no account—on the contrary". "The point is this, that the book is, as it were, a conversation between me and myself, in which I endeavour to arrive at the grounds of belief such as they seem to me to be." It would be more correct to say that the book can be read and understood by some sorts of ordinary people, but not by other sorts; it is not what is called a "popular" work. The topics over which it ranges are sufficient to show that: physical science, industrialism, capitalism, communism, materialism, business, personality, immortality, free will first, last, and all the time.

Eric Gill was an ordinary, simple man, a man in the street, both in his estimate of himself and in fact. "I am," he said, "an ordinary person who refuses to be bamboozled . . . What concerns me first of all is what man, the common man, the man in the street, the man in the workshop, the man on the farm, claims for himself. After all, I believe it is true to say that the philosopher and the prophet do not claim for man what he does not claim for himself." (*The Necessity of Belief*, p. 227.) He assumed no authority to teach: "The most I claim is to speak as one of the people, and as one for whom *vox populi* is *vox Dei*. It is not my voice, it is the people's voice. I claim that what I say is what mankind says. It is no little flock that proclaims man's free will. It is no minority of peculiar persons that asserts man's being" (*Belief*, p. 331). Worms are apt to get the best view of the roots of things,* and the important criticism of things as they are today comes not from princes and bishops, poets and politicians, but from "man the worm, man the proletarian, man the delectable whore". Early in 1939 the Royal Institution of Great Britain invited four well-known people, of whom Gill was one, to address its members on the relations of art and industry; and he told the assembly that it was a pity that a labourer or factory-hand had not been asked to speak as well (the address is reprinted in *Sacred and Secular*). On all sides we see men in revolt, and the principal instigators of rebellion in our time have been, not the professed revolutionaries, however important, but those "little men" who "wrote, in cheap books and parish magazines, or preached in nonconformist chapels, country churches or inconspicuous papist pulpits, the humane doctrine of responsibility for sin and the dual but undivided nature of man".

They were not conscious agitators, "but they did in fact prevent the entire submergence of the proletariat in the non-human system of industrialism. They did preserve as matters of common knowledge and common belief the common man's idea of himself: that he is a unique individual and uniquely valuable. If this idea persists as a commonplace of Christian doctrine, if Christianity persists as a commonplace profession, it is not due to the splendid writings, great speeches or heroic behaviour of one or more magnificent Christians—though such there were and such played their part—but to the widespread unheroic efforts of little men, little pastors, little sheep. There can be no rebellion without grounds for rebellion. It is the grounds of rebellion of which the little men have preserved the knowledge. There can be no rebellion except against wrong. It is the idea of right and wrong which the little ministers have kept alive." (*The Necessity of Belief*, p. 267.)

All this did not arise from any doctrinaire democracy, any sentimental regard for the masses, any invertedly snobbish contempt for learning and experience; Gill's comments on the suburbs were exceeded in pungency only by his comments on workers' ambitions

---

* In another place, he remarks that it is a long worm that has no turning.

to emulate the suburbs. No. Just as man's chief means to culture, worship and the contemplation of being have from the beginning been the necessity of providing himself with food, clothing and shelter—ordinary things—so wisdom, knowledge and understanding derive and ramify from fundamental truths discernible, whether through reason or revelation, by the ordinary man, man the tool-using animal, such a man as Eric Gill.

In England at the end of the nineteenth century there were thousands of obscure families like the Brighton Gills; Eric's schooling was rather below the average in such families; he had no advantage of upbringing and the rest that he did not share with thousands of other young men; he was for years no more than a letter-cutter and stonemason, living as such; when he found himself in a so-called superior environment, for example, among artists and literary people, he did not like it and cleared out; he had no high and overmastering ambition; he was not endowed by nature with any abnormal intellectual ability, he read widely, but mostly for recreation : in a word, he was quite an ordinary man—but one who used to the utmost his mind, his will and his heart.

This is one of the reasons why Gill's criticism is important. He was not like so many theorists who argue from the abstract to the concrete without any practical experience of the concrete. In the order of time, Gill started with the concrete; like the carpenter in Miss Sackville-West's poem *The Land*, he knew what it was to "hold down Reality, fluttering, to a bench" : when he expounded a philosophy of work and art, it was for once a working artist speaking. He slowly worked from the concrete back to the abstract and, used to dealing with real things, he found that abstractions too are realities, in the measure of their truth—and he handled them accordingly. It is sometimes necessary to screw a piece of wood tightly in a vice to keep it still : Gill found it is sometimes necessary metaphorically to screw an idea in a vice, for a similar reason and however impatient it may be of the treatment.

Eric lived for, worked for and spoke for and to his own kind. A simple fellow can read the writings of Eric Gill and find intelligible and convincing exposition of such daily and practical problems as God and man, matter and spirit, belief and science, personality, free will and responsibility, art, work and industry—all those things that are, whether we know it or not, of the first importance to every man jack of us. Gill could write and speak deliberately "on the level of ordinary human speech and thought", and so for the man Jack and the woman Jill, with no long words or technical jargon, no vague uplift or recondite notions, no metaphysical flights beyond the range of the kitchen and the bar, if only the kitchen and the bar would turn off the radio and pay attention thoughtfully for a bit: not these, but a straightforward examination of what are really everyman's problems, in language that everyman can understand, usually with illustrations that are at once familiar to him. And not only did Gill write what the ordinary person can read: he wrote what the ordinary person knows—but does not always know that he knows. Gill was not a moralist in the vulgar sense. He did not go around telling people what they ought or ought not to do, deciding what was right or wrong, sinful or good; he did not identify religion with personal rectitude alone. He knew perfectly well that they cannot be separated, that his own teaching on this, that and the other had immediate and far-reaching implications for personal morality; but his shyness, his humbleness and his fear lest he trespass on another man's job made him time and again repudiate any intention of talking about morals. His appeal was to good sense rather than to good will, and it was not till comparatively late that he found himself unable to keep silent when silliness, culpable ignorance, falsity or unlovingness had to be identified with sin and that he would refer simply to pertinent words of St James or St Paul or our Lord himself.

" 'Patriotism is not enough'—morality is not enough, Man is not merely a moral being. He is not merely moral or immoral. He does not merely will good or evil. He also knows true or false: at least he is capable of doing so. And not only does man know and will, he also loves." That was a common approach. In one of his attacks on the idea of the "leisure state" he declared: "It is not a moral problem. Leisure is not a problem because people are not good enough to use it properly"; it is an intellectual problem, of what to do that is worth doing. He deprecated the moral fervour that was mixed up with the arts-and-crafts and land movements: morally the handicraftsman or farm-labourer is in precisely the same position as any responsible chemist or engineer. When he deplored the deceits and shams of gothic-revival architecture he was accusing nobody of sin; his appeal was to reason—such things are foolish: "My indignation is not so much a product of moral rectitude as of intellectual exasperation". Nor did he fail to note the weak ineffectiveness of religious moralism: "Instead of doing anything about economics the moralists fulminate against the murder of unborn children and the selfishness of modern young people [in the practice of birth-prevention]. As somebody said: 'The drains are smelling—let's have a day of intercession'. And as another said: 'The economic depression is a good thing—it is sent to try us'." No wonder Pope Pius XI had to mourn that the people at large are estranged from the Church. It is not by moralism or formalist dogmatism, any more than by socialism or the first-aid of humanitarianism, that a sick world can be brought to health: "No 'welfare-work' in East London slums will supply religion with a reason of being, otherwise lacking. No distribution of property or nationalization of the means of production, distribution and exchange will produce Jerusalem in England's green and pleasant land if the earthly paradise have no City of God for its model. No truth, no good, no beauty will shine out of human handiwork unless the truth that 'whosoever will lose his life shall save it' be known, willed and loved". (*The Necessity of Belief*, p. 304.)

When Count Kessler visited Capel-y-ffin, Gill told him that since the war art had lost its first place with him, which had been taken by a search for the renewal of life. At Pigotts he was giving more and more attention to the problems of man in society, the question both social and religious of how persons can lead a whole, and therefore at least potentially holy, life on this earth. The titles of some of his writings from 1933 show this widening of interests, *Money and Morals*, *Unemployment*, *Work and Leisure*, *Work and Property*, *Christianity and the Machine Age*. He was always a most strenuous and fully-occupied worker, but latterly screwed out ever more time for books, articles and lectures directly or indirectly concerned with these themes. With, I believe, little conscious evangelical purpose, this son of missionaries and brother of the Friars Preachers expounded Christian principles and practice in places where they would otherwise hardly, or never, have been heard. He accepted invitations to speak or write, on this or that aspect of work and art or on social problems or on peace and war, indifferently for Catholics and Quakers, capitalists and communists, official bodies and obscure groups. This high-tide of lecturing came later, but it was at Capel-y-ffin that writing began to have a notable part in his activities, his pamphleteering, as he called it. His earlier publications were single essays; then came collections of articles reprinted from numerous periodical publications, many of them little known; and then longer single essays.

These writings give a clear and on the whole adequate account of Gill's ideas and arguments; and they are remarkable not only for their internal consistency but for their consistency and correlation as a whole: from the few paragraphs on Slavery and Freedom written in 1918 down to the posthumously published autobiography he was telling the same story, often in the same words. He was not afraid of repeating himself: "It has been said that I am one of those writers who can only keep to the point by returning to it. I may say in self-defence that there are many readers who can only remember the point if it is repeated often enough". In particular, certain pregnant sayings and quotations with which every reader of Eric Gill is familiar occur in the earliest writings as in the latest: such, for example, are "Look after goodness and truth, and beauty will look after herself", "Man is made up of body and spirit, both real and both good". The same basic ideas are always there—the nature of man and his relation to God, the Christian revelation, human responsibility and therefore the necessity of freedom, human sin and divine grace, man's work as a calling to collaborate with God in creation—and it seems to me that in general their application underwent but little real development. What did develop was Eric Gill himself; he saw the same things but saw deeper into them, he saw further and he saw more clearly, and in that vision he wrote about the same things again.

There can also be found in Gill's writings, especially the *Autobiography*, about as good a picture of what a man was like as can be got without knowing him in person—except in one particular: his actual style of writing and expressing himself was not always *l'homme même*, it was often misleading. It is sometimes thought by those who did not know him personally that Gill was intolerant, dogmatic (in the vulgar sense) and contemptuous of those who disagreed with him: an obituary-writer in *The Times* attributed to him a quite mythical "rich flow of invective". It is easy to see how readers formed this misconception: as he often admitted, in and out of print, his manner of writing could give an impression of cocksureness, of laying down the law. Indeed there could occasionally be detected a hint of William Blake's angel who "speaks with the confident insolence sprouting from systematic reasoning".

One contributing factor to this was Gill's constant desire to provoke discussion, not merely with himself, but among other people, as he frequently declared. He mentions another in a letter to G. K. Chesterton: "My trouble is that, being only an amateur writer and writing only at odd times, I have never been able to sit down and deal adequately with the whole business. Consequently I have only dealt with those things by which I have been stung, and therefore give an impression of one-eyedness". And he was always being stung.

On his writing up to the time he left Capel he gave his own verdict in the last letter he wrote from there to Father Chute: "I get more and more painfully aware of the fact that I ought not to be writing at all—not sufficient philosophical training. It's painful: every week I get the thing clearer in my mind, and last week's writing seems mostly tosh—or if not mostly, still, enough to damn it". These words point to the reason why the impression sometimes given by Eric's writing of a dictatorial, quarrelsome even cantankerous man, is so laughably wrong. He was in fact a really humble man, and his diffidence in all respects could be staggering. While never deferring to an opinion, by whomever expressed, unless he came to agree with it, he would ask and listen to the opinion of all and sundry on whatever topic turned up, even on technical matters of his own work. I have seen him bring engraving proofs in to the evening meal and ask for the criticism of all present—the family, visitors, servants: and next morning some of the suggestions of those inexpert critics were carried out. Since the publication of his autobiography there is no longer any excuse for thinking Eric Gill bumptious and intolerant.

Gill had hammered out in his mind and tested by practice certain principles, and these he put forward tirelessly for consideration and debate. But he hated to appear to be taking upon himself what he regarded as an office primarily of the clergy, and for that reason, as well as for the sake of first principles and of those who do not accept Christianity, he would appeal to natural reason as often as, or more often than, to divine revelation, to justice rather than to charity: charity he lived, his passion for justice was a fruit of his intense lovingness, and in more intimate private talk he would speak of God and of love more often than of either justice or reason. His intellectual judgements were downright ("We are told not to cast pearls before swine," he said, "and to adjudge persons swine in this sense necessitates making an intellectual judgement of them"), but

he was always scrupulous to try to avoid making, or seeming to
make, moral judgements of persons. I do not recollect ever hearing
him utter a word intended to wound, and time and again I have
watched him trying to find a worthy explanation of someone's
apparently indefensible action, or gently changing the conversation
when another's character or deeds were coming in for rough handling.

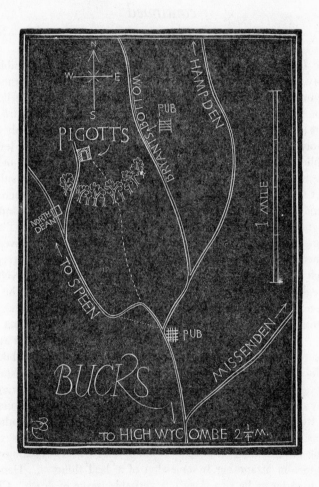

Chapter Ten

PIGOTTS

continued

Eric Gill's social principles can be summed up as responsibility, poverty, love of God. It should be plain by now that to Gill the one thing necessary was love of God and his Christ and a humble listening for the promptings of the Holy Spirit. As he wrote in *Work and Leisure*: "Man is a creature who loves. Ultimately he can only love the holy . . . Is the word 'holy' a stumbling-block (to the Jews a stumbling-block, to the Gentiles foolishness)? Why be afraid or shy of the word? Primarily it means hale and hearty, whole, unsullied, perfect and therefore of God—godly, sanctified, sacred; and therefore gay and light and sweet and cheerful and gracious. 'O taste and see how *gracious* the Lord is.' But gay—above all things gay . . ."

Man has free will. "The freedom of the will, whether proved by argument or not, is a fact of human experience, and to be accepted as such . . . Pathological states of mind apart—and let the psychologists enlarge the sphere of pathology as much as they can—the free will remains and man is master, captain of his soul". To have free will involves having responsibility, being responsible for what one chooses to do: "We know, we affirm, I know and I affirm that at the very core of our being, of my being, there is the fact of responsibility". Gill did not talk much about freedom or liberty but was constantly referring to responsibility, and the one involves the other: responsibility cannot be used unless there be freedom. He quotes Aquinas: "The free man is responsible for himself, but for the slave another is responsible . . . The highest manifestation of life consists in this: that a being governs its own actions. A thing which is always subject to the direction of another is somewhat of a dead thing . . . Hence a man in so far as he is a slave is a veritable image of death". Christianity imperatively demands responsibility: profession of it must be freely chosen by a free act, it must be lived equally freely. Where there is diminished responsibility there Christianity cannot be fully developed or fully effective.

Gill was sometimes criticized for apparently making too sweeping generalizations about the rich. The same objection can be, and has been, raised against many good Christians, such as St Basil and St John Chrysostom, and for that matter against the gospels themselves. He did not take upon himself to make moral judgements on rich people, whether individually or collectively; he was concerned with what St Paul was concerned with, that revolutionary threat and the truth which lies behind it, which Gill stated in as forcible a half-dozen lines as he ever wrote : "There is no idolatry so destructive of charity, so desolating, there is nothing which so certainly obscures the face of God, as the desire of money—the root of all evil. 'The root of all evil!' Did I make up that phrase? No; it is the word of God to man. The root of all evil, the *root*. The root of all *evil*." (*Autobiography*, p. 194).

"The principle of poverty," he declared, "is the only one consonant with the nature and destiny of man and his material environment and condition." What is meant by this poverty? Not, of course, indigence, destitution, evil poverty; but good poverty, that spiritual thing, explicit in Christian teaching, which bears fruit in human life and works. "To go without, to give up, to lose rather than gain, to have little rather than much—that is its positive teaching. Blessed are the poor in spirit; the humble, the common man, the common woman, simple women, mothers of children— 'How hard it is for a rich man to enter Heaven' . . . But it is only in love that this poverty can be embraced." "Is it not clear, beyond any possibility of doubt, that whatever other things may or must be said of the teaching of Christ and of the witness of his saints, it is the blessing of poverty which is the central fact of Christian sociology?" And our present organization, while it keeps many in dire want, insufficiency or grinding insecurity, holds up for our admiration and effort the pursuit of wealth and luxury; while many are ill-clad and ill-fed and ill-housed, many (and not only, or even principally, the rich) have a standard of living that is unnecessarily high. It was this, the standard of living which the middle class and the emulators of the middle class consider their due, that specially outraged Eric's doctrine of poverty : when a trade union might be expected to be discussing work it is found trying to shove or bolster up the standard of living, however much too high it may be already (see *The Necessity of Belief*, p. 61 et seq.). If money is the ruling factor in the state, if production for profit rather than for use rules in industry, the fault is ultimately ours, because money is the ruling power in our hearts.

Gill went on to expand his teaching on responsibility to that universal activity fundamental to all social life, the activity we call work.

Responsibility is of two kinds. There is moral responsibility for what we do and intend or refrain from doing, and there is intellectual responsibility for the kind and quality of what we make, "make" being understood in no narrow sense. Gill constantly returned to the theme of how deeply the idea of making properly enters into man's life and informs his work (as in the popular "What has he *made* of his life?"). "Deeds done, when viewed in themselves and not simply as means to ends, are also to be regarded as things made."

Work, says the dictionary, is "the exertion of energy, physical and mental" otherwise than for purposes of recreation. God has made the world and man such that work is necessary for life and, since nothing that truly subserves our life can be bad, there can be no form of necessary work which is in itself degrading. Nevertheless, an idea is now very prevalent that physical labour is bad, a thing to be avoided so far as possible, though even in the most mechanized conditions there must be a basic element of such labour. In a Christian society there should be no kind whatever of physical work which is either derogatory to human beings or incapable of being ennobled and hallowed; therefore, said Gill, "at every turn our object must be to sanctify rather than to exclude physical labour, to honour it rather than to degrade it, to discover how to make it pleasant rather than onerous, a source of pride rather than of shame . . . There is no kind of physical labour which is at one and the same time truly necessary to human life and necessarily either unduly onerous or unpleasant."

Industrial civilization fosters and encourages the notion that much manual work is, of itself, sub-human drudgery; when the working life of thousands of factory hands, shop-assistants, clerks, domestics, navvies and transport workers and labourers on our farms is considered, this seems to be true; and it appears obviously a good thing that, by the use of more machinery, more of this drudgery should be got rid of. Thus it has come about that people have come to believe that all physical labour is in itself bad. We seek to reduce it to a minimum, and we look to our leisure time for all enjoyable exercise of our bodies. (The contradiction has been overlooked that if physical exercise be bad in work, then it is bad in play also.)

"It should be obvious that it is not the physical labour which is bad but the proletarianism by which men and women have become simply 'hands', simple instruments for the making of money by those who own the means of production, distribution and exchange. And those who argue in favour of the still further elimination of physical labour on the ground that much manual labour is, of itself, sub-human drudgery are playing into the hands either of those for whose profit the mechanical organization of industry has been developed or of the communists and others who look to the 'leisure state' as the *summum bonum*. We must return again and again to the simple doctrine; physical work, manual labour, is *not* in itself bad. It is the necessary basis of all human production and, in the most strict sense of the words, physical labour directed to the production of things needed for human life is both honourable and holy."

Having through our cupidity and indolence degraded most forms of work, domestic and other, so that they are no longer to be viewed as pleasant, still less as sacred, having made men and women into "hands" and profit-making instruments, herded together in monstrous cities, "we turn round and curse the very idea of labour. To use the body, our arms and legs and backs, is now held to be derogatory to our human dignity . . . It is at the very base of the Christian reform for which we stand that we return to the honouring of bodily work."

The contempt shown for manual work has not been extended to those activities which in modern times are distinguished as the "fine arts"; on the contrary, their practitioners are excessively honoured, and a kind of mythology or mystagogy has grown up which Eric Gill castigated under the name of "art nonsense": he devoted a whole book, *Art and a Changing Civilization*, to what he called "the debunking of art". The isolation of something called Art (with a big A), especially pictorial art and the aesthetic chatter that goes with it, the putting of the artist on a pedestal as someone apart from

and above other men, the cultivation of an absurd artificiality called
the "artistic temperament", such things, he said, imply "a bourgeois
frame of mind, and are a notable product of a bourgeois society".

All the arts, whether "useful" or "fine", have their origin in
man's fundamental needs, to supply himself with food, clothing and
shelter, to pray to and praise God, to recreate himself; and accordingly Eric, putting aside all irrelevancies about emotion, self-expres-
sion, and the like, defined art simply by its earlier meaning, as "the
well-making of what needs making", thus vastly extending its scope
as commonly understood today. Time and again he quoted the words
of Ananda Coomaraswamy: "An artist is not a special kind of man,
but every man is a special kind of artist"; it was on the artist as
workman, as a "collaborator with God in creating", that his thought
on this matter was centred, the objective approach to work that has
been destroyed in so many arts. "I would rather have brick-laying
and turnip-hoeing done well and properly and high art go to the
devil (if it must), than have high art flourishing and brick-laying
and turnip-hoeing be the work of slaves." It was again to the common
man that he looked; his revolution was again away from the
specialist, the expert, professionalism, towards the ordinary person
and his needs.

I have no use at all for "art" as commonly understood today
. . . I would abolish the fine arts altogether. Music—let us sing
in church and at work and at harvest-festivals and wedding parties
and all such times and places. But let us abolish the concert-hall.
Painting and sculpture—let us paint and carve our houses and
churches and town-halls and places of business. But let us abolish
art-galleries and royal academies and picture-dealers. Architecture
—let us employ builders and engineers, and let them be imbued
with human enthusiasms and not be moved merely by the desire
for money or by merely utilitarian standards. Poetry—let those
who can write our hymns and songs and prayers. Let them write
dirges for funerals and songs for weddings, and let them go about
and sing to us or read to us in our houses. But let us abolish all
this high nonsense about poets who are "not as other men". And
let us abolish all the art-schools and museums and picture galleries. (*Work and Property*, p. 87.)

Fountain-pens, motor-cars and the like are as much works of art
as pictures and carvings, the bridge across the Saint Lawrence river

at Quebec would stand comparison with any medieval cathedral or castle; the difference between them is that the pictures and castles are the work of an individual artist—responsible workman—or a number of them working together, whereas the only artist concerned with the production of the motor-car or the bridge is the *designer*, architect, of it, the others concerned being mostly willing or unwilling proletarian hands. And each method faithfully reflects the philosophy and religion and life of a society : Chartres cathedral, simply as a building, could arise from none other than an ultimately spiritual background, the Canadian bridge is as clearly a product of the enthusiasms of the times in which we live.*

Work itself becomes a game, and the curse of Adam—"in the sweat of thy brow thou shalt eat bread"—is turned to blessing, for man has found joy in his labour and that is his portion. Thus, while the necessity remains and use is neither denied nor condemned, all things made become works of love, all deeds become things in themselves, all means become ends. This is the basis, the concreted and untrembling foundation of human art. This is man's response to his responsibility—that he freely wills what is necessary, he makes what must be into a thing he has chosen.

These are the things which the materialism of our time denies and derides. By its separation of work from pleasure, its divorce of use from beauty and of beauty from meaning, it has produced a real disintegration of humanity, and on the basis of its materialism there is no remedy for its sufferings but a more efficient organization of material. Let there be plenty for all and no parasites. Let all the milk be sterilized. They say : Let thought be free and let all work be commanded. We say : There is no such thing as free thought and let all works be free offerings. Materialism spells slavery . . . "Freedom is a concession of the state". (*Necessity of Belief*, pp. 330-1).

---

* It may be noted in passing that Gill did not entertain the delusion that the culture of the past was Christian in the sense that it was in any way a direct product of the Church or of ecclesiastics. Medieval bishops, priests and monks were clergy and customers, not workmen and producers (with individual exceptions, of course). "In fact, the civilizing power of man is a lay power—fostered, encouraged, nursed, petted by the Church but, in its own sphere, independent . . . [The Church] takes what she is given."

And the ultimate slavery and degradation of the artist is to be "freed from the necessity of making anything useful".

The more easy accessibility of Pigotts meant a pretty constant flow of visitors, but not often of the merely curious or impertinent kind that had been such a nuisance on Ditchling Common. An important consequence of this closeness to London was that Gill came into contact with and interested himself in certain wider aspects and activities of Roman Catholic life. While keeping in touch with many of his old associates he made new friends, among them several Dominicans, particularly John-Baptist Reeves; Thomas Gilby, a very lively and up-to-date Thomist; and Victor White, a disciple of C. G. Jung. Gill perhaps met Father Victor through his friendship with Dr Charles Burns, founder at Birmingham of the first municipal child-guidance clinic. It was the brother of the last-named, T. F. Burns, who brought Maritain on a visit to Pigotts about 1932. They had already met more than once in France, but this was their first meeting on Gill's home-ground. The two men had much in common, and Gill was deeply indebted to some of Maritain's writing, but they were markedly different from one another. The contrast was clear during conversation at table and after. On one hand the scholar, a man of deep learning and wide experience and interests, moderate and tentative in expression of his judgements; on the other, the enthusiast, an essentially simple man of vigorous and tireless mind, confident in his convictions within the narrower sphere of his particular practical interests but often at sea outside them. Making every allowance for language difficulties, I felt an atmosphere of some constraint, as if the two men were rather uncomfortable with one another.

There had been for some years a growing restlessness and discontent among some of the more educated and thoughtful of the Roman Catholic laity in England (the phrase sounds a little pompous, but the words describe them correctly). Some of the clergy shared it, and the fewness of their number was made up for by their ability. The movement was quite ununified, and touched on many facets of church life; but uneasiness about the accepted attitudes of Catholics to the society in which they lived and its problems was outstanding, and common to many critics who differed among themselves on other matters.

During 1928-29 this minority began to make itself heard through *Order*, "an occasional Catholic Review", issued through Bumpus, the Oxford Street bookseller. The promoter, T. F. Burns, was too busy to keep it going for more than four numbers, but it helped to break the ice. It was lively, critical and anonymous, though not irresponsible, whatever some of its more outraged opponents may have said about it; its principal targets were the Catholic press, Catholic education and the "schools question". The correspondence column was occasionally enlivened by a theological roar from a man-eating Dominican (the phrase was the editor's). Gill's contributions to *Order* were at once identifiable, their titles, style and content were as good as a signature: "Repository Art", "Twopence Plain, Penny Coloured", "The Right Mindedness of Modern Art".

A later quarterly publication was *The Colosseum*; it began in 1934, calling itself "the quarterly of action, not a polite review", and it was more solid, more ambitious and longer lived. It was edited by Bernard Wall, to support the idea of a sort of Christian revolution such as was then being advocated by, among others, Maritain, E. I. Watkin, Christopher Dawson and Eric Gill himself. Considerable differences of opinion emerged among its writers and readers, which were fully discussed in the pages of the review, and Gill was a frequent contributor to it throughout.* At this time there was a sharp division among young and critical Catholics as to whether they ought to "muck in" or "muck out", that is, whether they should join fully in contemporary life, or withdraw from that life as much as possible and "till their gardens".

In the autumn of 1934 there was a meeting of some of these supporters of the sort of ideas and policies represented by *Order* and *Colosseum*. It was held at the school run by the Dominicans at Laxton in Northamptonshire, and among those who attended were T. F. Burns, Father Thomas Gilby, Eric Gill, René Hague, Dr David Mathew (later archbishop), Vernor Miles, Father J. B. Reeves, Denis Tegetmeier, Martin Turnell, Bernard Wall, Evelyn Waugh. The following notes of the proceedings have been sent to me.

---

* Later Gill had a publication of his own. It was small and stencilled, and called The Gallery ("because the gallery is the place from which things are thrown"). It was short-lived; five monthly issues appeared, from December 1938. They contained four of his own contributions, over the signature E. Rowton.

All that I remember clearly are inessential things—Evelyn Waugh
sitting up in bed (we slept in the school dormitories) drinking the
port he had brought with him and smoking a cigar; the magnificent pork pie at breakfast, the largest I've ever seen, and the best;
a furious argument that went on for hours between Eric and me
on one side and Tom Burns on the other—a bitter argument:
about what? . . . There must have been, I think, about thirty of
us . . . it was very informal, no lectures or addresses, but groups
of people talking and talking. It was all vaguely about what's
called nowadays integrating church and world, and Catholics,
laity and clergy alike, being "with it" in relation to social problems, the arts, cinema etc. (This last simply meant Tom Gilby
talking a lot about Gretta Garbo—really with it—not like you
cads who call her Greeta.) The only concrete discussion centred
on the *Catholic Herald* . . . The whole tone of the week-end was
very much like Tom's *Order*.

It will thus be seen that this meeting (which some wag called the
"Laxton Synod") was of no particular importance, but the reference
to the *Catholic Herald* is relevant here. This weekly paper, which
for years had been published mainly for Irish exiles in Great Britain,
had recently come into the market and had been acquired by a
private person; John-Baptist Reeves was called in to direct the turning of it into a publication which should be a genuine newspaper
and genuinely catholic. Like all such undertakings its beginnings
were difficult; Father John-Baptist was full of enthusiasm for the
project and worked hard at it, but before long it became independent
of him. It was edited for some twenty-five years by Count Michael
de la Bedoyère, who made it an important element in the loosening-
up of the ideas of Roman Catholics in England, maintaining its
object of being a newspaper, and providing a forum for discussion
and disagreement. The *Catholic Herald* appealed particularly to
enterprising young people who were not interested in the parish-
magazine aspect of Catholic journalism, but could not stomach *The
Tablet* under the editorship of Ernest Oldmeadow, and found it too
judicious and conservative for their taste under his successor Douglas
Woodruff.

Since his letters to the *Chichester Observer* about the city's
market cross, Gill had become an inveterate writer of letters to the
press. The published volume of his letters gives a list of thirty-four

journals, letters to which are included in it. These are perhaps only a part of the whole, but even so the variety of subjects dealt with and of publications to which the letters were addressed is very large: the latter range from parish magazines and *The Sun-Bathing Review* to technical and professional journals, from national newspapers to *The Criterion*. But no publication received and printed so many letters as did the *Catholic Herald* during the last half-dozen years of his life.

The events of 1935-36 intensified the questionings among Roman Catholics, who were divided upon the matters at issue. So far as the Italian invasion of Ethiopia was concerned, most Roman Catholics in England were as shocked as the rest of the population, though there were a few who regarded it as manifest destiny that a European power, Catholic and Roman, should take over a barbarous and anachronistic African state. Opinion was more complex and more embittered about the Spanish situation. Roman Catholics in general regarded Franco as a crusader setting out to save his country from the tyranny and godlessness of Communism; but there was a minority of them who—invoking the Spanish Armada—saw him as an ambitious or misled man who had brought civil war upon his country and was endeavouring to impose a totalitarianism of the fascist pattern. One effect of these events was to re-direct attention to the whole question of war and its permissibility to Christians, to doubt which was almost unheard-of among Roman Catholics at that time. Stanley Morison and Francis Meynell had been conscientious objectors during the 1914-1918 war, which was regarded by their co-religionists as an astonishing aberration; and their organizing of an association whose prayers should support Pope Benedict XV's efforts for peace by negotiation earned them more obloquy. Now, in the summer of 1936, a society of Catholic war-resisters was founded in London. It was called "Pax", its membership was not confined to Roman Catholics, and no official ecclesiastical approval was sought. It was a loosely-knit association, the attitude of its members to war varying from the absoluteness of St Martin of Tours, "I am a Christian, and I am not allowed to fight", to those who approved of wars against Fascism or Communism but not others. This society, which still exists in England and the United States, was always small and apparently insignificant, but in fact its members did much to put conscientious objection against war on the map for Roman Catholics, and to support the work for peace of larger and better-known associations.

At the first Pax meeting which Eric Gill attended he noticed that one woman had brought her pet dog with her; he came to me in some alarm and said, "If that sort of thing is going to happen, this is not a society for me". However, his fears were overcome, and he gave Pax his active support; but he always had reserves about it—it had not got a sufficiently unified and rigid outlook for him. Repeatedly from 1936 onwards he spoke and wrote against war, on the platforms and in the publications of Pax, of the Peace Pledge Union, and of other associations of war-resisters—yet, though he freely used the term of himself for convenience, he was no pacifist as the word is generally understood. He held that taking part in warfare is not of itself and essentially at variance with a profession of Christianity, that the concept of the possible just war is a valid one, in the conditions commonly received (and often very imperfectly examined) by Roman Catholics and others: this position Gill held *ex animo*, it appealed to him as traditional, authoritative, reasonable and true. But the more he saw of the contemporary world, the more he learned about political and economic forces, the more that scientific means of warfare developed, so much the more he became disturbed in mind. He began to realize that, as Lord Grey had said, "War is the same word as it was a century ago, but it is no longer the same thing". The spiritual insight and logic of the medieval and seventeenth-century theologians had been applied to a quite different thing: is it possible to fulfil their conditions for a justifiable war in the new circumstances? Gill decided that it is not (and here he parted company from the great majority among those of his co-religionists who have given the matter a moment's thought). He still did not say that no war has ever been justified, that the use of military force is always wrong: he said that war as we know it today is such that no human being, much less a Christian, should take part in it; it has become bestial, inhuman, and to talk of patriotism and the defence of civilization by such means is irrelevant. "Modern war is a remedy worse than any conceivable disease"; it is no remedy at all for the congeries of diseases which afflict the world: it is an extension and amplification of them. Whatever high-minded, great-souled, public-spirited combatants may intend or do, war is supremely harmful to man's love of God and his fellows, to the spirit of truth and righteousness and justice, to human responsibility and to creative work: depersonalization is at its height and at no other time are men so stirred to undiscriminating hate and abandoned to irrational processes.

"What is the alternative of which we are so afraid? . . . Are we afraid of national humiliation, are we afraid to be humbled? But it is written 'Blessed are the meek, for they shall inherit the earth'. Are we afraid of poverty? But it is precisely poverty which as Christians we should welcome. There will be no peace, there can be no peace, while wealth, comfort, riches are the ideal we set before ourselves." This had been a foremost idea in his mind when he came back from Palestine: "It became clear that it is no use renouncing war unless we first of all renounce riches. That is the awful job before us . . . A whole world doomed to perpetual fighting—and no remedy but to persuade it to renounce riches. What a forlorn hope!" Indeed, Gill was interested as much in what he saw as the causes of war as in the strictly moral problem of war itself: all over his later writings are scattered references showing the inevitability of the sort of wars we have in the sort of world we live in—and we all help to make that world.

"Let peacemakers remember above all that it is no manner of good preaching peace unless we preach the things that make for peace— that even the love of our fellow men is no good unless it means giving rather than taking, yielding rather than holding, sharing rather than exclusive possession, confederation rather than sovereignty, use rather than profit. And it means the subordination of the man of business and the dealer and moneylender, both in the world and even more in our own hearts."

Gill's thought on war, coming later in life, is set out with less system and detail than his other dominant ideas. His insistence on the foulness and shamefulness in all departments of war as waged today laid him open to the charge that he was letting his feelings of disgust run away with him, and he was sometimes misunderstood in this way: it is therefore necessary to emphasize that he did not condemn war simply because it is horrible. It is a question of means: he denied that spiritual goods can be obtained by killing and hate and destruction, and he upheld the right of any man to refuse to take part in such an undertaking. "Could not Christ have called on twelve legions of angels to fight for him? And he did not. And shall we think to make a Christian triumph by calling up twelve armies equipped with all the products of our commercialism?—guns, bombs, poisons! (We can only obtain such things by calling in the financiers and borrowing their money.) Shall we thus 'make the world safe for Christianity'?"

In this context, of the horrors of war, it may be noted in passing that Gill's treatment of the problem of evil was too facile. He devoted a special chapter to it in *The Necessity of Belief*, and it contained some most valuable analysis and observations, especially the emphasis on the necessity of the distinction between moral and physical evil. There is also a third kind, which may be called spiritual evil, but to treat them, as he seems to do, as being in watertight compartments is bad psychology (and incidentally weakens his own arguments against modern war). The whole thing is badly over-simplified. "There is no problem of evil," he concludes, "there is only the intellectual difficulty of understanding the physical universe and the moral difficulty of withstanding our own appetites and lusts." But surely that precisely is the problem of evil.

By poverty Gill meant, where material goods are concerned, not less and not more than a reasonable sufficiency for decent human life. It need occasion no surprise that he saw the chief practical means to the restoration of the dignity of physical work, and of the quality of things made, in the ownership of property. He came to advocate as a practicable necessary reform the ownership of the means of production by the workers, *not* by the state; "workers" means all who work in a given enterprise, including the managing director if he works and if there is a job for him to do. This can be found set out in the essay on Work and Property in the book of that name and in another, Ownership and Industrialism, in *Sacred and Secular*; but here I follow mainly a communication to the *Catholic Herald* newspaper in which he summarized his argument.

The right to property, he wrote, is not primarily a moral right, one due to man on account of his free will, but is, so to say, an intellectual right, due on account of his intelligence: it follows from man's material necessities and intellectual nature, deriving not from his need to *use* things but from his need to *make* things. As a moral being purely as such, man has no right of private ownership; Gill quotes Pope Leo XIII and Aquinas on the duty to possess things not as one's own but as common. (Incidentally,

Christians, especially Catholic teachers, have made a big mistake in presenting the right to private property as apparently simply a matter of morals, "a thing good men believe in and bad men deny, and that's all about it". We have sought to defend the institution of private property by the very arguments which are our opponents' strongest line of attack: "the earth is the Lord's", his gift to us is for our "individual appropriation and public use" —and we have done our best to destroy both, and so allowed such miseries to be heaped upon man that the socialist says, "Destroy private property!" to which the communist adds, "And religion with it!", for it has been made to look as if the Church herself were on the side of big business and exploitation.)

It is, then, to man as workman, as an intelligent being who must manipulate things in order to make them serviceable, that private ownership is both necessary and a natural right, and only when there is full control of the means of production can there be proper and efficient manipulation. Unless the farmer own the fields (or has a tenure on terms nearly equivalent to ownership) he cannot exercise his best skill and intelligence upon them; unless the carver own the tools and stone, he cannot properly exercise his skill and intelligence therewith; unless the miner own the mine, individually or jointly with others, he or they cannot properly control the job of mining. This necessity of manipulation it is which gives the right of private property in the means of production: "The exercise of art or work, whether it be that of a craftsman or a manual labourer, is the formal reason of individual appropriation," as Maritain observes.

It is obvious that, as things are, the ground upon which alone a claim to private property in productive goods can be validly made has to a considerable extent been destroyed. The factory "hand" can make no claim to private ownership in his work, and the big machine industries and transport are no longer in any true sense private enterprises: they are (as their directors boast) public services. Hence the moral force of communism: what are public services should be publicly owned for the benefit of all. There no longer remains any rational and Christian objection to communal ownership, since the only reason for private ownership, the intellectual operation of the workman by which he imprints on matter the mark of rational being, has been destroyed by the development of machine industry.

The conclusion is inescapable. We cannot have any right to private property in the means of production unless we are prepared to abandon industrialism; most people are not so prepared, and even if they were, it would be impossible to return immediately to pre-industrial methods.

"Let us resolutely put away all dreams of that sort. Let us abandon the coteries of vegetarians and nut-eaters and artist-craftsmen . . . Politics deals with things as they are . . . Ownership is necessary to human happiness, to human dignity and virtue, and ownership means control. A share in profits is not ownership. Money in the savings-bank is not control of the means of production. The only desirable and at the same time the only possible reform of 'our world' is distribution of ownership." (*Sacred and Secular*, p. 168.)

Capitalist organization implicitly and communist organization explicitly lead to public ownership for private use. This is the exact opposite of Christian society, where there should be private ownership for the sake of common use. In our existing society we have degraded nearly all production and transport to being huge impersonal and therefore sub-human enterprises—and yet we have the insolence or folly to endeavour to maintain private ownership in the use of productive things, and to declare that this sort of private property is a principle of Christianity, which must be defended against ravening reds and subversive leftists.

Workers' ownership of the means of production, then, was what Gill put forward as a practicable, perhaps the only practicable, step towards the Christian society in which there shall be private ownership not asked for "on the selfish ground of private enjoyment, but for the sake of the good of things to be made and in order that the public use which morality demands may be a use of good things". The alternative we shall have to accept is in all probability some form of communistic industrialism and the leisure state, wherein man's intelligence will wither away in highbrow snobbery or mob vulgarity.

But "that alternative is no revolution, it is simply *progress*. In fact so-called revolutionaries are simply 'progressives'. They want, instead of the present world, the world which the present one *implies*. They want the same thing only more so—the same things only more of them . . . Merely to transfer ownership from private persons to the state is no revolution; it is only a natural development. Government by the proletariat is no revolution; it is only the natural sequel to the enfranchisement of lodgers. But to abolish the proletariat and make all men owners—and to abolish mass-production and return to a state of affairs wherein 'the artist is not a special kind of man but every man is a special kind of artist'—that would be a revolution in the proper sense of the word. And merely to proclaim an atheist government is no revolution—for that would be to make explicit what is already implicit in capitalist commercialism; but to return to Christianity would be truly revolutionary." (*Work and Property*, pp. 53-54.)

During these years Gill was living under considerable mental strain; he was in poor health, and working much too hard. Moreover, he seems to have been in a state bordering on real desperation. He could not understand why intelligent people were not at once convinced by his conclusions and the process of reasoning by which he reached them, and nothing he could do or say had any effect on this apparent obtuseness. For years he had lived with the conviction (and it was one not peculiar to himself) that the industrial-capitalist set-up of the Western world would shortly collapse under its own weight, complexity and human inadequacy—such collapse now seemed further away than ever. Gill's flirtation with schemes for currency reform, Social Credit and so on, brought no encouragement, and in a letter to *The Engineer* in 1935 he wrote that there is no remedy for the present state of affairs. "This civilization, like all others, must come to its term. And why not? Then we shall begin again—a new cycle: chaos, order, achievement, decay, disease, death. This view is only pessimistic if you think this life is all; I do not."

Meanwhile, from the publication of *Money and Morals* in 1934 he appeared to be becoming increasingly reckless in what he said and to whom he said it. His advocacy of the collective ownership of the means of production by the workers, as explained above, aroused the suspicion among many that he was going communist, and some of his careless and ill-considered references to Communism seemed to confirm the suspicion. This was particularly the case among Roman Catholics, and he aroused considerable opposition both privately and in the press, the critics including some of his own friends and supporters.

Particular exception was taken to his accepting invitations to send work to exhibitions arranged by Artists International, to writing in the *Left Review*, and to other associations with communist-inspired undertakings. On the face of it, this was an open disregard of the encyclical letter, *Divini Redemptoris*, issued recently by Pius XII, in which the pope warned Catholics against being inveigled into associating themselves with disguised communist activities. Individual Catholic persons and bodies asked Gill to explain how he reconciled his pertinent activities with this warning; protests about them were addressed to ecclesiastical authorities; and in 1937 the archbishop of Westminster, Cardinal Hinsley, was moved to take up the matter privately with Gill. There ensued a correspondence in which Gill set out his point of view moderately and with restraint, and the archbishop gently and firmly showed that nevertheless his activities were not compatible with the observance of papal directions, and were the cause of scandal to faithful Catholics. The upshot was that Gill promised that he would try to avoid such indiscretions in the future.

If for a time some communists were congratulating themselves on having hooked a big fish who would be a valuable ally (and some of them appear to have done so), they must also have realized that Gill would not be a docile one. There is a story that on one occasion he accepted an invitation to a gathering at which the guest of honour was to be some prominent communist figure. At the end of the proceedings one of the comrades asked him what he thought of it all. "I am puzzled," Gill replied. "This evening I have heard a lot of talk about liberty and throwing off chains, and then you go down on your knees and worship a bloody tractor."

A reproach often brought against Eric Gill was that apparently he did not pay enough attention to the cruelties and injustices of communists and their implacable opposition to all religion, or to the cruelties and injustices of fascists and nazis, and their subtle efforts to nullify the Church's influence. They overlooked that in his writing and public speaking he was concerned more with diseases than with symptoms. They were incredulous when assured that he did not believe that, fundamentally and potentially, the societies of Great Britain and the United States and France were much better than those of Russia and Italy and Germany; that, in effect, respectable democratic capitalist-industrialism was as atheistic, as destructive of responsibility and liberty, of decent poverty and the human person, of hope and love, as is communism itself; that its practical materialism had precisely the same effects as the dialectical materialism with which marxists opposed metaphysical and spiritual truth; that, in fact, totalitarian stateism, particularly in its communist form, was a logical development of the civilization of the democracies. No wonder, he said, communism seems the only just politics for the beehive state that most people seem to want and few try to prevent; for if all things are to be made by machines within a rationalized system there must naturally be more and more standardization.

Fascism and socialism and marxism, he declared, do not offer holiness: they offer more physical convenience and psychological satisfaction (by flattering human sensibility) in return for the obedience of their citizenry. They tell us they are going to cure a disease—by aggravating it. The socialist movement "offered nothing in the way of divine inspiration, nothing beyond the ideal of a world in which all should be hygienically and warmly clad—with a sort of B.B.C. 'culture park' looming in the background; as though to say : 'When we've properly got going with the love of our fellow men, then we'll see what we can do about culture and, well, you know, religion and art and stuff'." The marxists go one worse. "They have thrown away the God whom the capitalists profess to worship and do not, and have accepted the servitude which capitalism has developed and perfected but whose existence the capitalists deny. Thus they have not emptied out the baby with the bath water. They have retained the bath water while emptying out the baby. They have emptied out the Baby of Bethlehem only to swallow the foul and befouling bath water of London and Manchester." Gill challenged not simply the slums and misery of those cities, which are accidental to our materialism (are we not getting rid of them?), but its substance—its philosophy, its reversal of human and spiritual values. If capitalism is as irreligious as socialism, socialism is as inhuman and enslaving as capitalism. For all its lip-service to the spirit, its church on Sundays, and museums and art-galleries and "Shakespeare for the workers", "business" is materialist. "For all their real devotion to pure art, pure science, or pure what-not, the reformers are as much materialists as the men of business. The communists among them are clear-headed enough to recognize this; they are honest enough to proclaim it and glory in it."

"Workers, throw off your chains !"—and then put them on again.

No revolution that accepts materialism and its modern social incarnation, industrialism, can really be a revolution, Gill concluded.

It was, then, central to the social-revolutionary aspect of Eric Gill's teaching that industrial capitalism implies a way of life and work that is inconsistent with man's nature and with the Christian religion. Capitalism is a social theory based on the profit-motive, and its essence and object is production for profit; both labour and products have to be looked at primarily from the point of view of saleability, and not from that of their intrinsic quality and man's real needs. Its method is that of industrialism, which had three main processes, viz., the proletarianization of the craftsman, of the agricultural worker, and of the "small man" generally; the concentration of production in factories; and the use of machines, leading to mass-production by the division and sub-division of labour.

"Eric Gill," wrote Father Kenelm Foster, "holds things together. He is our great *pontifex*, bridge-builder, Spirit and matter, body and mind, knowing and loving: he distinguished them with exquisite clarity, and then held them together. He did it *in practice*; wherever he went he made matter alive with rational beauty. Why did he loathe industrialism?—fundamentally because he thought that *in practice* it separates what God has joined together, the body and the mind." That was indeed the main point among his many serious charges against industrialism: not its cruelty (for it had been realized that too obvious unkindness did not pay), but "the change which it has brought about in the nature of the work to be done and therefore in the minds of the men who do it"; it produces a world wherein "on the one hand we have the artist concerned solely to express himself; on the other is the workman deprived of any self to express". Gill did not assert that this was anything new in the world's history: the attempt to divorce art from work and use from beauty has been made—and resisted—from the beginning. But industrialism leads so clearly to the separation of mind and matter, which spells death to man, that death may be said to be its very object.

"It is only as persons that we serve one another, and when personal control is divorced from ownership it is only with great difficulty that men retain responsibility for the form and quality of what is done or produced . . . the men have no responsibility whatever, except a moral responsibility to obey the terms of their contract, i.e. to do what they are told. Thus the craftsman is finally degraded

—he ceases to be a person who in any way designs what he makes and makes what he designs; he is no longer even a hand: he has become a tool, a sentient part of the machine, and this without overlooking the real love of machines and the great skill and craftsmanship displayed both by machine-makers and machine-minders." "Our industrial set-up does not enslave the workers in any legal or technical or political sense. It does not necessarily maltreat their bodies or coerce their minds. It simply reduces the workman to a sub-human condition of intellectual irresponsibility.* It simply separates, divorces, the material and the spiritual." More and more workmen are being deprived of intellectual responsibility as regards their work, becoming automatons in it, prevented from being artists.

"And in their leisure, the time when they are not working they must be content to be amused; for industrialism has deprived them of the necessity of making anything useful." "The value of the creative faculty derives from the fact that that faculty is the primary mark of men. To deprive man of its exercise is to reduce him to sub-humanity . . . A man is as out of place in a factory as in a lightless dungeon . . . If the populations of our factory-towns were not constantly recruited from the country they would wither intellectually as certainly as they wither morally and physically."

Intellectual responsibility the concern of a few, or one; for the rest, obedience: the idea has become painfully familiar in other spheres besides industry.

The profit-making system, said Gill, produces things which, in their nature, because of the manner of their production, are unsuitable for the use of human beings: "We are making a bee-hive when we should have a house. We are making an apiary when we should have a motherland". The thing and its results have been summed up in words that might have been spoken by Eric Gill, but in fact came from Pope Pius XII: "In this age of mechanization the human person becomes merely a more perfect tool in industrial production and . . . a perfect tool for mechanized warfare".

Gill did not deny the impressiveness of the powers which industrialism has helped to confer on us, or seek to decry them. He had no fanciful ideas about the immorality of using machinery. "It is art-

* Gill quoted this aphorism so often that he made it his own. It originated with Father Martin d'Arcy, S.J.

nonsense to say that because the Forth Bridge is made of iron it is not a work of art . . . It is no more immoral to make things by machinery than by hand. It is immoral to make things badly and pretend that they are good, and no amount of 'hand' is an excuse for stupidity or inefficiency." The trouble is that machines are not simply complicated tools designed by workmen to help them in their work. "They are things designed to enable their owners to make things in great quantities in order to make great quantities of money. No definition of machinery and no description of machine industry can neglect these facts . . . The real distinction between tools and machines is discovered in the sphere of control and responsibility. Who is responsible for the thing made or the deed done?"

Eric Gill's indictment of industrialism has been widely misunderstood, and his sweeping generalizations of its evil effects sometimes gave understandable offence. When he said time and again that it reduces the workers to a sub-human condition of intellectual irresponsibility, the word "intellectual" was not always heard; when he said so often that the industrial population is dehumanized he did not always add that he meant dehumanized as workmen, as makers of things : machine-minding is often very skilful work and many mechanics are highly skilled and responsible workmen, but they are so in relation to the machine and not to the thing which the machine turns out. It would have been well had he more frequently and clearly stated his recognition of "the many men, and women, who in spite of the inhuman nature of their employment, retain the notions which properly belong to private and personal enterprise". Even so, from our own personal experience of people, we may think that he exaggerated, and in respect to contemporary actuality perhaps he did : but he was looking also to the future—and he was a far-seeing man.

Again, when in answer to the oft-made objection that "A man can be a good Christian in a factory", he replied, "Yes; and St Agnes was a good Christian in a brothel—but that was no reason why she should stay there," it is not surprising that the objector should not be silenced, for the analogy between a factory and a brothel does not go very far (quite apart from the historical question involved, which would not interest him). Of course he knew perfectly well, he never forgot, that Christianity can enable people to lead godly, righteous and sober lives amid any conditions : his point was that some conditions are more favourable than others. "A social order

cannot in itself force anyone to do anything, but it can be such as
to place many obstacles in the way" of those who would live in a
human and Christian manner: in a score of places (e.g. *Art Nonsense*, p. 132), he sets out briefly, clearly and cogently why the
conditions of industrialism are so bad in this respect, and it is only
common prudence to remove removable handicaps. His case is most
forcibly set out in *Money and Morals*, but its presentation there also
showed most manifestly an element of exaggeration. It is gravely
false, it is shocking, to say that "It is waste of time teaching Christian morals in the present condition of things", as he himself at
once goes on to admit; but his admission is too reserved. It is true
that the exercise of heroic virtue must not be demanded, and it
cannot be counted on; but the grace of God can. He is on surer
ground when he declares that "truth and error cannot permanently
lie down together and Christian morals cannot permanently flourish
in the same bed with a life contrary to nature".*

That just as right thinking precedes right faith, so a certain way
of living is the necessary preamble to Christian morals, is quite true
if rightly understood; but it can be distorted, and it is easy to overlook that if Eric set that "certain way of living" very high it was
because he was also looking at a very high and enlightened and
unrestricted standard of life and conduct. His search for perfection
was consistent and all-embracing. Moreover, on the psychological side, there was the factor of reaction. In his dealings with
his fellow Christians Gill was met on all sides by clergy, the shep-
herds of the flock, and other teachers, who seemed to him to seek
every excuse to avoid finding fault with industrial capitalism. Among
Catholics, in spite of the outspoken social encyclical letters of Pope
Leo XIII and Pope Pius XI, he did not find "clergy and laity all
agog for social or any other reform, and in general the clergy seem
to regard it as their job to support a social order which, so far as
it is possible, forces us to commit all the sins they denounce". What
seemed to him unbelievable, shocking and blasphemous was the
complacency of apparently the majority of Christians, not only about
the purity of their faith and practice, but also about the *kind* of
world in which they lived and which they had co-operated in making.

In any case, it seemed to Gill, that the Christians who ask the

* With Victorian appreciation of a good pun, Gill appropriated Belloc's
on *Magna est veritas et praevalebit*: "Truth is mighty and will prevail
a bit".

question, "Is communism (or capitalism or nazism or what-not) compatible with Christianity?" are approaching the matter from the wrong end. The proper question is, "Is Christianity compatible with the industrial and authoritarian development of society?" And the answer is certainly "No": for at the root of Christianity is the doctrine of individual personal responsibility. "Man is man all the time, and not only in his spare time."

In *The Problem of Pain* C. S. Lewis gave a timely warning against "making use of the idea of corporate guilt to distract our attention from those humdrum, old-fashioned guilts of our own which have nothing to do with 'the system' and which can be dealt with without waiting for the millennium". In *Christianity and Crisis* Reinhold Niebuhr wrote: "We do not find it particularly impressive to celebrate one's sensitive conscience by enlarging upon all the well-known evils of our Western world and equating them with the evils of the totalitarian systems". Substituting "capitalist-industrial" for "totalitarian" in the second quotation, no one who knew him or attentively reads his writings will imagine for a moment that Eric Gill stood in need of such warnings. He was a man of peculiarly searching mind and sensitive conscience. It is not given to everyone who sees the evils and abuses of industrial capitalism to see them in their setting so clearly or to examine them and their possible remedies with such precision as he did.

In the face of industrialism, it must not be obscured that the Christian religion has directly to do with only two things—sin and virtue. It can be applied to ploughing up pasture, or to poetry, only through being effectively applied to the matter of sin and virtue in farmers and poets. It can be applied to society only through the individual members of society: the disappearance of industrial capitalism and the establishment of some sort of Christian order could by themselves effect little for the kingdom of God. And so Gill wrote, "The holiness of God is something more and other than moral perfection"—but without moral goodness there can be no holiness at all, no wholeness. Eric Gill tried to live in the light of "Seek first the kingdom of God and his righteousness"* and he more and more

---

* In reading Gill it must be borne in mind that the Rheims-Douay version of the Bible which he often used has the word "justice" where the Authorized Version has "righteousness". This is rather misleading, since in current use the connotation of the word "justice" is almost entirely rational and juridical.

found the way to that kingdom to be through the word of St James, "pure religion and undefiled is this, to visit the fatherless and widows in their affliction and to keep unspotted from the world".

Gill had an accident early in 1937, falling off a scaffold in his workshop and breaking a rib; coming on top of a bout of illness shortly before, this reduced him to a rather poor state. With the object of setting him up again, a friend generously enabled him to have a holiday in Palestine with Mary. They stayed in Jerusalem; mostly with the architect Austen Harrison, who again took them on numerous expeditions including one to Cairo. They went there by air, and Eric wrote in a letter to a friend, "I enjoyed the flight very much—marvellous, wonderful, lovely, flying over the sea and Port Said and the Delta. What an astoundingly different kind of landscape from that of Buckinghamshire!" He found that Cairo too is very different from the Chilterns, "a corrupt and bad old city (I should think)", but he was delighted by its two chief mosques, and dutifully visited the Great Pyramid: "I went up and into its middle! Naught but exclamation marks will convey to you its amazing and marvellous mad grandeur! Did you like the Pyramids? Not half!"

While on this visit he made his one and only radio broadcast ("not so difficult or alarming as I'd imagined"), was commissioned to design Hebrew and Arabic founts of type for the government presses, and did a little inscription work. But he spent more time doing drawings of Jerusalem, and found this "a fine way of staying put and thus really soaking up the scene". His love, his reverence, for the City and the Land were as great as ever: once again he was overcome by the beauty of the Temple Area, "than which nothing, nothing, nothing could be lovelier, holier, more dignified, more humane or more grand". Jerusalem has been described as a city of iron under a sky of brass; to Eric Gill it was a city of stone lit by a radiance not of this world. Just before leaving he wrote to his benefactor, "We have had a truly wonderful holy-day, and I am now I think quite well and ready for the work that awaits my return".

G

Chapter Eleven

PIGOTTS

concluded

Towards the end of 1935 a number of people were dissatisfied with the work being done on the interior decoration of the Roman Catholic Cathedral at Westminster, and an appeal was made to the archbishop to stop the work in order that the whole thing might be examined afresh. Eric Gill was among the signatories to this appeal; later on, he was asked, together with two other artists, one of whom was his relative Colin Gill, painter and mosaicist, to make suggestions. Eric's replies to this were at first all in terms of whitewash, in the literal sense of the word. But he came to realize that few people concerned could be brought to appreciate the virtues of so simple a solution; so he evolved a scheme whereby the half-dome at the east end, the great dome over the sanctuary, and the saucer domes of the nave should be covered with nothing but plain gold mosaic, varied only by a suitable inscription in large roman letters behind and above the altar. Such a scheme might well be calculated to appeal to the harassed authorities and at least some of their critics; and perhaps it did, for in a letter to Graham Carey on 1 January 1939 he refers to the possibility of "doing the mosaics over the choir"; but the coming of war a few months later put the whole matter in abeyance indefinitely.

But this was not before Gill had been commissioned by Cardinal Hinsley to do another work in the cathedral. This was to carve an altar-piece for the chapel of the English Martyrs, in the north aisle; it was to consist of a large crucifix, with supporting figures of St Thomas More and St John Fisher, Bishop of Rochester. Sir Thomas More had had a small menagerie when he lived in Chelsea, including a monkey, a particular pet of his. When Gill designed the reredos, he found he had a small space to spare behind the figure of

More, and he filled it with a little monkey, who clung to the skirt of his master's gown. In doing this he was not only indicating a characteristic of More, but was following an age-long tradition of Christian iconography, for instance St Hugh of Lincoln's swan, St Gertrude of Nivelles' mouse, St Jerome's lion, St Antony's pig.

At the time of Gill's death he had nearly finished carving this altar-piece, to which the finishing touches were put by Laurence Cribb. It remained in the workshop at Pigotts throughout the 1939-45 war, and afterwards was removed to the Cathedral, and set up in its place. What happened then may be given in the words of Mr Tegetmeier in a letter to the press: ". . . No sooner had the carving been put in place than the monkey vanished (overnight, as it were), as if it had taken flesh and fled, overawed by the grandeur of his surroundings. No explanation was offered. The architect in charge was absent at the time. Neither Mrs Gill, her husband's executor, nor Mr Laurence Cribb, his colleague, who had the task of finishing the work *in situ*, was advised or consulted. None of them knows what motive prompted the peremptory order in obedience to which the monkey, beautifully carved, returned to dust". The motive for this deed has never been divulged, and the name of the person responsible for its being done has never been made public. Mrs Gill wrote to the Archbishop of Westminster, Cardinal Hinsley's successor, respectfully asking for an explanation; the letter was acknowledged by a secretary, and no more.

Gill would not have been shocked by a customer exercising his right of altering the work of art he had purchased. In 1936 he received a letter complaining of alleged mutilation of Michael Angelo's paintings in the Sistine Chapel; in the course of his reply, Gill wrote: "speaking as a sculptor, I maintain that if a man buys from me a statue and does not like the shape of any part of it, he is quite at liberty to remove that part or alter it or do anything he jolly well pleases. All this talk about the sanctity of the work of artists, as though it could be claimed that artists were directly inspired by the Holy Ghost, is, I think, flat nonsense". (Letter 259.) But he would have been shocked by the state of mind of the persons responsible at Westminster, and by the discourtesy with which the thing was done. Whatever the motive may have been, there could be no excuse for such insensitive mutilation, and no excuse for such bad manners.

The above occasion was not the only one in which an image by Gill was treated with disrespect. At the request of the Roman Catholic priest at Glastonbury, Francis Burdett, he made a Madonna and Child to go over the west door of St Mary's Church there. Some years later Father Burdett being dead, this was removed and replaced by an image of a more familiar pattern. Several people in that part of the country who were interested in such things heard of this— Gill's carving was then lying neglected in the garden of the convent school—and talked of trying to buy it and restore it to suitable use. However, they had been anticipated: it was bought by a Cambridge don, Mr Mortlock, and adapted as a headstone over his wife's grave. The Glastonbury Madonna can now be seen in the cemetery there.

Nine years after it was first proposed that he should be nominated, in 1937 Eric Gill was made an Associate of the Royal Academy, and this was only one of several public honours. He was an Associate of the Royal Institute of British Architects, LL.D. *honoris causa* of the University of Edinburgh, Associate of the Royal Society of British Sculptors, and one of the first recipients of the honour of Designer for Industry then newly instituted by the Royal Society of Arts. Some even of his friends did not know of these recognitions, which he regarded simply as manifestations of the uncritical kindness of the public bodies concerned. There were some people who were not gratified by his acceptance of official honours, just as they were shocked by some examples of his lack of "teetotalism"; they said he was selling the pass, being spoiled by success, unmindful of his own principles. These were the intransigeants among those who had called themselves his followers. As a wit remarked— precisely, I believe, in relation to a follower of Gill—"God sends disciples to geniuses to keep them humble".

Gill gave ordinary people data (however inapplicable as things are) whereby they could live in a humane, just and civilized society; monuments of stone and engravings which they could understand and take pleasure in; fine public inscriptions; and straightforward, readable printing types. Moreover he wrote, and he wrote not only with a precision corresponding to that of his lettering (the comparison is Coomaraswamy's), but usually in a colloquial, conversational way; this was spontaneous and unstudied and makes an immediate appeal to the reader who is indifferent to literary airs and graces. It is ironical that one of his gifts to us in most frequent demand was tombstones. But this need not be taken for a sign. It was an inevitable consequence of the times in which he lived that to a large extent Gill's messages, in whatever medium conveyed, came mainly to the notice of people of good education and cultured tastes, with corresponding interests. The irony of this limitation of his audience is the more marked because his underlying but avowed concern was not with art but with man, and this needs to be always borne in mind in reading what Gill wrote or considering what he made. He aspired to be a spokesman of the inarticulate and unconscious masses, not as masses but as individual persons. To what limited extent he may have succeeded in being this is a matter of opinion; but when he claimed to be stating "what any man or woman knows", he himself added "but does not always know that he knows".

Nevertheless, Gill had, and in a measure has, a following larger and more varied than some have supposed. An obvious example is among printers of all sorts and conditions, for whom his name commands the respect given to a master in their own trade. Of quite a different kind were those people who were sufficiently interested in the conditions under which they lived to be attracted towards some form of community life, usually rural. These regarded Gill with reverence as an exemplar of what they aspired to. This, as we have seen, rests on a misapprehension of Gill's real attitude in this matter. But the set-up as it actually existed on Ditchling Common gave some justification. Then there were the young Roman Catholics who on the one hand were impressed by Gill's outspoken and consistent profession of Christianity and on the other welcomed his equally outspoken criticisms of some of the clergy; they welcomed, too, his open championship of such causes as that of conscientious objection against war. In the thirties there were many people who, knowing little about political and economic theory and actualities, were yet revolted by what they were told was going on in Italy, and Germany and Russia, while feeling that the set-up in Great Britain was ineffective, unenterprising and onerous. Some of these were attracted to Gill because, without understanding it fully, they got the idea that here was a man who was preaching an alternative which really did put the people and their personal needs first, last and all the time. And Gill made a strong appeal to the scattered individuals in all walks of life who, genuinely or merely as a pose, were unconventional; they knew him principally through casual refer-

ences or "stories" in the popular press, and regarded him as a great
non-conformist, who was ready openly to denounce humbug of any
sort.

But Gill achieved fame in the first place as an artist, and as an
unusually articulate one. As such he attracted attention outside the
circles of other artists, art critics, and artistic coteries, and here
again the attraction was often his non-conformity. Perhaps I may
here take myself as an example. I was ten years younger than Gill,
but at the time I first met him I had lived on my own in the world
for a dozen years, and I was by then fairly well formed. I had been
brought up in a professional family, in which thought and intelligence were given their full due, and the existence of the arts was
recognized, first place being given to the arts of speaking and writing. The attitude which I encountered to the arts and artists was a
source of puzzlement to me; it was a manifestation of what Gill
later showed me to be "art nonsense". I was a voracious reader; but
when, for instance, I came upon a reference to Shelley as "gold-
dusty from tumbling among the stars", it at once struck me as the
most utter rubbish. I could not understand why it was accounted
more honourable to paint pictures to be hung in galleries than to
make chairs and tables or horseshoes (or why trade wholesale should
be more worthy of respect than trade retail). I was, in fact, here and
elsewhere, up against the idea that the painter or the poet is not as
other men. I just could not see it. I loved music, and buildings, I
was not indifferent to painting and sculpture—but could not see how
the people who did these things really differed from anybody else.
But everybody seemed to agree that they were different, and that
their work must not be judged as other work was judged; the whole
thing really was a puzzle. I tried to solve it by doing some relevant
reading, but I could not understand the language—jargon, it seemed
to me—and thought of the writers. And yet it was impossible to
believe that great works of art of any kind were made simply for
the benefit of art critics and enthusiastic amateurs. When I met Gill,
I heard for the first time explanations of it all that made sense,
explanations moreover that came from a working artist and not
simply from someone who talked about art or beauty. In particular,
I saw that art is simply the well making of what needs making, and
that the artist is *not* a special kind of man, but that every man
should be a special kind of artist; and I add that this does not seem
to me to be inconsistent with a quality which has been called

"gratuitous" inhering in some works of art in the narrower sense.
Ideas about other things, which had hitherto existed in my mind
only as dim apprehensions or uncertain opinions, were first formulated for me by Gill, and he showed me why. There must have been
a lot of other young chaps in the same sort of maze as myself, to
whom Gill's writings showed the way out.

But over and above all this there was the attractiveness of the
man himself as a human being. Most of the sorts of people referred
to above never met him, nor heard him speak, but that attractiveness shines through all his more general writings.

In 1938 Gill reached his fifty-sixth birthday. That is no great
age; but a lifetime of tremendous industry lived with unflagging
energy and high spirits was beginning to tell, his responsibilities
were not lessened and the burden of ill-health was increasing. In a
letter written to Father Chute six weeks before his birthday, there
is an unmistakeable undertone of "towards evening". He writes:

> Every day, with us as with you, has its pint and a half trying
> to squeeze down into a pint pot.* The sooner it's over the sooner
> to sleep . . . and yet on the whole life is worth living even for its
> own sake, and as you know and I know, I am one in a thousand
> for blessings flung upon me. It doesn't get easier though, and the
> noise and rush and inanity of the life of our civilization get
> plainly and rapidly worse. However this place is, in spite of the
> beastly little cars and the telephone, still an oasis in which the
> little children, for all their yearning after aeroplanes and motor-
> cars and cinemas and other gadgets, can and do grow up sweet
> and good, and they do. Petra's four are truly lovely and Joanna's
> two too. Michael Hague, aged 6, is now revelling in a new small
> bicycle—you ought to see his real joy in it and on it. "Oh I
> am glad, I am glad," he shouts as he rushes around. He went for
> a ride on the real highroad with René the other day—he on his
> tiny bike and René behind on his. It reminded you of the eighteen-
> nineties in Battersea Park when bikes first came in and you and I
> or our fathers and mothers went on them for joy! Petra's young

---

* To mention writing alone, during 1939-40 Gill wrote one full-length
book and over thirty booklets, pamphlets, contributions to periodicals,
and other fugitive pieces, excluding letters to the press.

Adam has got an aeroplane with real red and green electric lights. It's attached by a sling to the ceiling and flies round and round in the dark room amidst shrieks of delight. But still the cows give milk and the garden vegetables, and pigs squawk and breed. And still the noise of hammer and chisel on good stone resounds in the shops.

That is the writing and disposition of an ageing man, but it is only one aspect of Eric at this time. In the same letter he anticipates going shortly to Geneva to superintend the setting up of the finished monument there, and wonders if it would be possible to meet Desmond at Rapallo and "get up-to-date again in our reminiscences and prophetic utterances"; and he speaks of the amount of correspondence and other writing that he has to do, at least two hours of it every morning, so that "if I get four hours carving done before dark I'm lucky".

Ever since his first visit to Palestine a certain change or shifting of emphases had been slowly taking place in Gill's religious outlook. To take one example of it: it has often been remarked that Gill looked for rules and regulations and was happy to accept them from a competent authority. Early in our friendship he surprised me by saying that he willingly observed any disciplinary rule from the church authorities; but if they forbade something not as a matter of discipline but on the grounds that it was essentially sinful, there was always the likelihood that he would not be able to see why it was sinful, and so would want to argue about it. Years later he told me that his attitude had altered somewhat: he had begun to be doubtful of the desirability and usefulness of disciplinary rules, and to be wary of the ingenuities of casuists and canon lawyers. Precisely after his return from Palestine and in the context of the legitimacy or otherwise of war, he wrote, "I had been misled by the romanticism of my childhood and youth. And I had been misled by the logic of medieval Christian theology". At the same place in the *Autobiography* he alludes to the policeman-like frame of mind of many of the clergy and their apparent conviction that the spirit kills but the letter makes alive (so that you would think getting to heaven was a business of "going by the book"); and he goes on to emphasize that such attitudes are aberrations and are condemned by the teaching of the Church herself. Side by side with this there went a questioning, even a doubt, about his own method of teaching, the continual appeal to human reason and reasoning. Eventually he wrote, in the year before he died, in *The Cross and the Plough* :

> The best and the most perfect way is the way of love. This applies not only to life but also to teaching. The best and most perfect way to inculcate, for example, the virtue of honesty is to show that love implies it. It is probable that no other method can ever be successful; for though we are rational beings, inasmuch as we are persons . . . yet we use our reason so rarely and fitfully and with so rash a carelessness, without training or discipline; we follow our prejudices and predilections with such confidence and impudence that any appeal based upon rational argument is unlikely to be successful. Moreover the lovely has a wider reference than the reasonable : what we love we do not merely desire—it is something that, whether consciously or not, we recognize to be right as well as good, not only desirable but also as it ought to be; and the fact that this recognition is arrived at by that leap of the intelligence that we call intuition, and not by discursive reasoning and the painful process of thinking it out step by step by logical argument, seems to show that reasoning is both unnecessary and absurd.

Just as great changes took place in the Roman Catholic Church at the Gregorian reform of the eleventh century, again at the era of the friars and the universities of the thirteenth, yet again after the Council of Trent in the sixteenth, so far-reaching reforms began to be observable by all in the second half of the twentieth century. Some of these changes and new emphases were anticipated by Eric Gill individually—so far as that was possible—in his personal life and convictions, for instance, in the matter of public worship. Others of the changes would no doubt have been less welcome to him, in so far as they may seem to blur the edges of what to him was plain, clear-cut and certain. In one matter of fundamental importance to him he was on the losing side. Whatever deposit of theory may remain, the Roman Catholic Church has in practice accepted the pluralist society : the Gospel has to be proclaimed within the framework of society as it actually exists, without reserve or *arrière pensée*. Up to a point this is what Gill did, but never wholeheartedly or without reserve : his ideal was always and openly a unanimous society. He was always beating his wings against the bars of the

H

cage of contemporary piecemeal society which separated him from this ideal.

Eric Gill found in the Roman Catholic Church a religious society which was unanimous in its affirmation of traditional Christian teaching concerning God and man and the principles of human conduct that go with them : a society moreover which claimed to teach these things with an authority divinely guarded from error in that teaching. With the religious foundations thus secure, Gill was in quest of a wider unanimity. It is impossible to say to what extent he actually expected to find it among Catholics; but it cannot be questioned that his hopes, or expectations, were disappointed as regards social, economic and other matters to which he gave so much thought. He found that, outside formulated and defined matters of faith and right living, Catholics were as much at sixes and sevens as other people, and that their opinions and convictions more often than not were divided along the same lines, were influenced by the same considerations as among their neighbours who were not Catholics, sometimes not Christian. It looked to Gill as if Catholics in general were indifferent to the implications of their faith outside wholly religious and ecclesiastical concerns.

Responsibility. Poverty. Peace. These were the themes Gill recurred to again and again and again. Whatever his theme, those or others, he argued from ultimately Christian principles, hammering away at their consonance with right reason which obliges all mankind. But it does not seem that his co-religionists gave him any readier hearing than did other people. Many Catholics made the strange boast that as citizens and members of society they were no different from their fellows, people whom in other circumstances they were prone to dismiss as being in the outer darkness of misbelief or unbelief. Early on, Gill was told of the large northern industrial town he was visiting that sixty per cent (or whatever the majority was) of its inhabitants were Roman Catholics. "I should never have thought it from what I have seen of the place," he replied drily.

It is worthwhile recalling the mysterious passage in the letter which Gill wrote to William Rothenstein at the beginning of 1911, two years before he became a Roman Catholic. "There is a possibility that religion is about to spring up again in England. A Religion so splendid and all embracing that the hierarchy to which it will give birth, uniting within itself the artist and the priest, will supplant and utterly destroy our present commercial government and our present commercial age. If this is true it is good, if not then we are of all men most miserable." Thirty years later there was certainly no sign of a religious revival in the terms of that passage. Gill may have forgotten that he ever wrote it, but it still represented his ideal of a unanimous, church-guided society. His own share in the misery to which he had referred (in St Paul's words about Christ rising from the dead) was brought about by the blindness of men rather than by the insufficiency of the Church.

It used to be said that when people join the Roman Church their doubts are resolved and all their questions answered without any more trouble. To this Gill would reply, "When I became a Roman Catholic it was certainly not the end of questioning; the difference was that I now learned to ask the right questions". He learnt that lesson thoroughly, and on occasion would disconcert questioners by his use of it. One such occasion was when he was asked to contribute to a symposium on "Why I became a Roman Catholic". He declined to do so, on the ground that it was the wrong question: it should have been "Why I remain a Roman Catholic".

In view of what has just been said above, this reply could be misconstrued. It could be understood as meaning that Gill had been disillusioned by his experiences in the Roman Catholic Church, but that in spite of them all he remained a member of that church, and that his reasons for doing so would be of more interest than the reasons for which he joined it. In fact, there was no "in spite of" about it: he remained in the church for the same reasons for which he had joined. The possibility of doing anything else never entered his head. He did not try to identify the church with the general run of her members, or any school of thought or party, any more than he saw her as the pope or the bishops or the clergy at large; he saw her as a whole, and a whole of which he was part. She was Christ's church, a living thing which teaches the necessary truths about man's first beginning and last end, wherein fallen and divided mankind is united, restored and divinized, particularly in the sacramental meal which commemorates and continues the redeeming sacrifice of her Master and Lord. No simply human assembly can do these things; she is divine. Her members on earth, members not in the sense of a club, but as a hand of the body or a branch of the tree, visibly or hiddenly united with her, are human: she is human. Of what can be said against the Roman Catholic Church on her human side he was only too well aware—but "the world" was painfully apparent, even to the length of apostasy and betrayal, among the first Twelve themselves, yet who now would choose the alternative of following Herod and Pilate?

Eric Gill, then, did not look on his failure to convince more Catholics, and others, of the truth of his convictions about work and art, property and industrialism as due to some defect inherent in the Church or to innate perversity among her members. His eventual conclusion on this matter has been set out above when, after half a lifetime of appealing to the processes of human reason, he wrote, "The best and the most perfect way is the way of love. This applies not only to life but to teaching . . . reasoning is both unnecessary and absurd".

Desmond Chute was one of the first to comment on the fact that Eric Gill's enthusiasm was aroused particularly by the beauty of the constituent details of natural objects and the organic aspects of things. He had a passion for observing the relationship with one another of things and ideas, and for trying to find such a relationship where none seemed to exist. Thus he would compare the beauty of machinery with the beauty of skeletal bones and crystals and insects' wings.

This however did not mean that he was devoid of appreciation of the co-ordinated wholes. Study of the structure of a flower did not blind him to the setting in which it was as a speck of dust, in admiring its motive action he did not overlook the perfection of the whole machine. So far from being indifferent to landscape, as has sometimes been suggested, he had a heartfelt love for the bare contours of the South Downs and for the hills and valleys of the Welsh mountains; evidence of this has already been given from his own writings. He was a vigorous and all-observant walker and continued to be so in the Chilterns so far as work and health would allow. There was the walk up to the escarpment overlooking the Vale of Aylesbury on which a drink could be had at the pleasantly named Pink and Lily. A favourite short stretch was to the pub kept by Ramsey Macdonald's daughter, Ishbel, at Speen across the fields from Pigotts. On one occasion I accompanied Gill on this walk together with a stranger who had called. This young man talked incessantly on a subject that interested Gill not at all, and he got more and more restless. When presently the configuration of the ground separated us momentarily from our companion Eric whispered to me, "For pity's sake keep this chap in play for me—I want to say my prayers".

For many people a visit to Pigotts was an escape into the country, remote from the city's grime, turmoil, tyrannies and distractions; for others it was a place beleaguered—too many trees being felled or lopped, lanes becoming roads and roads becoming highways, villas and shacks creeping along the bottoms, tracts of grazing and arable abandoned to await "development". But for all alike the attraction of Pigotts itself remained unspoiled. The range of buildings round the grass plot that once had been the farmyard, secluded among the beech trees; the orchard in front of the house, with the lawn which was a tennis court until it became the grandchildren's playground (they also had a brick shelter with an entrance so small that grown-ups could go in only on their hands and knees); pigs and a cow, poultry and dogs, and the huge piles of logs and brushwood behind the printing-shop; children scampering about everywhere and enjoying themselves; people living a reasonable sort of life and enjoying themselves too. They had their troubles of course; but who has not?

If one sound more than another characterized Pigotts, it was "the noise of hammer and chisel on good stone", resounding from the two stone-working shops. Lawrence Cribb, in succession to his brother Joseph, continued to be Gill's principal assistant throughout the Pigotts period. Gill did not want a large staff. "If I had 5 men working under me," he said, "I should no longer be a stone-carver, but either the head of an office or the overseer of a factory." Of the other assistants and apprentices who worked at Pigotts, the late Anthony Foster, David Kindersley and his nephew John Skelton became well-known when they emerged from the anonymity that ruled during their training. His men loved and respected their master as a man and as a fellow workman, who took endless pains over everything he did and required them to do the same. The discipline of the workshop was strict: it goes without saying that Gill would not tolerate short-cuts or dodges to cover up mistakes; but he was always reasonable and understanding—he was too conscious of the mistakes he made himself to resent it when other people made them.

Mr John Skelton's apprenticeship lasted only a very short time; it was cut short by the master's death. His own carving, then, is not a product of training in the Gill workshop. But this short time enabled him to experience something of the efficacy of Gill's seemingly easy-going but well disciplined methods.

For a month Skelton was set to drawing alphabets, varied by odd jobs, some of which had nothing to do with stone-carving, such as mending a broom handle or shifting coal. On one occasion a letter he had drawn brought from Mr Gill the remark that the two downward strokes were not of equal length, to which Skelton replied that he had not measured them. Gill's response was typically playful, and firm: "Neither have I. But I have an e.gill eye." Under that eye Skelton made the pedestal for a small statue, and his first lettering job was a stone to be let into the floor of Pigotts' kitchen, indicating the four points of the compass. Gill was evidently watching him carefully, especially for such pointers as tidiness and orderly method, for on the strength of these preliminaries he reported to Skelton's parents that their son was a very acceptable and promising pupil.

Gill went round to each pupil or assistant twice a day to see how he was getting on, encouraging, criticizing, pointing out how a mistake could be turned to good use or something good made better, all very quietly; disapproval of any kind might be expressed by no more than a shrug of the shoulders. That quietness was characteristic: no excitement or fuss, no malice, an apparent casualness not only in comment but in doing. For example, this careful man paid his new apprentices' pocket money from cash kept in the pocket of an old rain-coat hanging behind the workshop door.

As a stone-carver himself, John Skelton's opinion is that his uncle had too many irons in the fire, that he spent too much time and energy on other things, perhaps particularly on writing and controversy. He believes that had Eric Gill given his undivided attention to stone-carving, especially in the round, the resulting work would have gained him fame as a sculptor far greater than he has in fact today.

By the end of 1937 the great carving for the League of Nations building was nearly finished, and the seventeen sections of which it was composed packed up for transport from Pigotts to Geneva. Gill, accompanied by Anthony Foster, was to follow them to put final touches to the monument when it was in position. Even after the work was formally commissioned in April 1935, there had been such delays in official procedure that Gill was hampered in even starting the work; so in June he wrote to Anthony Eden himself. He set out in some detail particulars of the design and the ideas it was intended to convey, and appealed for Mr Eden's support in getting things moving. The contents of this letter seem to show that Gill hoped to enlist Mr Eden's personal understanding of and sympathy for the design of the monument, without which procrastination and waning interest might result in its being abandoned altogether. Mr Eden replied very appreciatively almost at once, and Gill wrote again sending detailed drawings with copious explanatory notes. But in spite of this encouraging exchange, it was a further ten months before the contract was signed, May 1936, and Gill could begin work.

The central panel of the Geneva monument, thirty feet long by eight high, is almost entirely filled by "a naked figure of a man reclining, a vast and grand figure of Man with hand outstretched and the tip of his finger touching the tip of the finger of God which is coming down from above". Clearly this was suggested to Gill by Michelangelo's painting of the creation of Adam in the Sistine Chapel in Rome. Gill's idea was to adapt this to signify those things which were the League of Nations' immediate concern, a re-creation of man. The spaces in this panel are filled with lettering, two significant quotations: words meaning "He has created him in the image of God" and these lines from "The Wreck of the Deutschland",

> THOU MASTERING ME
> GOD, GIVER OF BREATH AND BREAD
> WORLD'S STRAND, SWAY OF THE SEA
> LORD OF LIVING AND DEAD—
> OVER AGAIN I FEEL THY FINGER
> AND FIND THEE.

Gill made the suggestion that the attention of visitors to the monument should be drawn to the words "Over again I feel thy finger"; and the idea of man's re-creation, by turning again to God, and offering himself and all he has and does is further emphasized in the two smaller lateral panels. Of the one Gill wrote that it would contain "figures of animals, trees etc, moving as though drawn by an invisible Shepherd towards the centre panel". Gill's "etc." are shown to include the services of such things as electricity and mechanics. The words on this panel mean "He has placed him over all his works", because the created world is God's gift to man. On the other side panel, Gill wrote that "there would be represented Man's gifts to God, and obviously these gifts would be ourselves, and I would carve a group of children, again moving towards the central panel as though drawn by the invisible Shepherd". The accompanying inscription means "We are his people and the sheep of his pasture". With the exception of the quotation from Gerard Manley Hopkins all the above texts appear in Latin, because, as Gill emphasized, they are universal statements; it was suitable to include the English quotation because that is the language of the donors of the monument.

In grandeur of conception and scale, combined with technical excellence of execution, no doubt the Geneva monument is the most impressive of all Eric Gill's carvings. Moreover, each smallest detail of the design had been thought out with the greatest care so that its meaning should contribute to the total meaning of the whole. A striking example of this is the way the head of the recumbent Man breaks the top line of the centre panel: this was because Gill did not want the panel to be simply a picture frame into which the figure of a man is neatly fitted, but rather "the universe itself into which man does not completely fit". The monument as a whole can be seen as the last words in stone to human society of a man who at an early age had grasped the concept of "mission" and made up his mind that life is more than art. It is therefore the more interesting to find that in 1937, when the Geneva work was well under way, Gill still held the judgement on his own work first made a dozen years before: in a letter to Graham Carey he repeated that in his opinion the black marble "Deposition", carved at Capel-y-ffin, was the best thing he had ever done.

Gill as sculptor was constantly plagued by people who either accused him of working in by-gone "styles", or wanted him to do so. Among the last, was the bereaved lady, "jaunty, horsey, distinguished" (the epithets are Chute's), who turned up in his workshop on Ditchling Common and said that she wanted a tombstone "in the Egyptian style". Chute, alone in the workshop, was bewildered; the lady explained herself. "Like that," she said, and pointed her stick at a small crucifix carved in relief on a headstone. A serious critic who accused him of archaism provoked an unequivocal and sufficient answer in a letter to The Criterion in 1934. "The implication is that I am working in a primitive style on purpose—because I like it," he wrote. "The facts are quite otherwise. *I work the only way I can . . .* That I have ever worked deliberately in a primitive or archaic manner is not true; I took to carving after ten years as a letter cutter, and, having no 'art school' training and having never drawn from 'the life' in my life, my carvings were inevitably of the kind Mr Penty calls 'even archaic'." In the *Autobiography* he declared that at the time he began to carve he was the only man in England who was a stone carver in the strict sense: "For stone carving properly isn't just doing things in stone or turning things into stone, a sort of petrifying process; stone carving is *conceiving* things in stone and conceiving them as made by *carving*. They are not only born but conceived in stone; they are of stone in their inmost being as well as their outermost existence". There is nothing esoteric about all this. Anyone who looks attentively at Eric Gill's stone carvings can see what he means, and what Father Chute was driving at when he wrote that Gill was a maker of *stone objects*. The claim to be the only stone carver in this sense was justified: Gill was almost certainly "the first artist in this country, after a lapse of some generations, to work directly on the stone (that is to say without clay models* and the rest)", as David Jones pointed out in *Blackfriars* (February 1941). That this is now again common practice among sculptors is very largely due to Gill's original influence.

It is to David Jones again that we owe some knowledge of Gill's considered attitude to his own work, primarily as a stone cutter but without doubt applicable also to other of his activities. Gill said to him in effect, "What I achieve as a sculptor is of no consequence, I can be only a beginning. It will take generations, but if only the beginnings of a reasonable, decent, holy tradition of working might be effected—that is the thing". Mr Jones does well to comment, "The astonishing thing is that within certain bounds, and in spite of all deficiencies, he achieved what he did achieve—the relative success is the surprise, not the obvious limitations".

* Surprisingly enough, some people were so undiscerning of Gill's mind and character that they attributed to him a belief that modelling in clay was positively wicked. It is therefore worth while to repeat Gill's repudiation of such nonsense in a letter to *The Times Literary Supplement* (Letters, 189) about a specific example of this. "I have never said or thought that modelling was sinful or even silly. On the contrary, I have frequently said and written that carving and modelling are two arts, each having its own proper good qualities."

There were people who admired or were interested in Eric Gill and his work as stone carver, engraver, letterer, but with the reserve "It's a pity about this Roman Catholic thing". They had failed to recognize that without his Christianity he would not only have developed into a different sort of man, but would have used his talents very differently. For some years after he became a Catholic, particularly after he was received as a Dominican tertiary, he had concerned himself with learning to pray, trying to distinguish which should be his among the disciplines prevalent in the church at various times and places. His difficulties were solved early in 1922 following a visit, with Hilary Pepler and others, to the Carthusian monastery at Parkminster and a correspondence with one of its monks. The practice of much earlier centuries, and the experience of such men as these, greatly helped him to reach the conclusions which he discussed in a letter to Desmond Chute. "It has come to be supposed that the conventional, the hieratic, the formal, is a dead thing and that there is life only in the naturalistic and idiosyncratic . . . Just as you cannot certainly paint a good picture by going to an art school and learning a 'method', that it is not 'art' you can be taught but only technical things (e.g. to keep your hand and your brushes clean and your lines clear)—so you cannot certainly walk with God by following a 'method' but must wait upon him as a lover—singing beneath his window—waiting for him in the snow —and that the only things you can be taught are technical things —to keep clean."

"Lord, thou knowest that I must be very busy this day; if I forget thee, do not thou forget me." Gill called that a perfect prayer. He was a very busy man, every day and all day. One forgets. What then becomes of "pray without ceasing"? Year after year Gill's daily life was led in a prayerful and contemplative spirit, he went about his business in the presence of God. Such a continuous, un-selfconscious, habitual offering of all one is and does to God is the realization of Eric's own words, that "we are all so many sweet-hearts to God. Are we going to fob him off with borrowed kisses, with even the best Elizabethan lovesongs? Would he not rather have the vulgar endearments which are our own?" Deliberated prayer became more and more a matter of "the conventional and hieratic", represented by daily Office and participation in the Eucharist. Throughout his life as a tertiary he was faithful to the daily short Office in its Dominican form, consisting mostly of

psalms, reciting or singing it with his fellow-tertiaries on Ditchling
Common, and in a measure at Capel-y-ffin, saying it in private at
Pigotts. There one of the most familiar glimpses of Eric Gill as one
passed from the house to the workshops or into the open air was of
him sitting motionless before the altar in the chapel.

Scattered up and down Gill's writings are many references to
public worship and to appropriate buildings and furniture; and as
always he went down to first principles. Public worship consists of
various forms of religious service, made up principally of Biblical
material, corporate actions to which the individual personal worship
of the participants is essential. A church is essentially simply a
shelter for the worshippers together; an altar is a place of sacrifice
and a table at which men eat; crosses, candlesticks, "stations" and
the rest, these are furniture and should be kept to the minimum
required by practical considerations. Himself a maker of statues, the
fewer Gill saw in a church the better he was pleased, since the altar
is what matters and the direct approach to God that it involves. He
advocated simplicity and plainness for several reasons, not the least
being that plain buildings and furnishings are the only kind that
this age can do really well. Time and again he emphasized that what
is good, and therefore beautiful, need not be costly, and what is
costly is often not good.

Gill was particularly concerned for religious chant and its singing
by the people at public worship. In 1935 he wrote a short article
called "Plain Chant and the Plain Man". He began with a description of the plain man: "The plain man is one who lives in an
ordinary way as a human being. He is free from fads and fancies.
He's not specially grand or peculiar. He's not moved by theories or
eccentricities. Really he's the normal man—penny plain, not two-
penny coloured. He lives according to nature. He's neither highbrow
nor high art. He's not a museum specimen—he'd wither in a glass
case. If you make him selfconscious his virtues decay. He is a man
of tradition, he follows the fashion but contributes to its changes.
He is a rational soul but doesn't bother about it." Those who knew
Gill closely will recognize here an unintended description of what
he hoped for himself, and of what in so large a measure he was. He
went on, "And as is the plain man, so is his plain chant. Plain
chant is not a peculiar music suitable only for chamber concerts at
which music is *performed* [or suitable solely for the use of monasteries and convents]. The thing to remember about the chant of

the church is that it is not *the* chant or *a* chant; it is simply chant. It is the singing natural to the human voice, it is not the voice of organs or of trumpets or violins, but the voice of men . . . the natural way in which speech, untrammelled by the exigencies of musical instruments, is sung".

Gill was distressed by the state of public worship which he found in so many Roman Catholic churches in England in the earlier part of this century. The majestic mysteries of religion, the outpouring of Christians' worship of their Creator and Saviour, seemed sometimes deplorably casual or mechanical, carried out in a setting disguised by commercial fripperies and by externals deemed devotional, in which the assembled faithful were left to fend for themselves in whatever way their private devotion prompted. He realized that such a state of things could not be remedied by piecemeal attempts to introduce such novelties as congregational singing, or that any alteration of long and deeply-rooted habits could be other than slow. But even when a boy at Chichester, his interest in buildings in general and churches in particular had brought with it a dim apprehension of the relationship between their shape and their use, and he now became increasingly interested in one reform in church building which would have real significance in itself and help towards bringing about an important change of attitude, namely, the removal of the altar from the east wall and the putting of it in the midst of the congregation. In 1937 he had an opportunity to put this into practice in some degree, when the head master of Blundells School at Tiverton, Doctor Nevile Gorton, asked him to re-make the interior of the school chapel. Gill agreed, and took the boys of the school into partnership. Extensive alterations were made, and the result to which these all contributed was to bring the altar into a cleared space much closer to the congregation; it thus became the focal point of the building, visible to all, whereas before it had been remote and obscured. The new altar itself was a plain stone one, each of its four sides being designed and carved by boys. Thirty years later, across southern England there are to be met middle-aged men with clear recollections of the enthusiasm that Eric Gill inspired in them at this time and of the experience of working under his direction. Subsequent events were less gratifying. After Doctor Gorton had left Blundells to become bishop of Coventry, the authorities of the school, bowing before the malcontents in a lively controversy, had the new altar taken away. These unnamed gentlemen have their place with the unnamed priest of Glastonbury and the unnamed prelate at Westminster.

A by-product of all this was Gill's essay, "Mass for the Masses", published in 1938 in *The Cross and Plough*, and in *Orate Fratres* in the United States, revised and reprinted in *Sacred and Secular* (1940), which was in substance an enlargement of the original explanatory address which he gave at Blundells School. It is his manifesto on behalf of the central altar surrounded by the worshippers on all sides, thus enabling worship to be more understanding, more whole-hearted and more united. He wrote to John O'Connor, "I am at present completely one-eyed about it. I see no hope whatever . . . until the Mass is brought away from the mystery-mongering of obscure sanctuaries separated from the people . . ." Father O'Connor was not the man to disagree with this, for he had just built an octagonal church in Bradford which exactly met Gill's requirements, so that the sacrificial Supper was offered "not only for the people but by them and in the midst of them". In 1937 one would have had to have gone a long way to find another such in English-speaking countries, though in some other lands the need for this apparent innovation had already begun to be recognized. But more was to follow.

Doctor Lawrence Youens, the bishop of the extensive Catholic diocese of Northampton in which Pigotts is situated, was well disposed towards Eric Gill, at a time when members of the episcopal bench were prone to be especially suspicious of him because of his seemingly ambiguous attitude towards communism. Soon after his accession to the see Dr Youens proposed that Gill should take charge of the design and building of a church which should exemplify the principles set out in "Mass for the Masses"; this church was required at Gorleston on the Norfolk coast near Yarmouth. Gill responded with delighted alacrity, but he did not lose his head. He had been a draughtsman in an architect's office, he was a tireless critic of the work of architects, but these were not sufficient qualifications for building a church. So he went to an architect in High Wycombe, Mr John E. Farrell, and enlisted his help as a partner in the enterprise; the combination was a happy one, and work was begun just before Christmas in 1938, Messrs J. Middleton & Co., of Great Yarmouth, being the builders. Gill wrote that the building was "bound to be judged by all sorts of false canons. No one will believe that we designed the job from the altar outwards". Yet so it was. With the exception of the provisions for artificial lighting and heating (which Gill accepted without demur and without enthusiasm) the whole thing was the work of local bricklayers, tilers and carpenters, though the altar, its crucifix and the font were made in the workshops at Pigotts.

The building is not circular or polygonal, with the altar in the middle, but on a traditional cruciform plan; the altar is in the crossing of the nave and transepts, but with the congregation accommodated not only in the nave but also behind the altar and in the wide transepts, that is, on all sides of it. The building material is hand-made multi-coloured bricks from Norwich, the interior walls being plastered and coloured white, and the windows filled with clear glass. Even after the lapse of thirty years and a great decrease in the buying power of money, it is instructive to note that this church, accommodating 300 people and made of best quality materials, cost only about £6,700, a little less than the contract price.

Whatever adverse criticism could be justly brought against this building, there is no doubt that it established the credibility and importance of its governing feature, the altar in the midst of the congregation. While it was still building, Gill himself wrote that "though I know it will be good in some ways (and those not the least important) I think it quite likely that it will be gawky and amateurish". And "if ever we get another church to do," he added, "we shall have learnt a lot from this one". At the opening of the church in June 1939 no reserves were expressed. A canon of the Northampton chapter, pleasingly named Squirrell, preached a sermon which Eric called "a hard-headed discourse, full of piety and sweetness", endorsing and recommending all that the builders had done, and at the subsequent luncheon Bishop Youens repeated this approval, which was shared by many of the clergy present, especially the younger ones. Gill summed up : "But, of course, it is one thing to supply the bones—it is another to make them live—so we must not crow too soon. Anyway, it is undoubtedly a great triumph to have established—at least in this diocese—the notion that it is the right thing to do and apostolical to place the altar in the middle of the church and that it represents Calvary in the middle of the world."

In *Social Justice and the Stations of the Cross* (1939), which Desmond Chute called his spiritual testament, Gill wrote: "The sufferings of Christ on the cross are not the chief thing . . . The chief thing now to be thought of is that he is lifted up . . . , shown to the world." For years Gill had been giving his attention to the earlier tradition of Christian iconography in relation to the representation of Christ crucified. In this, the figure was shown not as a dead body, naked and mangled, but as living, robed, crowned, reigning and ruling from the Cross. So early as 1926 he had made an engraving of this kind, suggested by a photograph of the Volto Santo at Lucca. From later years there are several examples in stone, such as that on the Sibell Lumley Wyndham memorial at Clovelly, and the English Martyrs altarpiece in Westminster Cathedral. It can be seen again in the Calvary group high up on the outside of the east end of Saint Thomas's church at Hanwell in Middlesex, which he carved at the request of the architect, Sir Edward Maufe, in whose opinion it is one of the best things Gill ever made. It was Sir Edward again who after Gill had carved the John the Baptist, and the diocesan arms for Guildford cathedral, commissioned from him an outside crucifix for that building too.

This work also was to be on the eastern end of the building, which stands at a commanding height on Stag Hill, overlooking the town. The exact design had not been settled when the architect happened one morning to hear on the broadcast "Lift Up Your Hearts" the words, "The eternal God is thy refuge, and underneath are the ever-lasting arms", which at once he suggested to Gill should be taken as the framework of the design. Eric agreed, but he carried the idea further, and the design for the crucifix developed into a great symbol of the Holy Trinity. "The idea is," he wrote, "that the Incarnation means, God with us . . . That being so, God may be said to present himself to us in Christ, and so the design represents the hands of God holding up his Son. At the top, because the church is dedicated to the Holy Spirit, and for the sake of completing the Blessed Trinity, there is the traditional symbol of the Dove." Here again the figure is living and robed, because the idea was not to represent Christ as victim, but as the risen Lord come into his kingdom.

During the last few months of his life this great conception was very much in Gill's thoughts, and he was hoping to make a start on it as soon as his health should improve. But early in August 1940 he heard from Sir Edward Maufe that certain difficulties had been raised about the design, and, shortly afterwards, that the work was to be postponed, ostensibly on financial grounds. Gill continued to hope that it would be possible for him to begin it in the spring. On November 4 he wrote briefly from hospital to Mr Lawrence Powell; it is the last letter in his Collected Letters, perhaps the last letter he wrote, and it ends with the words, "I hear from Ed. M. that he's still hopeful that the big ☩ will be done . . . and I hope I'll be here to do it".

It was not to be. Nevertheless, this work of Eric Gill is in its place at Guildford cathedral; for after his master's death it was carved by his pupil, Anthony T. H. Foster, and Gill would have been pleased by the way in which his design was carried out.

The final stage of the uneasy period between the wars was in full flux by the time the Geneva carving was finished. At the moment of the Munich crisis in September 1938 I had an appointment to meet Gill in London. When going to keep it I unexpectedly came upon him in High Holborn; characteristically, he was looking into a shop window, entranced by its display of useful gadgets and neatly-fitting boxes and files. We went off to lunch, and I asked him the question that everybody was asking everybody else; he replied in an almost airy way, "War? Of course there's not going to be a war—there's no money in it for anybody". My breath was taken away by this example of Gill's simplicity of mind, almost naivety, and I made no reply.

A few weeks later, Gill and I were in Glasgow together; we had been asked to speak on behalf of the War Resisters' candidate, Laurence Housman, in the election for the Lord Rectorship of the university. The audience was extremely disorderly, and Gill (whose voice had very little carrying power) was hardly heard. I, by hardening my heart and being rude, forced some sort of hearing. "The difference between the two speakers," commented a Presbyterian minister afterwards, "was that Gill was forgiving those hooligans all the time, whereas Attwater did not forgive them till he had finished." This was very characteristic of Gill; but it would also be true to say that he was reduced almost to silence by astonishment that intelligent young people could come to a serious meeting only in order to make a din and throw things about.

Both the principal opponents, the Liberal Sir Archibald Sinclair, and a Distributist candidate, polled more votes than did Housman, thus reversing the result of the previous year's election when the Pacifist Dick Sheppard had beaten the three other candidates (including Winston Churchill) by a handsome majority. The 1938 election was interpreted as a verdict against the foreign policy of Chamberlain and Halifax, which shows (if any demonstration be needed) how relative popular Pacifism is. Looking back, it seems strange that I think Gill, and certainly I, were given no information beforehand about the local political background of the election; otherwise I feel sure we should have spoken somewhat differently from the way we did.

There had been a meeting in the previous year which I recall because of a few words which illustrate Gill's aptitude for the right touch. It had been arranged in his Stepney parish by the vicar, Father John Groser. The audience was very mixed indeed, and there were three speakers, Alick West, Herbert Read, and Eric; I cannot remember what any of them said, or even what the meeting was about, but no doubt it was something relevant to the relation of art to society. What did impress itself on me was the way these speakers addressed their audience : the first one began "Ladies and gentlemen," the second one began, "Comrades"; Gill began, "Ladies and gentlemen, comrades, brothers and sisters . . ."

One of the longest series in Eric Gill's printed Letters is addressed to Graham Carey in the United States. The first is dated 31 March 1928, and is a business communication concerning the wooden bed-head which Gill had been commissioned to carve for him. Over the years which followed, their correspondence became more and more discursive; agreements and disagreements were discussed, and many common interests were uncovered. Gill and Carey exchanged puzzles and problems, read one another's writings, and Gill did more work for Carey, whom he found to be a perceptive and therefore valuable critic. By 1937 a firm friendship had been established, and this friendship by letter became ever more close and affectionate during the remainder of Gill's life.

Graham Carey, ten years younger than Gill, was a native of New England and resident there. From a very early age the idea of making —the making of things—seems to have been dominant in his existence. As a boy, he read *Ivanhoe*, and remembered only a floor of beaten earth and lime which is mentioned in it; he read Schiller's

Das Lied von der Glocke, and remembered only the pouring of the bell metal; he read about Mount Everest, and remembered only Buddhist monks making paper in a mulberry forest. His play was the making of things out of the natural materials of the New England countryside—mineral, vegetable, animal. In the ethnological museum at Harvard, he was fascinated by the tools and other things made by the aboriginal Indians. It did not occur to him that these were beautiful and holy, for beauty was a quality he had heard predicated only of objects in picture galleries and art museums, most of whose exhibits he found very uninteresting. As for holiness, in his own words that was "rather an affair of ancient martyrdoms and dark corners of dusty modern churches, and nothing to do with things made by human hands". But later on Carey took an honours degree in fine arts at Harvard, and he continued to read Ruskin during four years of the first world war in France and Macedonia (presumably this has no connexion with his commanding officer's calling him "the worst officer in the American army"). Still later he was, like Gill, an architectural draughtsman, then a worker in stained glass, and for ten years a silversmith.

It was natural that such a man should be drawn to the ideas of Distributism, and from the 'twenties he was an avid reader of Chesterton, Belloc and Arthur Penty. It was in *G.K.'s Weekly* that he first came across Eric Gill, who had written there an article about art and making entitled "What's It All Bloomin' Well For?". Here was the light Carey had been groping for, but it was not till 1930 that he visited Ditchling Common, strongly attracted by St Dominic's Press and the working community. He rented Hopkin's Crank there for the month of August. Gill was by then settled at Pigotts, and here eventually Carey was able to meet him briefly—"an unforgettable evening, night and morning". What Carey saw and heard during this time confirmed his enthusiasm for the right making of things, and increased his distaste for human societies wherein the natural resources of the earth were grossly wasted and destroyed, wherein the life and values of primitive peoples were dismissed with contempt and the animal creation treated with disrespect.

Carey learned much from Ananda Coomaraswamy, whom he knew well in Boston; he studied Maritain's *Art et Scolastique*, and he gradually built up for himself a systematic philosophy of work. After reading a public lecture Carey had given, Gill wrote to him in 1937 that "there seems to be nobody in England (unless you think

I fill the bill) who is doing the same work that you and Coomaraswamy are doing on your side". Carey did much to make Gill's work and ideas more widely known in the United States, and since his death has kept his name before the public there, especially through the Catholic Art Association, and its quarterly illustrated review which he edited, now called *Good Work*.

At a time when Gill's health was steadily deteriorating and he was harassed by other difficulties and uncertainties, Graham Carey gave him generous help and encouragement; and the correspondence, understanding and affection between the two men made the friendship an important element in Gill's last few years. Indeed, Carey's interest and solicitude made Gill feel that there might be still one more "escapade" to be undertaken—the removal of the Gills *en famille* to the United States. Eric was taking this suggestion seriously from the spring of 1939, and it had nothing to do with the migrations across the Atlantic which war was to multiply a few months later; it was rather connected with Graham Carey's own quest for "a cell of good living" which he was hoping he might be able to establish in Vermont. That the United States was in some respects a better country than England for such attempts had been recognized by him and others for some time.

Clearly the first thing to be done was to find a way whereby Gill could make an extended stay in America, to explore, observe, receive impressions and reach conclusions for himself. One way to do this was to try to get a commission to build a church in the States, and to this end he wrote an article on the Gorleston church which was published with illustrations in the *Christian Social Art Quarterly* in the autumn of 1939. Negotiations were also begun for the organization of a lecture tour by Gill. One of the difficulties encountered here was that people interested in Gill's work wanted lectures on such subjects as sculpture, drawing and wood engraving, whereas Gill wanted to talk about the menace of industrialism. In any case, the war had begun, and the impossibility of the scheme at that time—obvious from the start, in retrospect—became clear. Moreover, Gill was really ill, and in a letter to Carey in July 1940 he called the tour off.

During the first six months of the war Pigotts underwent a rapid reduction of its male population and a corresponding slackening of working activity. Evacuees from a Marylebone slum came, and went; "perfect dears," Gill wrote, "a little girl of 11, 2 younger sisters, and baby brother". By November Gordian Gill had gone into the R.A.S.C. (later he was to be one of those who got away from Dunkirk). René Hague joined the R.A.F. and work was suspended in the printing shop. Of the stone-carvers, only two were left, Laurie Cribb and an apprentice. Eric himself was engaged on the Guildford cathedral work, mainly in the open air and in very bad weather, and then on the altar-piece for Westminster cathedral; he was worried by his financial position, and was wondering for how much longer there would be any work for him to do. Pigotts was uncomfortably near the headquarters of Bomber Command, which no doubt accounted for the first dropping of enemy bombs nearby in the May of 1940.

Many people, torn between their repudiation of all war and what appeared to be the compelling and not merely nationalistic necessity of overthrowing Hitler's Germany, turned to Eric Gill for advice in their quandary. To them he would set out explicitly and plainly the various possible appraisals of the conflict and his own judgement of what practical course was appropriate to each; but the questioner had to decide for himself, the responsibility was his—an appeal to conscience must be an appeal to one's own conscience, and not to somebody else's. Eric's own attitude to the war was predictable, but nevertheless it was not understood, or was dismissed as the vapouring of an incorrigible theorist. This was partly his own fault, for in his written or spoken references to the subject he does not appear to have made any effort to modify his habitual modes of expression concerning the matters involved. As so often, he did not understand the motives and passions of his critics, and moreover his knowledge of the antecedents and causes of the war was extremely limited and one-sided—he knew little history, and confessedly cared less. It is no wonder that he was rebuked for being "unhelpful" at a time of human crisis; but he was not trying to be helpful in that sense. What he *was* driving at he made clear in a letter to Coomaraswamy : "The aftermath of hate and vengeance will, I imagine, be irreparable . . . I myself am much occupied by trying to help to spread about the ideas which must be the basis of peace, if there should ever again be such a thing". But he could see only one enemy where there in fact were many, for he adds, "obviously there can never be peace until the world is rid of its allegiance to commerce and finance".

The time that could be spared from earning his living and keeping up Pigotts under war conditions was divided between a variety of activities: in spite of almost unbroken illnesses of one sort or another, the last fifteen months of Eric Gill's life were as unremittingly busy as ever. He was, in his own words, "pretty well entangled in pacifist doings", particularly with the Peace Pledge Union and with producing for the Pax Society a leaflet setting out the concept of Conscience, which was intended to help their judges even more than the conscientious objectors they judged. He kept up his usual general correspondence, wrote other letters to the press, and made a new translation of the daily Office of prayer used by Dominican tertiaries: "the existing English trans. are abominable—both nonsensical and, as regards hymns, nauseating". It was intended that this should be printed by Hague and Gill, but it has never been published. Early in the summer of 1940 he visited Capel-y-ffin, making arrangements for some tree-felling, and visited his brother Dr Cecil Gill in Cardiff. Later he undertook shorter expeditions to Birmingham and to Oxford, where he stayed with his Dominican brethren at their house of studies.

These activities were carried on between the bouts of illness; he spent much time in bed or convalescing. It was during these times of enforced inactivity that he carried through, as it were on the side, a work to which other men would have to devote all their attention and all their working hours over a long period: he wrote his autobiography. He had been asked to write this by the publishing house of Jonathan Cape, and had replied that it couldn't be done, but that he could and would write what he called an "autopsychography". He set to work on this in April 1940 and must have written without pause or check, and with little reference—perhaps no reference at all—to diaries, letters or other records, for he delivered the typescript of 100,000 words in July. On St Dominic's day, August 4, sitting in the garden at Pigotts, "it's my third day down and I'm more or less stuck in a chair with a rug round me," he wrote to an old friend. "Really [the book] amounts to 'a search for the City of God', but of course I can't give it a fine title like that. I wish you were here that I could discuss innumerable points with you. Dr Flood kindly, most kindly, did all the typing for me and kept me on the theological rails. Leastways I don't think he passed anything that he thought wrong—but he made very few adverse criticisms. It feels to me as tho' I ought really to die now. I don't know how I shall be able to face the world after stripping myself more or less naked as I have done." There are similar references to death in the same context in other letters at this time, but without any sign of premonition, or of a wish that it might be so.

Having once been persuaded to do the job, Gill did it thoroughly, honestly and delightfully. The *Autobiography*, which was first published on 20 December 1940, is different from much recent autobiography. He did not foul the nest of his own upbringing. There are no anecdotes of the distinguished people he had met, his introspection was never morbid or directed towards self-justification, he does not prattle or gossip. In essence, it is not a record of doings and happenings; he called it a record of mental experience, "for nothing particular has happened to me—except inside my head". From another aspect, it may be called a hymn of thanksgiving, and the word "hymn" is deliberately used, for it abounds in passages of pure lyricism. More often than not these passages spring, directly or indirectly, from a thought about his home. On the last page he wrote:

> If I might attempt to state in one paragraph the work which I have chiefly tried to do in my life it is this: to make a cell of good living in the chaos of our world. Lettering, type-designing, engraving, stone-carving, drawing—these things are all very well, they are means to the service of God and of our fellows and therefore to the earning of a living, and I have earned my living by them. But what I hope above all things is that I have done something towards re-integrating bed and board, the small farm and the workshop, the home and the school, earth and heaven.

A record of mental experience—and so the prospective reader might suppose that the book before him is a highbrow work, with a lot of talk about the soul, lofty abstractions and philosophical terms, and no getting down to the realities of daily life. Not at all. "I preface this book with the statement that man is matter and spirit, really both, conjoined and inseparable. The record will be concerned with the spiritual as informing the material, and with the material as manifesting the spiritual." On the title-page are printed the words *Quod ore sumpsimus* . . . This is the beginning of a prayer in the Mass, having reference to the sacramental body and blood of Christ. Gill is using it here with wider reference. "What we have taken with our mouth," that is, all bodily, sensual experience, *pura*

mente capiamus, "may we receive with a whole mind". Matter and
spirit, both real and both good, distinguishable from one another
but not separable without disaster. "The senses are a kind of
reason"—Gill didn't say that, but St Thomas Aquinas. The autobiography is greatly concerned with that truth; and we see that
the prayer on the title-page was fulfilled: he was a man of whole
mind.

To read this book is to hear Gill talking, answering objections,
gently touching out sillinesses. The old tag comes true—"Who
touches this book, touches a man". Gill did a lot of writing all
through his life, and it has sometimes been made a matter of reproach that he kept on saying the same things, often in the same
words. When a man thinks he has got hold of an important truth,
he may well be called to go on repeating it to an unbelieving world.
In the autobiography we meet them all again: the iniquity of
industrial capitalism; the importance of a prosperous agriculture and
a satisfied rural community ("the country must be said to exist to
support the town," but such places as London or Birmingham "are
not towns in any human or holy sense"); the sham of politics "as
the word is understood in our time and in what are called democratic
countries"; the insubordination and tyranny of commerce; the desire
of money, the root of all evil; the ordinary necessity of private property in real things; the wickedness of modern war, "a totally
different business from that envisaged by medieval theologians"; the
nonsense of Art with a big A and the aesthetic chatter that goes
with it; the responsibility of the human person for his own deeds,
especially his own work; the artist as workman, the workman as
artist; the primacy of spirit, and the truth of the Christian revelation. But there is a difference. In the *Autobiography* these things
are no longer expounded as it were for our enlightenment. Rather
are we shown how these convictions came to force themselves upon
Eric, not only by a process of abstract reasoning but also by the
total various activities and experiences of a full life.

Eric Gill's *Autobiography* is a remarkable work, a piece of deliberate, honest, but unlaboured self-revelation. And there are no
long words or recondite notions; it is written throughout on the level
of ordinary speech and thought, humorous and witty, serious but
without portentous solemnity; Gill was the most friendly of men
and charming of companions, and he simply talks to the reader. For
twenty-five years Eric Gill lived unswervingly in the light of "Seek

ye first the kingdom of God and his righteousness . . ."; because of this, other things have been added to other people too. Among these his autobiography has a unique place.

After a brief period at the end of the summer during which he was able to get about and make several visits, Eric on October 10 went into hospital in High Wycombe for X-ray examination. He was back at Pigotts after a few days, where he was visited by his doctor brother Cecil. Eric was now known to be suffering from lung cancer; the situation was fully discussed by him and Cecil, and he agreed to a modified surgical operation. Eric was in good spirits and for three weeks busied himself with clearing up affairs before again going into hospital. On October 30 he wrote a long letter to Graham Carey, his last to him. It ended, "I'm in bed at the moment waiting to be called to go to hospital. I don't think there's serious danger of life in this operation, but, just supposing the Lord God wills otherwise, please know that I love you very much and thank you dearly for *your* love. May the good work go on and may we meet in heaven. God bless you".

On November 4 Eric was admitted to the Brompton Chest Hospital, then accommodated at Harefield House. The operation was successfully carried out on November 11, and he seemed to be making satisfactory progress. But there was a sudden relapse. During a heavy air raid, Eric Gill died a few minutes before five o'clock in the morning of Sunday, 17 November 1940. He was nearly fifty-nine years old.

There was only one burial-ground near Pigotts, adjoining a small Baptist chapel at Speen, and Eric had arranged some time before that he should be buried there. In spite of war-time difficulties, a considerable number of people, including three Dominican friars, gathered for the funeral on November 21. Eric's body lay in the Pigotts chapel, where the Requiem Mass was celebrated by the parish priest of High Wycombe, Father Frederick Lockyer, and served by Cecil and Gordian Gill; the anthem In Paradisum, "May angels lead you into Paradise" was sung by other members of the family. The body was carried to its resting-place on a straw-strewn farm cart. Hilary Pepler carried the processional cross; with him walked the grandchildren (some of them were Hilary's as well as Eric's). So they all passed down the tree-lined hill and up the road to Speen.

At the graveside, after the committal, a hymn much loved by Eric
was sung: it was "Jerusalem the Golden".

> O sweet and blessèd country,
>   The home of God's elect:
> O sweet and blessèd country,
>   That eager hearts expect.
> Jesu, in mercy bring us
>   To that dear land of rest;
> Who art, with God the Father
>   And Spirit, ever blest.

Mary Gill survived her husband for twenty years, and died at
Pigotts on 22 March 1961. In 1944 she had said to the young
American soldier whom she befriended, "I can't imagine Heaven
without Eric".

INDEX